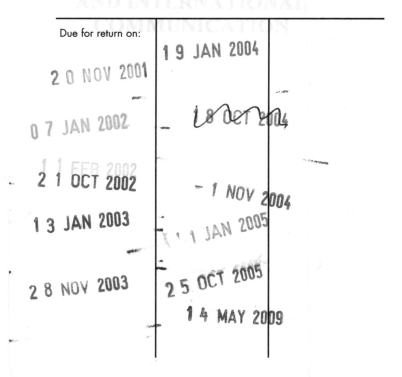

D1427659

ETHICS IN INTERCULTURAL AND INTERNATIONAL COMMUNICATION

Edited by
FRED L. CASMIR
Pepperdine University

LAWRENCE ERLBAUM ASSOCIATES, PUBLISHERS
1997   Mahwah, New Jersey   London

Lawrence Erlbaum Associates, Inc., Publishers
10 Industrial Avenue
Mahwah, New Jersey 07430

Library of Congress Cataloging-in-Publication-Data

Ethics in intercultural and international communication / edited by
   Fred L. Casmir.
      p. cm. – (LEA's communication series)
   Includes bibliographical references and index.
   ISBN 0–8058–2352–2 (cloth : alk. paper). —
   ISBN 0–8058–2353–0 (pbk. : alk. paper)
      1.   Intercultural communication—Moral and ethical aspects.
   2. Communication, International—Moral and ethical aspects.   3.
   Communication in international relations—Moral and ethical
   aspects. I. Casmir, Fred L.   II. Series.
   HM258.E797   1997
   175—dc21

                                             97–29452
                                             CIP

' Books published by Lawrence Erlbaum Associates are printed on
acid-free paper, and their bindings are chosen for strength and durability.

The final camera copy for this work was prepared by the author, and therefore the
publisher takes no responsibility for consistency or correctness of typographical style.
However, this arrangement helps to make publication of this kind of scholarship possible.

Printed in the United States of America
10   9   8   7   6   5   4   3   2   1

Contents

Acknowledgments

The editor gratefully acknowledges the contributions of Hollie Muir, graduate assistant, to the completion of the manuscript. Along with Hollie, deep thanks go to Craig Bowman, Darlene Kirtz, Dora Pember, and Tara Saunders of Pepperdine's Academic Project Design for technical computer support in readying the book for publication.

Foreword

Values, morals, and ethics form the foundations for interactions in any culture. Their acceptance by members of a culture, as well as adherence to them in practice, make human societies possible. That is the case because all three provide a basis for predictability as we build and maintain societies together. Values, morals, and ethics exist both as written or orally transmitted rules which cultures and societies have found important to their continued existence. Such rules help to create an atmosphere of stability as well as one in which cooperative processes of change and adaptation are made easier or less threatening. It is for this reason that they commonly become part of value systems passed on from generation to generation.

Whenever cultural consensus breaks down, it tends to be the result of changes in values, morals, and ethics. In such situations attempts to force the concepts of one group on another, or worse, to destroy those who will not accept a new set of standards for behavior and interactions, are not uncommon. There is also the destructive factor of forcing the value systems of a colonizing (political, economic, technical, etc.) culture or society on another, because the dominant or conquering culture sees the other as inferior and in need of a *better* value- and ethics-system, and most likely in need of better morals. In such cases positive human interactions, especially constructive dialogue, are replaced by bloody confrontations, hate, lasting resentment, and generations of wasted energy, resources, and human development.

Rather than seeing culture, as well as morals and ethics, as never changing, constant, or frozen, one basic concept behind the chapters in this volume is the fact that cultures do change, that morals do change and that ethics do change. However, of equal importance to the authors is the fact that if change and adaptation for human survival are primary concerns in the development and maintenance of any culture and its value systems, then we must consider how such change can be brought about in a non-threatening, cooperative, mutually beneficial way. It is at this point that communication scholars, and especially communication scholars concerned with INTERcultural and INTERnational communication, can make an important contribution both to our understanding and in our attempts to answer the question: "What kind of communicative interaction can make the process of change and the development of moral and ethical systems most productive and responsive to the needs of all those involved?"

It is for that reason that the concept of dialogue will be repeatedly used in the discussions and in some of the models included in this book. Such a dialogue is made more difficult when it has to take place across cultural or political lines of demarcation or division. Differences become more readily apparent, or are more readily supposed to exist, when we deal with those who can be easily identified as being *different* from us. Thus important dimensions for misunderstandings, confrontations, and serious conflicts are added to what, in many cases, are already common difficult processes of interpersonal or group interactions within any one culture.

Intercultural and international communication, as a result, requires careful consideration of the values, the morals, and the ethical systems undergirding human interactions. That fact becomes readily apparent if we define communication as that which takes place, symbolically, between human beings as they do things together. Differences in standards related to age, gender, culture, status, and geographic location are only some of the most important contributing factors. To find ways not only to dialogue, but to define problems *together* and to work out their solutions *together*, is one of the most serious challenges human beings face for the foreseeable future. It will require the creation of applicable and acceptable value- and ethical-systems which can assure some predictability and stability in our emerging world of global interactions.

Fred L. Casmir
Malibu, California

. . . and so, finally, I dedicate this book to all those who understand that ultimately human beings are not capable of making themselves or their environment perfect, but who, nevertheless, are determined to leave the world a better place than they found it, always striving to improve the conditions of others even as they seek to improve the intellectual, moral, and spiritual foundations of their own lives. As I see them, they are the ones who will not allow age, gender, race, or ethnicity, nor the boundaries of states, to become barriers as they make the ultimate ethical motto "Do unto others as you would have them do unto you" a reality in their efforts to continue the human dialogue.

Fred L. Casmir
Malibu, California

Some Introductory Thoughts ...

Fred L. Casmir

Pepperdine University

The challenges faced by communication scholars as they deal with ethics and ethical systems are often different from those faced by colleagues in other academic areas. My own definition of *communication,* as that which takes place *between* human beings—symbolically—as they do things *together,* is indicative of that difference which is based on a focused concern with symbolic process and dialogue. Although all of us, during our lifetime, may enter into or join various ethical systems or environments, it is self-evident that ethics, and ethical- and value-systems, are the *creation* of human beings. Indeed, even their modification or change depends not on some inherent capacity of the systems, but on the actions of individuals, or actions by individuals in concert. Our concern in this volume, as a result, is not merely with *description* or *identification* of extant ethics or systems of ethics as end-states, though that is an important subject for some. Nor is our interest primarily focused on the cultural, social, or individual factors identifiable as *parts* of extant systems. Rather, our focus is on the *dynamic process* which is involved in building, maintaining, and even destroying systems of values or ethics.

As Hewitt (1989) has pointed out, in the more stable societies of the past, social order was an expected, shared norm and that included norms of ethics. We were bounded by traditions and a sense of community, and our identities and securities were directly related to institutional involvements. As we became more involved in and aware of our almost daily interactions with those who belong to other, different cultures, sub- and co-cultures, including individuals from formerly remote parts of our world and the resulting changes in our life-space, a sense of insecurity and a feeling of chaos emerged.

1

The awareness of our changing environment has brought to the fore the necessity of understanding how we can best cope with the resulting confusion, confrontations, and feelings of malaise. As Folts (1973) put it "Communication is the major vehicle through which we can cope with, control, and manage change" (p.121). Weick (1987), as a scholar who focused on the processes involved as humans organize their common efforts, was also aware of the fact that "Interpersonal communication is the essence of organization because it creates structures that then affect what else gets said and done and by whom" (p. 97). It would be difficult to find a clearer identification of the role of communication as an activity or process *between* human beings, as they accomplish tasks *together,* including the building and maintaining of systems of ethics. Equally important is the realization that such structures, organizations, institutions or systems, once we develop them have a profound impact on *how we* do things *together.* At the same time, I agree with Heifetz (1993) who wrote, "By accepting change as natural process and choosing to manage it, we're really choosing life over entropy" (p.3). Managing change effectively and beneficially for all involved is probably the major task facing us at the end of the 20th century, and it is truly a survival challenge.

The continuation of human existence, of human creativity, of human value systems, and many other related factors is part of the process of choosing life over entropy. As I discussed in an earlier contribution, although we may continue to survive biologically, without the ability to communicate we lose those distinctive human features which make up our cultural, social, symbolic, interpersonal and aesthetic life-space (Casmir, 1978). I continue to insist that *anything* that limits or hampers our communication–survival processes is dangerous to the future of the human race.

When we look, specifically, at the building and maintaining of systems of ethics and values, the communication scholar's insistence on directing "one's attention to neither the self nor the other but to the actual happenings between men" (Poulakos, 1974, p. 212) is of major importance. The fact that the "'between' or 'relationship' involves much more than the 'mere sum of two individual entities,'" rather that it is the "interhuman force which sustains dialogue" (Poulakos, 1974, p. 208), accentuates the focus of my own concerns as I work with this volume. If one accepts Dewey's (1929) dictum that to learn to be human is to "develop through the give and take of communication..." (p.154), and the idea that "the individual does not behave in isolation from his social environment" (Etzioni, 1967, p. 2), it becomes even more vital to look at the dynamic processes involved in the building of ethical and value system.

Rousseau (1991) understood that "We balance unity with separation, vulnerability with safety. We constantly renegotiate, and when negotiations break down, relationships break up" (p. 6). That balancing act is not easy, but it is, of course, the fear of breakups or breakdowns that is at the root of ethics- and value-systems. Attempting to bring about consensus and adherence to any systems can be seen as one important means of keeping human beings *together*. Through communication we, essentially "...confirm the basic unity of common life" (Brownell, 1950, p. 241). Communication can thus be developed into a meaningful process or form of expression for those human beings who choose to engage in a mutually beneficial, supportive process (Casmir, 1978).

Our contemporary world appears increasingly to be torn asunder. It is a world in which neither individuality nor community can be as easily defined or accepted as in the past. It appears to many people as if in "olden days" we could more readily base concepts of community on the idea that we were "living in mutual relation with one another" (Buber, 1958, p. 45). What is often forgotten, is the fact that whatever mutual relationships had developed in the past, did develop over many centuries. What can become dangerous is any tendency to use our often imperfect perceptions of the past in any attempt to simply *copy* or *resurrect* those old times and their systems of ethics and values. What does appear to be necessary is recognition of the idea that the time has come for some *renegotiating of value- and ethics-systems*—which will be informed by the past and which are made urgent by the need for future human survival.

All that is new in contemporary or future change does not need to be feared *if* we accept the perspective espoused by Arnett (1992) "that with the knowledge that new insights come when both parties bring their uniqueness to the conversation" (p. 78). I might add, that that is especially the case if "both" parties can feel secure in the knowledge that the systems of values and ethics which emerge out of such conversations truly belong to all who produced the change.

Out of the contemporary insights by our colleagues in the natural and social sciences which relate to chaos theory, I would conclude that if human beings accept and manage change, it does "develop a set of new behaviors that assist them either to reduce the amount of stress in their lives or to cope better with the stress they do experience" (Merry, 1995, p. 129). Burack (1993), writing primarily about contemporary organizations, makes the more generalizable observation that "proactive responses require awareness of change forces and dynamics and their impact on the individual or organization" (p. 8) I would include systems of ethics and values among those parts of our life which need that kind of understanding and willingness to be proactive in their change. After all, such systems have never been as static or as much of a controlling force as many of us believed, or would like for them to have been. Otherwise, such aberrations as the horrors associated with Adolf Hitler's rule in Germany, or lies perpetrated by presidents of democratic countries, simply would not have occurred.

Merry (1995) provides an important warning when writing about "old dysfunctional ways of adaptation that are unsuitable to the changed circumstances" (p. 129). What appears to be unchangeable is the *need* for systems of ethics and values—but that need should not be confused with the idea that we consistently maintain, or even should maintain unchangeable value- and ethics-systems. Nor can we actually hope to maintain unchanged the old, familiar systems as the one and only answer for human needs. That is especially the case if we wish to survive in the changing environments of human history. As matter of fact, in the human life-process even "history becomes a proactive tool rather than a record carved in stone" (Burack, 1993, p. 40).

I certainly do *not* want to be understood as advocating some sort of oversimplified and apparently easy *situational* ethic, and I certainly do not advocate change for the sake of change. Nothing could be further removed from my concerns as a communication scholar who seeks to develop an understanding of the means used by human beings, in an *ongoing dialogue*, to create and maintain community through the creation and maintenance of value- and ethics-systems. Attempts to simply overthrow old orders and their value systems abound in human history. None more dramatically illustrates the destructiveness of such efforts than the French Revolution, which never was able to build a common ethical or value system based on dialogue.

On the other hand, I do accept the notion that chaos can create opportunities that are not present in any slow-moving organization or sociocultural environment (Flander & Moravec, 1994). Chaos *can* widen the spectrum of options and forces, leading to new and necessary points of view (Nonaka, 1988). As we create new structures out of chaos to meet human needs which go beyond mere biological survival or the maintenance of traditional systems, however, Bergquist's (1995) concept of "structures in which people view themselves as a part of a whole, complex systems, structures in which the whole is greater than the sum of its parts" (p. 5) contains, for the communication scholar, both the foundations of "ancient truths," and the inevitability of human efforts to restructure meaningful relationships as the need arises. Becker and McCall (1990) remind us that "meaning is constructed in the process of interaction. Society *is* the process of symbolic interaction" (p. 6), a concept which undergirds much of what I am trying to identify here as foundational concepts for those who will be reading our book.

Whichever way one defines ethics, and whichever past, present, and future considerations one brings to the subject, Elliot (1986) provides one meaningful summary for what I wanted to say in the preceding pages "It is partly through our collective or common knowledge of...human interest stories that our social ethos emerges. Their stories become part of the lore of our civilization, and that aids in helping to become one people...not just community of knowledge but community in the sense of sharing the world together" (p. 28). I invite you, the reader, to look for the discussion and illustration of these concepts in the pages to come.

We, as communication scholars, have undoubtedly been slow when it comes to dealing with ethic- and value-systems that need to be renegotiated and built *across* the dividing lines of cultures and the boundaries of states–or *inter*-culturally and *inter*-nationally. But as the need for such an effort becomes clearer in our minds, communication scholars surely do have an important role to play in focusing on the ongoing, emerging symbolic processes *between* human beings, as they build their future *together*.

REFERENCES

Arnett, R. C. (1992). *Dialogueic education: Conversation about ideas and between persons.* Carbondale, IL: Southern Illinois Press.

Becker, H. S., & McCall, M. M. (Eds.). (1990). *Symbolic interaction and cultural studies.* Chicago: University of Chicago Press.

Bergquist, W. (1995) *Building strategic relationships.* San Francisco: Jossey-Bass Inc.

Brownell, B. (1950). *The human community: Its philosophy and practice for a time of crisis.* New York: Harper and Brothers Publishers.

Buber, M. (1958). *I and Thou.* New York: Charles Scribner's Sons.

Burack, E. H. (1993). *Corporate resurgence and the new employment relationships.* West Port, CT: Quorum Books.

Casmir, F. L. (1978). *Intercultural and international communication.* Washington, DC: University Press of America.

Dewey, J. Barnes, A., & Buermeyer, L. (1929). *Art and education.* Merion, PA: Barnes Foundation Press.

Elliot, D. (1986). *Responsible journalism.* Beverly Hills: Sage Publications.

Etzioni, A. (1967). *The active society: A theory of societal and political processes.* New York: The Free Press.

Flander, G., & Moravec, M. (1994). Out of chaos, opportunity. *Personnel Journal, 73(3),* 85-90.

Foltz, R. G. (1973). *Management by communication.* Philadelphia: Chilton Book Company.

Heifetz, M. (1993). *Leading change, overcoming chaos.* Berkeley, CA: The Speech Press.

Hewitt, J. P. (1989) *Dilemma of the American self.* Philadelphia: Temple University Press.

Merry, U. (1995). *Coping with uncertainty.* Westport, NY: Praeger Publishers.

Nonaka, I. (1988). Creating organizational order out of chaos: Self-renewal in Japanese firms. *California Management Review, 23,* 57-73.

Poulakos, J. (1974). The components of dialogue. *Western Speech, 38,* 199-212.

Rousseau, M. F. (1991). *Community: The tie that binds.* Lanham: University Press of America,

Weick, K. E. (1987). Theorizing about organizational communication. In F. M. Jablin, L. L. Putnam, K. H. Roberts & L. W. Porter (Eds.), *Handbook of organizational communication* (pp. 97-122). Newbury Park, CA.: Sage Publications.

ETHICS AND INTERCULTURAL COMMUNICATION

Fred L. Casmir

Hall provides common ground for the issues to be considered in the following pages. More than merely defining terms, the first chapter addresses central issues and explores the connections between the interwoven subject matters dealt with in this volume: Ethics and communication in intercultural as well as international settings.

Although not all intercultural communication involves international dimensions, that is, individuals from different areas of the world or representatives of different states or nations, all international communication includes vital intercultural aspects because of the differences in background brought to interactions by the participants.

In this first section of the book, it is our intention to explore the fundamental issues related to such interactions. We wish to bring into clear focus the fact that differences in culture, ethnicity and gender are some of the most crucial areas which have to be considered if we are to provide some understanding of the need for ethical, mutually beneficial communication and interpersonal interactions in the decades ahead.

Intercultural communication scholars tend to focus their efforts on the interactions between individuals of culturally diverse backgrounds, individuals who may not necessarily be assumed to be official representatives of their respective cultures. On the other hand, in many if not most international interactions, individuals may not only come from culturally diverse backgrounds, but they are commonly assigned or are seen as having representative status—that is, they do not merely speak or communicate for themselves but but for others from their same geographic, ethnic, or gender cultural group.

Both by example and through the review of some traditional as well as more recent scholarly work, Hall provides vital insights and can draw some initial conclusions on the basis of the examples he cites. As will be true in all of the chapters to follow, the very paucity of sources dealing directly or extensively with ethics in relationship to intercultural and international communication makes it necessary to provide more than case studies, or the development of a volume which can assume common foundations. It is the ultimate purpose of all of the authors to provide a basis for dialogue, to address foundational, conceptual issues which must be dealt with before we can meaningfully deal with specific cases.

One more concept does need to be stressed at this point. This book deals with *Inter*-cultural and *Inter*-national communication. That requires all of us contributing to the volume to do more than describe various ethical problems or communication situations in different cultural settings. It is our intention to address issues which must eventually be dealt with when individuals from varied backgrounds are called upon to find or develop ways of interacting with one another in non-threatening ways. What happens between people as they symbolically interact with other human beings in order to find mutually beneficial solutions to the vexing problems of our complex contemporary lives, is, after all, a major concern of intercultural communication scholars. In that effort it is especially important that we address emotional issues and deal with personal convictions, as Hall does. After all, in order to address ethics in communication practically, we must recognize them as an extension of personal convictions, or we condemn ourselves to study them as idealistic, theoretical constructs which never touch our lives or those of other human beings with whom we must interact.

To indicate immediately that this book is not only interested in the more abstract, or theoretical aspects of ethics in intercultural communication, Elliott provides us with an opportunity to come face to face with a specific situation in recent history. The Kobe earthquake and subsequent events connected to it, serve as means for focusing Hall's contributions even more specifically. Human beings in dangerous or at the very least problematic situations face some of the greatest ethical challenges imaginable. Thus it is fitting to address our concerns against the background of such an event.

While this volume is not intended to "survey" all areas of ethical challenges we face in intercultural and international communication, Steiner's chapter serves as a reminder that we have only slowly allowed ourselves to deal adequately with many of the differences between human beings which result in communication challenges of various types. The relationships of men and women in our world offer us great opportunities as we strive to reshape our thinking and our actions. The balance which Steiner brings to her contribution, furthermore, serves as a strong reminder of the fact that ultimately we need to find ways to plan, work and accomplish together. If we do not succeed in that effort, intercultural and international communication will once more become, or remain, a mere tool for dominance of one race, gender or group over another.

Casmir's attempt to provide a specific model for achieving mutual benefits through a communicative, interactive building process represents a challenge to go beyond the description or identification of problems suggested by cultural divergence. He offers an ethical alternative to traditional persuasive, dominance enhancing approaches which have been common in much Western communication. Reviewing past efforts and traditional models becomes a means for critically exploring the alternative of dialogue. Intercultural and International dialogue, it is suggested, can encourage individuals to create together both the standards and goals for mutual efforts which thus become more than a simplistic fifty-fifty sharing process in human interactions. At the same time, Casmir's model reminds us that, like all worthwhile efforts, such communication must be seen as a long-term, ongoing, careful process requiring hard persistent work—as is true of all relationship-building.

Culture, Ethics, and Communication

Bradford J. Hall
University of New Mexico

George Elliot (1977) commented in her novel *Middlemarch*, that "Sane people did what their neighbors did, so that if any lunatics were at large, one might know and avoid them" (p. 3). Alas, in today's world we may seem to be surrounded by lunatics. As the world has continued to evolve into what some call a global village, it is evident that our neighbors not only differ from us, but they differ from each other as well. These differences make it easy to conclude that those who are different from us are tricky, insensitive and improper. Indeed, consistent problems with our intercultural relationships may suggest that our neighbors are worse than insane, they may be downright unethical. How are we to deal with such a situation? Although the strategies of avoidance and name calling referred to by Elliot are still popular responses, there seems to be a growing awareness that in the long run these do not result in the type of community in which we (as humans) enjoy living. This chapter, and this book as a whole, is one effort to deal with the sense of "insanity" which results from our interactions with different cultures and different ethical systems by focusing attention on the foundation of all communities–communication.

Before considering the role of communication, however, I review some general perspectives on the concept of culture and present a working definition of culture for this chapter's discussion as well as an initial comparison point for the chapters which follow. Next, I consider the nature of ethics and their relationship to culture and some of the resulting challenges and controversies that exist concerning this relationship. Then I turn to the issue of communication and its relationship to the challenges presented by the culture/ethics connection. I also discuss the benefits which can be garnered when we approach these concerns from a communication perspective.

CULTURE

The term *culture* and what constitutes culture has been, and I suspect will continue to be, a much debated subject. The consequences and implications that result from explicitly defining culture have inspired some to deal with these challenges by expressly *not* defining culture at all (Martin and Nakayama, 1996). Although such a route allows for great flexibility in use of the concept, I think it is important for both the reader and the author to be clear in what is and is not being discussed. Therefore, while the discussion of culture in this chapter will not resolve all past disagreements, it is intended to provide an explicit frame for the present discussion. It will also provide a departure point to help readers better understand the use of the term in the chapters which follow.

The study of culture has become an important part of many different disciplines, including anthropology, communication, education, law, linguistics, psychology and sociology. The history of the concept of culture and the subtle implications the various definitions of culture have conveyed within each of these disciplines could be the subject for an entire book. The modern use of the term culture may be traced to the anthropologist E. B. Tylor and his book *Primitive Culture* (1958) which was first published in 1871. Tylor (1958) defined culture as "that complex whole which includes knowledge, belief, art, morals, law, custom and any other capabilities and habits acquired by man as a member of society" (p. 1). Over 80 years after Tylor's initial work Kroeber and Kluckholn (1952) identified 160 different definitions of culture. I am sure that number has grown considerably during the last 46 years because the concept of culture has become increasingly important to our study of humankind.

For the purposes of our discussion I deal with the complexities of the concept of culture through the use of an implicit taxonomy of the term suggested by Philipsen (1987), which I believe encompasses enough diversity to have cross-disciplinary application. In addition, I use Tylor's (1958) original definition as a comparison point throughout the discussion.

Philipsen (1987) articulates three different ways that the concept of culture is used in the current literature on intercultural communication. First, culture is a *code* or a system of values, meanings, premises, images of the ideal, and so forth. Tylor (1958) suggests this in his reference to the "complex whole" made up of such things as community specific knowledge, morals, and so forth. Culture from this perspective is not tied to specific behaviors or artifacts, rather it is made up of the intersubjective resources available for generating a given meaning or meanings from observed behaviors and artifacts, thus turning behaviors into actions and artifacts into items used in action. Geertz (1973) captures the essence of this "cultural" process when he explains how the sheer movement of closing and opening an eye takes on meaning as a "wink" within certain systems of sense-making. Further, the meanings, values, appropriacy, etc., associated with winking in general and with any specific instance of winking are governed by the system of meaning shared by a group of people. Winking and other such recognized actions are communicative resources through which humans are able to build and maintain communities. These resources constitute a system of their own, thus making culture a system of its own, rather than simply another variable in some other system.

This cultural system operates at the level of "common sense" and, although often tacitly taken for granted, it is intersubjective in nature and thus public. Carbaugh (1990) also notes that this system is "deeply felt." In other words, it delineates the nature and scope of appropriate feelings and their objects. Studies, then, that attempt to identify cultural particulars may in fact be seen as merely identifying common sense. The difficult aspect when dealing with intercultural communication is recognizing and appreciating that there are as many common senses as there are communities (see for example, Griefat & Katriel, 1989; and Hall & Noguchi, 1993, 1995).

Recently in a graduate class we discussed a variety of articles dealing with different cultural communities. One of the classes' favorites was Basso's (1990) article on how the land may be said to stalk the Western Apache, shooting them and thus helping them to live better. Basso's (1990) work is a classic ethnography written in the form of a mystery. Although Basso (1990) notes that he visited with a number of Western Apache, he goes into great detail about his relationship with one primary informant, Nick Thompson. Through a series of related interactions with Nick, Basso gradually uncovers and reveals to the reader a series of clues which solve the mysterious and confusing statements made by various Western Apache about the land stalking them and shooting them. During the second hour of discussion, we turned our attention to an article dealing with the term "communication" and the cultural understandings which surround that term in what may be considered middle class America (Katriel & Philipsen, 1981). Katriel and Philipsen (1981) use the intensive study and interviews of two particular women, as well as a number of informal observations and discussions over the course of a year and the study of a popular talk show to uncover cultural meanings associated with the term "communication." The class discussion quickly turned negative. "How could the authors make such broad claims for a country so big and a people so diverse?" After all, the in-depth interviews and analyses of personal journals had only used *two* people. One of the international graduate students stopped the flow of negative comments by noting that it was interesting to her how defensive and ready to qualify findings everyone was when an article dealt with the students' own culture. I used this opportunity to compare the methodological similarities of the Katriel and Philipsen (1981) article and the one by Basso (1990). I also noted that Katriel was an Israeli, not an American. Both of these observations almost instantaneously seemed to make Katriel and Philipsen's study appear better. The findings were then more closely analyzed, and we found that not a single student disagreed with the authors' interpretations as they related to what may be viewed as a mainstream, largely white, American community.

Afterwards, I did overhear one of the students grumble to another that Katriel and Philipsen were "just lucky this time, as it was pretty much just common sense." The implication seemed to be that Basso's (1990) work on the Western Apache was not equally based on common sense. This white, male, middle-class student still had trouble seeing the Western Apache cultural system and the American cultural system as essentially different manifestations of the same thing. The former was seen as exotic, whereas the other (articulating his own culture) was seen as just the mundane way the world is. This sort of thinking is reflective of what I call the "zoo" approach to intercultural communication. When using such an approach we view the study of culture as if we were walking through a zoo admiring, gasping, and chuckling at the various exotic animals which we observe. One may discover amazing, interesting and valuable information by using such a perspective and even develop a real fondness for these exotic people, but miss the point that we are as culturally "caged" as others and that they are culturally as "free" as we are.

A second approach to culture is to view it as a *conversation* or a patterned representation and enactment of a people's lived experience. In other words, culture is an ongoing creation of the everyday activities of interconnected people. The notion of interconnected persons is a loose one. It does not mean that I, personally, have actually interacted with all these people. Indeed, some of the people with whom I am connected have long since died or have not yet been born, and my connection to them may be mediated by a number of other individuals. However, we may still be said to be connected in the sense that we share certain types of problems and responses to those problems that have been worked out and modified over time. These patterns of reactions may (and typically do) change over time, but they do so in ways which are connected to the past and responsive to the sense-making systems noted above. In this way, culture is constantly being created and recreated in our daily lives in ways which constrain us and yet simultaneously allow for creativity.

Finally, culture is viewed as equivalent to *community* or a named human grouping which provides for social identity and the sharing of communal memories. This ties back to Tylor's (1958) notion that culture is inherently tied to membership(s) within a society. Such a perspective encourages the recognition that virtually everyone may be said to be multicultural in the sense that we all belong to different family, work, school, religious, ethnic, political, or other groups. That insight should help us to avoid the simplistic conclusion that every individual is a member of just one culture. A group-membership focus thus allows us to discuss culture more easily by using diversified group labels.

However, the very ease with which we may use group labels can itself become a problem. The danger of reducing culture *simply* to group membership is strikingly exemplified in this personal account by Friedrich (1989):

> In my interviewing class I had been using an instrument called "The Dove Test," created by a Watts social worker named Adrian Dove, to illustrate the impact of environment on what people know. Mr. Dove had generated about twenty questions that lower-class blacks living in Watts could answer, but most other people could not. On the day before I intended to use the "test," I discovered that I had misplaced the answers. So I hurried over to the office of the only African American graduate student in the program, Bailey Baker, and asked him to help me generate the correct answers. With a sly smile on his face, he asked me why I thought *he* would know them (p. 3).

Too many times membership in a certain racial or ethnic group is assumed to imply a shared interpretive system or "culture." Group membership (racial, national origin, or otherwise) does not guarantee the shared knowledge, or shared morals, noted by Tylor (1958) in his original definition. The implication is that, although culture is necessarily tied to membership, it is not the membership per se that is the culture. Rather culture is those elements which create, maintain and transform social memberships.

Culture implies community, many communities in fact, communities that exist at all levels of human society. These communities provide a stage on which the patterns of the past, the practicalities of the present and potential prospects are played out. These ongoing dramas are made sense of under the loose direction of what I am calling culture, a community specific system of common sense which facilitates shared meanings and coordinated actions. It is a system which is interdependently related to human interaction and which includes standards for appropriate and effective human interactions.

Culture, as a system of sense, inherently functions as a constraint on what is socially enacted and understood. My point can be readily demonstrated by citing an old elementary school joke, which I use in certain courses, that relies on the development of a system of answers to questions based on the principle of rhyming. The joke begins with questions which have obvious answers, all of which rhyme. Finally, the last question, "What do you call the white of an egg?" changes this systematic pattern by asking a question to which the correct answer is not a rhyming word. Invariably I get the answer "yolk" because it rhymes with a preceding word. Seconds later the groans start as people start to realize that they have been tricked into giving an answer which they know to be "wrong." After this exercise we discuss how even a simple rhyming system constrained or blinded them from seeing something that otherwise would have been obvious. What is often left unsaid is the equally important realization that it is a much larger and complex system that makes this teaching device possible in the first place. It is this larger cultural system that makes some of the earlier answers so obvious and it makes possible the realization that "yolk" is an incorrect response. After all, "yolk" has a conventional, not a necessary connection to the physical part of an egg which is yellow, not white.

Just as any system of formal linguistic variety such as Portuguese, Thai or English involves arbitrary but conventionally powerful connections, so do the systems of common sense known as culture. When these cultural systems go beyond distinguishing what is sensible and nonsensical to include judgments which attribute value and worth to individuals and their actions, then they may be said to be involved with ethics.

ETHICS AND CULTURE

Nilsen (1966) wrote that ethics is the systematic attempt to answer "questions about the good, right and wrong, and moral obligation" (p. 10). Ethics refers to that which articulates standards by which action may be judged good or bad, right or wrong. Culture, as a sense-making system, necessarily implies ethics. The ethical aspects (standards of right and wrong, good and bad) of any cultural system function as a form of quality control for the community. Those who wish to be members in good standing within a community and receive all the rewards that such full fellowship may imply must present their behaviors in a way which is supported by that community's system of sense. Ethics then, and rightly so, tends to be viewed in terms of systematic constraints on those actions which are acceptable, appropriate and worthy of approbation. Two examples drawn from research within different cultural communities will help to illustrate this point and provide a basis for further discussion.

Basso's (1979) discussion of a form of joking among Western Apache, in which they pretend to be a "whiteman," provides one clear example of how ethical dimensions are interwoven into any cultural tapestry, constraining what can be seen, heard and felt. One of the examples of such joking that Basso (1979) both presents and explains in some detail is the following exchange that occurs at L and K's home after L responds to a knock at the door from J:

J: Hello, my friend! How are you doing? How are you feeling, L? You feeling good?
[J now turns in the direction of K and addresses her.]
J: Look who here, everybody! Look who just come in. Sure, it's my Indian friend, L. Pretty good all right!
[J slaps L on the shoulder and looking him directly in the eyes, seizes his hand and pumps it wildly up and down.]
. . .
J: Sit down! Sit right down! Take your loads off you ass. You hungry? You want some beer? Maybe you want some wine? You want crackers? Bread? You want some sandwich? How 'bout it? You hungry? I don't know. Maybe you get sick. Maybe you don't eat again long time.
[K has stopped washing dishes and is looking on with amusement. L has seated himself and has a look of bemused resignation on his face.]
J: You sure looking good to me, L. You looking pretty fat! Pretty good all right! You got new boots? Where you buy them? Sure pretty good boots! I glad . . .
[At this point, J breaks into laughter. K joins in. L shakes his head and smiles. The joke is over.]
K: indaa? dogoyaada! ('Whitemen are stupid'!) (pp. 46-7).

Let us consider for a moment what turns the above into a humorous exchange. Certainly there is exaggeration in the joking sequence, but more important than that for our purposes is that many of the things which are either nonsensical or wrong and, therefore, seen as legitimately laughable are perfectly sensible and socially correct within the "whiteman" culture being referenced. Take for example the systems of sense surrounding the use of a person's first name. J's frequent use of L's name is inappropriate among the

Western Apache who view one's name as personal property and refrain from "borrowing" that property too often. In contrast the "whiteman" often uses the first name as a sign of interest in and concern for the other person. I have seen advertisements for more than one business which tout the fact that they know their customers by name and promise to use that first name every time you do business there, thus capitalizing on that particular cultural understanding of first name use.

Furthermore, the Western Apache prefer to come and go from social groups unobtrusively, whereas in many communities in the U.S. that would be considered rude. You might ask yourself, if you arrived at a party and the host did not make a point of greeting you and introducing you to those already there, or, when someone left your party and did so without making the rounds to say good-bye, what would you think? There are also the questions about one's health and if the guest would like something to eat or drink. Such questions and comments are frequent, expected and appropriate in many other communities, but not common in Western Apache culture. The list could go on, but the point here is that the joking in this case not only makes use of violations of common sense (good manners) among the Western Apache, it reinforces the guidelines for future behavior if one does not want to come across badly or as a marginal member of a community. These social dos and don'ts are but outcroppings on the deeply felt and deeply patterned cultural landscape of the Western Apache. They reflect and constitute standards which are used to evaluate the worth of actions. These standards constrain what can be seen and understood when one is asked about one's health or repeatedly called by her or his personal name (is this polite and caring or intrusive and stupid?).

Generally, standards and values such as those just noted are not expressed in direct opposition to other cultural communities, but they are often most noticeable in multicultural situations. Fitch's (1990/91) detailed discussion of her experiences at large Colombian social gatherings is illustrative of this point. She noted that when someone attempts to leave such a gathering, the Colombian hosts inevitably performs what she came to call the salsipuede (or leave if you can) ritual. The hosts would ask why the guest would have to go and then upon hearing the reason come up with some way to discount that reason and convince the guest to stay (quite different from the Western Apache). Through ethnographic research she discovered that this practice reflected and honored the importance of interpersonal connections (not the specific relationship, but interpersonal ties in general) among the Colombians. Indeed, after convincing the guest to stay the host may not even directly interact with that person again until they finally manage to leave. Still, for either the host to respond to the guest's announced intention of leaving by saying, "Well thanks for coming. We were so happy to have you and we'll see you later," or for the guest to refuse to stay at least a little bit longer would be very rude and it would have serious social consequences. Fitch (1990/1991) was first made aware of this informal and seemingly spontaneous ritual because it contrasted with her own common sense ways of leave-taking, yet such actions are merely part of the Colombian common sense. The Colombian common sense, like all common senses, is infused with ethical standards for what is important, right or wrong, good or bad.

The leave-taking actions of both the Western Apache and the Colombians in the settings described above form a constraint on what can appropriately be done without invoking a sense of wrong-doing or indicating a rejection of basic cultural values. Such cultural constraints, and the lack of individual freedom they imply, are often the sources of critiques by scholars. For example, Cronen, Chen and Pearce (1988) describe and analyze an episode of talk which occurred around a Chinese family's dinner table (including father, mother, teenage daughter, and her uncle and aunt). The particular episode in question involves a statement by the uncle about youth with which everyone knows the teenager disagrees. At the end of his statement the uncle makes eye contact with the niece. She returns it, smiles slightly and looks away. Her father then responds to the uncle, while she continues to remain silent.

This episode is then contrasted with a hypothetical one involving similar participants in a North American home. In this case it is expected that the teenager would respond to her uncle's challenge directly, thus appearing to be more liberated than her Chinese counterpart. However, Cronen, et al. (1988), go on to explain how the Western teenager is in fact very constrained in her options. They illustrate how the uncle's comment is likely to convey a challenge to the teenager's individuality or personal identity and that she must somehow respond in a way which defends herself and yet shows respect for the adult at the same time. They argue that these conflicting demands put the niece in a bind and constrain rather than free her communicative choices. Cronen et al. (1988) evaluate such a situation negatively because they maintain that the highest goal of communication, that of liberation, is not being met.

Although a cultural system of values may be shown to constrain the choices of individuals if they wish to maintain a positive identity and membership within the community, what is often not seen in cases such as those discussed above is that the individual is also empowered at the same time that he or she is constrained. The North American teenager is allowed to express her feelings out loud, and perhaps work through and make sense of those feelings in an active verbal exchange with adults. The outcomes of this exchange may be either positive or negative, but she is empowered by her culture to engage in the process in ways which are mutually understood and accepted by those around her. The same could be said about the Chinese teenager. She may also be portrayed as being dominated by the adults and put into a position of relative weakness. Yet, as Cronen, et al. (1988) point out, the niece's silence shows respect for her position in the family while not denying her stance on the issue under discussion. Her silence also prevents the uncle from being able to explicitly argue with her and the issue is dropped. It is the cultural system of which she is a participating member that allows for this mutual respect and understanding.

The systems of meaning described by both Basso (1979) and Fitch (1990/91) are systems which enable the members to nurture relationships in productive and meaningful ways, just as much as they are systems of constraint. Edmund Burke (1955) captured this paradoxical relationship in writing about the French revolution when he argued that rights and responsibilities could never be realistically separated. Liberation or empowerment requires not unlimited choices and freedom, but a system of constraints which allows for productive action and interaction. Just as traffic laws not only constrain us, but make relatively safe travel possible, ethical systems must be recognized as essentially both constraining and empowering. Part of being culturally competent is knowing what you can do because of the particular pattern of constraints on meaning that exist within a community. Part of the task for any researcher of culture is to explicitly identify the system that creates those possibilities.

That culture implies ethics and that these ethics serve not only to constrain, but to empower individuals in their social lives serves as an important foundation in dealing with the question of culture and ethics. It changes ethics from some sort of anchor weighing down intercultural interactions, to a series of musical notes which can generate intercultural harmony.

However, important as the realization that culture necessarily implies ethics is, much of the debate surrounding culture and ethics is focused on the question of whether ethics implies culture (or community specific systems of common sense). There are two strongly held opinions on this question. On one hand, there is what is frequently referred to as the universalist position, which answers the question with a resounding, "No!" On the other hand, there is the relativist position which answers this question with an unrelenting, "Yes!" The debate between universalist and relativist stands has marked the discussion of ethics and culture since at least Plato's time (Fleischacker, 1994), and has probably been part of such discussions for as long as they have existed. Extreme formulations of each of these positions have been used by those opposed to them as strawmen to demonstrate the correctness of their own approach. Because of the historic impact of these positions, it is worth taking some time to review the stands of each and some of their implications. I have no expectations that my discussion will resolve the long standing controversy, but hopefully it will help to clarify some of the implications of each position and establish a common ground for productive discussion.

The universalist position maintains that ethics go beyond the cultural limitations of any one cultural system and thus do not necessarily imply culture. In its most extreme form the universalist position maintains that there is a single set of values and standards of action which is applicable to all cultures, and that there are universally correct and incorrect ways for these values to be enacted. The value of respect for others is a case in point.

Brislin, Cushner, Cherrie and Yong (1986) report an incident in which a Japanese student, Mariko, living in the United States, is volunteered for a task by a fellow student from the United States. These students had become friends as the semester progressed and when the professor asked for two volunteers the American raised her hand and also suggested that Mariko could be the other one. Mariko knew that the timing was bad and that she would not be able to do it, however, she did not want to be disrespectful to the professor by telling him "no" directly and in front of the whole class. So, she indicated the potential problem by responding in a hesitant fashion and noting that she might not be skilled enough for the task. The American student immediately reassured the professor that Mariko was perfectly capable and indicated they would do it. When the professor looked to Mariko for confirmation she seemed to agree. Mariko did not show up for the appointment. Frustrated, the American queried Mariko and found out that she had known about other commitments when the volunteering was done. The American student was very upset about the lack of respect shown by Mariko by not being more "straightforward" in her earlier replies.

The problem with the extreme universal position is that Mariko's behavior could be perceived to be both disrespectful and respectful. Yet if there is truly only one right way of doing things, this cannot be the case. For the American student, volunteering Mariko to help out and then to back her up when she expressed doubts was a sign of respect, whereas Mariko's lack of straightforwardness about a timing conflict was a sign of disrespect. For Mariko, respect was shown to the professor by avoiding a direct refusal to a request, especially in public. It is somewhat like the different leave-taking styles of the Western Apache and Colombians noted earlier, one unobtrusive and the other extended and elaborate. Both may be said to be showing proper respect to the guest. Given the different operating cultural systems, two very different sets of behaviors may rightly be seen as both displaying respect and being disrespectful.

Furthermore, being completely straightforward and honest is not always a sign of respect in American society. If one has a co-worker who has had a very discouraging week and in an effort to lift his or her spirits gets a new haircut, it would generally not be seen as a sign of respect to blatantly tell him or her that the haircut really does not look good, even though one may sincerely believe that it doesn't. Those favoring a relativist position would use situations such as these to show how mistaken it is to assume that there is somehow only one correct way to respond. Assuming that universally there is only one right way to do things is the cornerstone of ethnocentrism and a key element in many devastating conflicts.

The polar opposite to such a universalist stance is complete cultural relativism. I use the term cultural relativism here to emphasize that I am dealing with a community rather than an individual system of ethical relativism. I do this in part because the focus of the book you are reading is on cultural rather than individual issues, and also because even those who have written in favor of relativism admit that the existence of a completely individual ethic system must by definition destroy human *society* (Hauerwas, 1983; Kale, 1991). There must be some shared understanding of what is right and wrong for a community to exist. Indeed, Bilmes (1986) maintains that the essence of morality or ethics is that it necessarily goes beyond the self. The strong relativistic (culturally based) position, then, is simply that each cultural group has its own value system and can only be judged and evaluated by an insider. In support of the relativist position and in opposition to a universalist perspective, Howell (1982) maintained that, "The concept of universal ethics, standards of goodness that apply to everyone, everywhere, and at all times, is the sort of myth people struggle to hold onto" (p. 187). One extreme conclusion of this stand would be that there is no cross-cultural or universal basis that can be used to evaluate a community.

There are two common responses to this cultural relativism. One is that by its very definition a completely relativistic stance is impossible. The reasoning behind this claim can be seen in Howell's (1982) use of the word "myth" in regards to those who do not share his relativistic view of the world. The use of the word implies a belief that any community that disagrees with his stance is wrong. Such a reaction indicates a belief in a universal social reality that goes beyond specific cultures, thus implying an objective base from which the intelligence and insight of one community may be compared to another. Thus, Howell's (1982) use of the term myth is condescending toward other cultures. Carbaugh (1988) noted a cultural dilemma of a similar nature in his work on cultural norms revealed in the popular *Donahue* talk show. An explicit social rule for the communication on that show was that, regardless of how controversial, any *personal* opinion was acceptable. Donahue would defend this right for any and all. However, at the same time there was another informal rule that one could not acceptably hold an opinion that implied that others should also hold it. Thus, my opinion could only be valid so long as I did not assume it should hold for others. Such an exception, of course, allows for the rejection of many personal opinions and implicitly demands conformity in the way opinions could rightfully be expressed. In a similar manner, universalists would argue that absolute relativism is caught in a vicious cycle which continually denies its own basis for existence.

A second common response is to point out the social dangers of a relativist position. For example, Swidler (1986) shows how a relativistic philosophy lies behind the "culture of poverty" debate, subtly keeping people in positions of low economic and political power. After all, the argument goes, they don't want better, right? Others point to such communities as the German Nazi or certain white communities in South Africa, both of which developed cultural beliefs that supported persecution and discrimination in such extreme forms that the world in general has agreed in its condemnation of their actions. If I were truly and completely relativistic in my outlook, I would have to agree that these communities and their beliefs were just as valid as any other cultural community's beliefs. Such a stand is as potentially dangerous and untenable as the strong universalist stance noted above. Herskovits (1972), a strong advocate of relativism, rejects the notion that cultural relativism is a doctrine of ethical indifference and that all things should be tolerated. However, he does not go into detail on what criteria he would use in deciding what to tolerate and what to change. Even if one refuses to discuss or think about what this basis is, there is some standard being used when the Nazi or some other cultural community is evaluated either negatively or positively by people outside of that specific community.

In recent years more and more writers who maintain a "relativistic" outlook also identify some value or ideal upon which communities may be judged. For example, Cronen, et al. (1988) note that all cultures are incommensurable, yet they advocate cultural critiques based on the notion that all communication should be liberating. Kale (1991) and Hatch (1983) both argue for a relativistic perspective that is grounded in the universal need to respect the worth and dignity of humans. Steiner's (1997) work in this text "rejects ethical schemas that could or would justify acts that increase the oppression of women" (p. 2). I suspect that one would not have to look long to find cultures whose ethical systems could be argued to oppress women.

Whatever the basis for the lack of indifference or tolerance, these "relativistic" approaches are no longer only community specific. From a universalist's perspective, a relativistic stance simply allows people to blame others for having biases while subtly nurturing some of their own. Certainly both relativism and universalism may become tools to be used in condemning other human beings.

Based on this brief review of relativistic and universalistic philosophies, three points seem worth noting. First, behaviors do not have inherent meanings, but rather particular meanings are dependent upon specific systems of shared sense-making. Thus, the meaning and/or correctness of a behavior cannot be known or judged without understanding the culture from which it stems. It is important that behavior should not be confused with action. By behavior I refer to the sheer motion and physical movements engaged in by humans, whereas action is behavior that has been infused with meaning (see Burke, 1969). A single behavior may in fact constitute multiple actions. Thus, Mariko's nod of agreement to the professor may be respectful or disrespectful depending upon which cultural system one is applying.

Second, there are values which are appropriate in determining the worth of actions across cultures. These values, however, have an open texture to them and are not necessarily connected to particular behaviors. Again, the distinction between action and behavior is crucial here. Meaning cannot be separated from culture. Therefore, we can only determine the worth of actions, not behaviors.

Finally, universalism and relativism are not dichotomous. Indeed, ethics may be viewed as a compound of universalism and relativism. All ethical systems involve a tension between what is universal and what is relative. It is this tension which both enables and constrains creativity and stability in human societies. The challenge, then, is to understand the nature of this compound and its implications in intercultural settings.

One of the dangers of viewing the debate between relativism and universalism in terms of a dichotomy is that it encourages a type of simplification which distorts our understanding of culture and leads to misunderstanding and unnecessary conflict. Whether one takes a completely universalistic or relativistic stance, the need for a detailed dialogue and discovery process is often covered up. Edward Hall (1983) warns of the dangers in missing the subtleties within other cultures. Too often discussions surrounding ethics and culture do just that. For example, a colleague from India recently told me about a loan officer who had asked him what it (the loan) was worth to him, when he was applying for his loan to come to study in the United States. This was after months of frustrating and unsuccessful efforts to obtain the loan. In discussing this situation he noted that, although he was very well qualified for the loan, it was common practice to give the loan officer some funds on the side in order to obtain the needed money. Thus, the clear implication of the officer's statement to him was, "You'll get the loan if you're willing to pay me enough on the side."

Let us consider this situation from both a universalistic and relativistic stand point. From a universalistic viewpoint one might immediately assume that the loan officer's comment reflects a corrupt practice. As such, it should be exposed, condemned and corrected. A somewhat more laissez-faire approach might be to nod and note how interesting such a practice is, but silently maintain that no matter what one says, it is simply still a bribe and, like the proverbial rose, smells just the same, regardless of what you call it. In either case, further discussion and discovery is preempted by the fact that one already claims to *know* what act such a behavior constitutes.

From a relativistic position I would respond by quickly and fully accepting as fact that giving money to the loan officer in order to get the loan is perfectly all right because it is a common and accepted practice in India. Even if I recognize the importance of the humanistic principle as does Hatch (1983), I may easily argue that such a practice does not physically damage another human, so it is just as valid as any other practice. I may then go to my intercultural class and teach them that in India it is okay and perfectly normal to pay a loan officer money on the side in order to get a loan. By doing so I may even create the impression that it is seen as unethical if I don't give the official some money on the side. This may appear to be a more culturally sensitive response, but it also oversimplifies the situation and still discourages discovery and discussion by positioning any attempt to explore the worth of such an action as ethnocentric.

In the example noted above my colleague did not pay the loan officer anything. Even though he knew that such a practice was appropriate in one sense, it still seemed unethical to him and he did not want to get his loan that way. In an e-mail correspondence with another person from India the idea that, although a "bribe" may be a common and accepted practice, it is still unethical, was also supported. My colleague eventually got his loan after his mother talked to an uncle who was a high ranking bank officer. My colleague did not know that this discussion had occurred until some time later, because his mother knew that he had wanted to resolve this matter strictly on his own. Certainly, his concern for using connections would have been shared by one of my undergraduate students this past semester who became quite upset at the Colombian leave-taking article by Fitch (1990/91) which I discussed previously. This student was very concerned that Fitch (1990/1991) had discussed the importance placed on interpersonal connections in too neutral a way. She maintained that this emphasis on connections is what had led to all the corruption in Colombia and that the article's focus on understanding rather than correction was a travesty. My student's stance implied that it was a clear-cut case and that no further discussion was necessary. Yet, it is interesting to note, for example, that the Colombian president has experienced much grief in his public life from other Colombians because of the nature of such connections. We are forced to conclude that to assume that interpersonal connections, or individual rights or some other valued aspect of a culture functions without a system of constraints in relation to other culturally valued aspects is to miss important cultural subtleties.

Both the relativist and universalist could, of course, use this information to claim, "See, I'm right," but both would miss my point. Regardless of whether one's stance is universal or relativistic, viewing these approaches as a dichotomy encourages one to ignore the subtleties of other cultures and limits discussion and understanding. On one hand, you and I may gain an often unconscious smugness from the feeling that we and our group are the only ones that really understand what is going on, thereby eliminating any need for discussion. On the other hand, one may patronize that culture, automatically treating any discussions related to the relative worth of actions as threatening and, therefore, strive to avoid them.

As easy as it is to slip into a simplistic way of thinking about the ethical systems within cultures, it is perhaps even easier to forget the extent to which we personally are part of the discussion. During a graduate seminar one of my international students became quite incensed at the presentation of another student. The presenting student had done an analysis of an educational entertainment program designed to help encourage family planning and combat HIV and the AIDS epidemic occurring in Tanzania. The presenter had raised some concerns about the effect of some of the content of the program on Tanzanian culture. The program encourages a "modern" versus "traditional" approach, which involves some common Western practices such as encouraging women to not remain at home with the children all day, but to go out and develop financial independence (see Swalehe, Rogers, Gilboard, Alford, & Montoya, 1995). In addition, she also presented some evidence that Tanzanians actually perceived the spread of the AIDS virus to be less pressing than a variety of other social concerns and suggested that some of these "pressing" problems need to be dealt with first. The graduate student, who is part of a research team involved with the entertainment education project, just could not believe that anyone could be critical in any way of what was being done through the use of the program. "We are saving lives here," was her response. She stressed that regardless of how the native people saw it, AIDS prevention was the most important issue facing that country today and that it was time people recognized just how important it is.

My point in considering this instance is not to determine the relative importance of AIDS prevention, the worth of women with young children working outside the home, or even the worth of entertainment education. Indeed, this particular project has included many efforts to make its pro-social messages and presentation resonate with Tanzanian culture. Instead, I want to focus for a moment on the graduate student's reaction. I believe that the strength of her reaction was due to a perceived threat to her identity. She is an international student with an intercultural focus, engaged in helping with an intercultural project. To suggest that this project, in which she is involved and which she supports, may in some way not be one hundred percent culturally pure and sensitive threatens her self image. In this case, the student strongly identifies with the goals of the project, thus encouraging a more explicit and emotional response. However, even when there is no specific project identification involved, I believe that one of the complicating factors that emerges in any discussion of cultures and ethics is that people's identities are intertwined with the outcome of these discussions.

At the end of 1995 I conducted an all-day workshop on organizational communication and diversity. The workshop was just one in a series in which roughly twenty-five community leaders from education, business and government were participating. These workshops were done with an eye toward developing personal leadership skills and building interpersonal and interorganizational connections. The county in which these leaders reside is marked by a high degree of cultural diversity and cultural tension. The leaders themselves represented a variety of community backgrounds including Native American, African American, Hispanic, Chicana and Anglo. In addition, there was a fairly even mix of males and females involved. As the discussion progressed, one of the Anglo males commented that he felt that the notion of multiculturalism was really just a power play to try to cover up inadequacies and gain undeserved influence. He felt that it resulted in division and decreased productivity in an organization. At the time I was inwardly amazed by the blatant ethnocentrism and ignorance of his remarks. They proved to be a trigger for a long, thoughtful and, based on later feedback, valuable discussion often marked by tension and personal experiences.

I believe that this person's comment negatively distorted the situation, but not because the concept of "culture" could not be used as part of a power play, because it can be. Notice that I am talking about the "concept" of culture here. Culture, as it was defined earlier as a system of common sense, is what allows his comment to be meaningful and, for some, to be a description of the way it is. The term "culture," as he used it, referred not to the common-sense cultures of which many different ones were represented in the discussion, but to a group membership. Tajfel and Turner (1986) explain how one's self image is made up of not only personal aspects, but social identifications as well. Threats to these social identifications often result in defensive action. The workshop participant viewed the idea of cultural communities as competitive. Although I personally enjoy and value athletics and other forms of competition, "cultures," as I have defined them, are not in competition with one another. The workshop participant's focus on group membership rather than "culture" effectively blinded him from understanding the culture of the other. Thus, discussions of ethics are complicated because they have implications for both our personal and social identities and desires.

One may say in a discussion of ethics, "Let's be rational here and logically think through all the implications involved in the issue," but, due to the implications of such discussions for identity, all of them are inherently emotional. Even a statement such as the one in the previous sentence demanding only logic reflects an emotional attachment and commitment to a proper way of interacting. I have seen people become quite emotional in their insistence to keep emotion out of a decision. When we deal with ethics, the evaluations of what is right and wrong, good and bad, and worthwhile, we are dealing with concepts which have implications for who we are and how we see ourselves and others. Even the vigor with which the universalistic and relativistic perspectives are argued may in part be accounted for because the answers have implications for the images people have of themselves. Emotion and identity, as a result, are always going to be part of such discussions, and any effort to eliminate them from our discussions will be futile.

In summary, the relationship between culture and ethics is problematic for three major reasons. First, the very notion of culture, as described above, implies the existence of an ethical system. Cultural systems tend to be viewed only in terms of what they constrain ("a problem"), however, they also function to enable action. Indeed, shared meaning and coordinated action is impossible without such a system. John Lennon sang a song in which he asked his listeners to imagine a world with no right or wrong. Such a world is a mirage. It may appear nice from a distance, but inherently lacks the substance necessary for community life. Debates on ethics and culture which ignore this necessary tension between control and empowerment within ethical systems will never progress much beyond name calling. Second, relativism and universalism are not separate stances that can exist in isolation from each other, rather they are a compound that brings life to an ethical system. Like the tree limb which can bend in the wind, together they are both flexible and strong, in isolation they are both rigid and weak. Understanding the nature of this compound and its implications for meetings between those of different cultures is clouded by efforts to eliminate either perspective from the scene. Third, issues of ethics and culture are inherently tied up with issues of identity which affect us personally and, therefore, cannot be understood or dealt with unemotionally.

COMMUNICATION, CULTURE, AND ETHICS

As noted earlier, this book is about more than culture and ethics. It is about communication and how the study of communication can help us understand and deal with issues related to culture and ethics. As I consider what the study of communication may bring to such issues, I am reminded of Plato's *Gorgias* (1967, translated by Lamb), in which Socrates questions the worth of rhetoric and its place in society. He argues that, while such things as law, medicine, painting, mathematics and so forth have substance, rhetoric has no substance, but is merely the means to create an illusion of substance. A similar complaint could be made in regards to the role of communication and communication scholars in dealing with the issues of ethics and culture. One may argue that the study of these issues seems to "belong" to philosophers, anthropologists, psychologists, sociologists, and others. My response to such challenges, whether it be in our present time or in Socrates's day is that the question itself reveals a common, but deep misunderstanding of rhetoric and/or communication. It assumes that communication has no real substance. It envisions communication as a neutral container through which meaning is transferred from one person to another. Communication is viewed as a mere vehicle of thought and intention.

Although I recognize that communication has great flexibility and may be a force for good or bad, it is much more powerful and influential than the simple container metaphor suggests. Perhaps because communication is so pervasive in our lives (it is a part of every interaction) it is easy to miss just how influential it is. Instead of viewing communication as a simple container of which we all happen to make use, it may better be seen as fibers through which the fabric of our lives is formed and woven together in recognizable patterns.

To get a better understanding of how communication relates to the issues of culture and ethics, I will discuss some of the characteristics of communication and their implications for our current concerns. In the foreword to this book, Casmir (1997a) defines communication "as that which takes place, symbolically, between human beings as they do things together" (p. 2). Although, as with culture, there are many definitions which could be used, the one by Casmir is both detailed and broad enough to provide a good base from which the importance of communication for these issues can be understood.

As Casmir's (1997a) definition highlights, communication is fundamentally symbolic in nature. The term symbol is derived from the Greek terms *bolos* or "to throw" and *sym* or "with or together" (Simpson & Weiner, 1989). That which is symbolic, then, may be understood as that which has been simply thrown together. Two things are connected in such a way that one thing is brought to mind by the existence of the other thing. This connection, however, is not a necessary one. It is arbitrary. When I use the symbol "chair" it brings certain physical entities to mind, but that symbol does not *have* to bring that to mind. For many individuals "silla" would serve that function and "chair" would not bring any particular thing to mind. It is fairly easy for us to see that such differences in symbol-use across communities may prove to be a challenge, but one may be tempted to argue that the path to understanding is fairly clear-cut since we are dealing with the same physical object. However, symbols do not simply refer to physical, tangible objects. Frequently they allow us to connect and understand a world for which there is no physical referent point. Take for example the Japanese symbol "Amae." There is no single English symbol equivalent to the emotion suggested by that term (see Doi, 1973). On the other hand, there is no equivalent symbol in the Japanese language for the English term "privacy" (Baker & Gudykunst, 1990). The concepts understood by the use of such symbols may be very sensible to members of one speech community, but quite nonsensical to another. The articulations of ethical systems are replete with terms which refer to that which is intangible, thus forming a fertile field for misunderstanding and frustration.

Given the arbitrary nature of symbols, one may begin to feel like Humpty-Dumpty in Louis Carroll's (1934) *Through the Looking Glass*, who felt that it was all right to use symbols whatever personal way his whims dictated. However, as Casmir's (1997a) definition suggests, these symbols are inherently connected to humans doing things together. The formation and maintenance of communities requires that symbols go beyond personal whims and are shared across individuals. This general agreement establishes powerful conventions. Because they are arbitrary, these conventions may change over time, such as with the symbols "pot," "gay" and "myth." However, the conventional force is powerful enough that if one violates the connections suggested by it long and often enough, one becomes ostracized from that community and may even be locked away from those more willing and able to follow convention.

Returning to Casmir's (1997a) definition, communication is what takes place as humans are doing things together. By implication, together refers to something shared versus something in isolation and that which takes place may be viewed as action, or in other words meaningful behavior. When humans communicate they make promises, complain, develop friendships, persuade others and engage in many other actions, all of which imply the creation of a certain set of meanings. For if there is no meaning created, there cannot be said to have been communication or vice-versa. We established earlier in the chapter that any meaning we derive from behaviors is filtered through a system of sense which is negotiated and shared across individuals. We called this culture. This does not mean that communication cannot take place when there is no shared culture. Indeed, meaning may be generated in intercultural encounters just as easily as in intracultural encounters, but the amount of shared meaning may vary dramatically.

Therefore, when we talk about communication we are talking about action (see Austin, 1962). It is a type of action which does not involve a single or necessary connection between the behavior and its attached meaning, making creative change possible. However, this change is not easy because, although the connections are arbitrary, they are accompanied by a powerful communal pressure. If one wants to relate to others and maintain membership within a particular community, one must know and use these arbitrary connections in ways similar to others around them. Without an understanding of both the arbitrary and conventional nature of the symbols which form our communication with one another, one may easily view the system of symbols with which we deal too lightly or as too fixed. Understanding the nature of communication, then, becomes a vital part of understanding any human action or interaction.

A key question for our present purposes centers around the relationship of communication to culture in general and to ethics in particular. This relationship can begin to be understood by considering a typical approach in the social sciences. One common way of understanding the ethical aspects of culture is to focus on the norms (social rules) and values (social ideals) of a community. When issues related to culture and ethics become a concern it is usually because of a perceived difference between the cultural norms and values of the communities or individuals involved. Therefore, the question may be reworded as, "What is the relationship between norms/values and communication (action)?"

One view of this relationship is that it is essentially causal in nature. If a particular community feels strongly about a particular norm or value, then it is expected that members of that community will act or communicate in ways which adhere to these values and norms. Thus, as one learns the important and agreed upon values and norms of a community, one can explain, predict and manage interaction across cultures. A concern with such a perspective is suggested by considering such value research as conducted by Sitaram and Cogdell (1976). Their research indicates that efficiency is a primary "Western" value, whereas hospitality is only a tertiary one. Thus, one would expect that when issues of efficiency and hospitality conflict in the "West," that efficiency would always win out. Without taking the time and space to elaborate, I trust that my readers can fairly easily think of examples where "Westerners" don't act in the most efficient manner for the sake of hospitality.

A similar problem in understanding was revealed in one of my student's surprise at discovering that some Japanese students she had been visiting with had some goals that were very personal in nature, after all "they're collectivist, aren't they?" As scholars interested in social relations we may recognize the problems of such simplified thinking, but too often our own research and theorizing treat norms and values as if they were clear cut causes of certain behaviors and choices (see Bilmes, 1986, for a fuller discussion of this point).

Bilmes (1976) presents an ethnographic report of a Thai village which elaborates the type of concern noted above and which bears on our understanding of this relationship between norms/values and communication.[1] His study reports on the group decision-making process in a Thai village. The village was working on a large communal building and was trying to raise community funds to finish the structure. In the beginning, village members had agreed to all give a certain amount of money. Due to a variety of circumstances, including the fact that not everyone had given the amount requested, the building was not completed and more funds were needed. The headman of the village made a public plea for people to give even more than originally proposed so that the building could continue. His brother opposed this plea by pointing out that those who had paid already should not be asked to pay more until those who had not paid their fair share had done so. The headman responded by noting that the others could not be forced to pay and that each person had freedom of choice in this matter. The discussion continued. On one side were admonitions grounded in the value of equity and norms for following agreed upon rules, and on the other were norms allowing for freedom of choice and the value of generosity. Later a similar event occurred between the village Abbot and the ex-headman. The Abbot was offended by some of the ex-headman's questions regarding money and a debate between the value of accountability and trust ensued.

---

[1] The implications of Bilmes' (1976) work for the connection between norms/values and communication was first suggested to me in a conversation with Gerry Philipsen.

According to Bilmes (1976), each of the values and norms referenced, freedom, equity, trust, accountability and so forth, were widely accepted and strongly advocated by the members of the community. However, these values and norms were being presented in opposition to each other. The discussions among village members both in and out of the meetings constituted a negotiation over which norms and values were appropriate in these particular circumstances. Bilmes (1976) argues, and I concur, that, although specific details may differ, community accepted norms and values may be brought into opposition with each other. For example, I grew up hearing that, "he who hesitates is lost," and that one should "look before you leap." Potentially these statements would allow me to be praised or blamed regardless of my behavior. Perhaps one of the most classic examples of norms and values being used in opposition to each other is in political debates. I remember being surprised by a course activity presented by Haig Bosmajian in which the norms and values of two United States presidential candidates were compared in isolation from their specific source. One could not tell from the list from which party they came. During the debate many of the norms had been positioned in opposition to each other, yet each candidate used important values and norms of American society (often the same ones, just at different times) to show why they were praiseworthy and their opponent was blameworthy.

One potential conclusion that could be drawn from this example is that I am arguing for a situational ethic. I am not. Although understanding a particular situation is crucial to understanding action (keeping in mind our behavior/action distinction), and is, therefore, part of ethical judgments, a "situational ethic" is problematic. A situational ethic creates an image of sensitivity and tolerance, but at its very core it is destructive to community and morality as these exist in any culture. An ethical system that is grounded in an "it all depends" attitude, quickly degenerates into ethics of personal desires, which, as noted earlier, destroys the very basis of community. Discussing the general idea of morality and ethics, Durkheim (1965) maintained that, "Everything which forces man to take account of other men is moral, everything which forces him to regulate his conduct through something other than the striving of his ego is moral" (p. 365). Situational ethics do not necessitate such a consideration, and, therefore, are inherently flawed as a basis for moral decisions. As vitally important as situational understanding is in productively applying ethical systems, the ethical system itself must have the power to override individual circumstances and desires if it is to provide a solid foundation for community.

If the fact that norms and values can be positioned in opposition to each other does not lead us to advocating a situational ethic, what does it suggest? In short, it leads to a fuller understanding of the relationship between values/norms and communication. Values and norms cease to be viewed simply as independent variables causing particular patterns of communication. Davies and Harré (1990) argue that, "The possibility of choice in a situation in which there are contradictory requirements provides people with the possibility of acting agentically" (p. 59). The positioning of norms/values in tension with each other creates the contradictory requirements mentioned by Davies and Harré (1990). Tensions, oppositions and quandaries are part of all cultures. No culture is so simplistic that it can avoid such challenges. These tensions, which occur naturally because of the very nature of communication and community, provide a foundation of choice and accountability. Humans are not simply cultural robots. If this were not the case, any discussion of how to deal with or handle cultural conflicts would be pointless.

Katriel (1986) describes the dilemma faced by an Israeli (Sabra) war hero, Ben-Yehuda. On one hand, there is a strong norm in the Sabra community for toughness and not admitting any weakness by questioning the value of war time actions. On the other hand, there is a strong norm and value placed on speaking *dugri*, or speaking-up about what one feels in blunt, straightforward ways, regardless of whom it bothers. Although she was a war hero and seen as the epitome of the toughness norm, she had many questions about the war and the way it was handled. Culturally she was faced with contradictory requirements. Katriel (1986) uses this case-study as an illustration of the power and nature of dugri talk in the Sabra community, but it also illustrates inevitable tensions which arise in all cultures, but which are often ignored if we deal in too shallow a manner with the relationship between cultural values and norms.

Values/norms are recognized as resources for communication, for making sense, for creating community and for establishing one's personal and social identity. This relationship can be further understood by considering in more detail the metaphor in which our lives are viewed as a piece of tapestry in the making. When tapestry is woven on a loom it is done through the use of two types of fiber. One is called the warp and the other is termed the weft. The warp fiber is attached to the loom and then the weft fiber is put on a shuttle and interwoven in and around the warp. Although it is typically the weft fiber that is seen and is what creates the design of the fabric, the warp fiber provides a base or resource without which the weft fiber would quickly unravel and fall a tangled mess upon the floor. Communication may be said to be the weft fiber of our lives, whereas norms/values are the warp fiber. Both types of fibers are necessary to create a beautiful and sturdy cloth. Without the warp, the weft would lie in confusion on the floor, yet it is the weft fiber that forms the patterns (relationships) of our lives and makes the warp meaningful in terms of its use. The warp fiber does not always have to be of the same type and texture, yet such differences must be attended to in the weaving of the weft. When adjustments are made in the weft due to the differences in the warp, beautiful cloth can be produced, such as ribbed material. Like all metaphors, this one can be stretched to the point of distortion. Hopefully, however, it helps the reader to grasp the vital, interdependent nature of the relationship between communication and norms/values.

Understanding the relationship between values/norms and communication as one that is essentially sense-making in nature rather than causal, is valuable because of the perspective it provides when approaching ethical clashes across cultures. For example, consider the controversy over the decreed death sentence on Salman Rushdie by the Ayatollah Khomeini in 1989. On one hand, there was shock and general condemnation of this lack of respect for freedom of speech, while on the other there were some who attempted a culturally sensitive reaction, declaring that we could not impose our standards on others and that under Islamic law the death sentence could be justified. Fleischacker (1994) was referring to these two reactions when he noted that:

> Neither of these attitudes takes Islam [and its cultural system of ethics] to be a conception of the good. The first rejects it in favor of what is supposed to be a higher standard of behavior; the second, by refusing to apply any standard to Muslim behavior except internal ones, reduces it to a pointless code, void of interest or meaning to those not already immersed in it. Neither attitude, moreover, requires a deep enough engagement with Islam to determine whether Khomeini's interpretation of it has to be accepted as correct (p. 153).

Fleischacker (1994) goes on to explain that there were other possible interpretations of Islamic law which, while not changing the offensiveness of the book, could have avoided the death sentence. He further wonders what would have happened if Western countries had tried to send a delegation of Islamic scholars to try to negotiate the interpretation of this event and the death sentence. I am not trying to say that such an effort would have proven successful in terms of having the death penalty revoked. The difficulty of this situation was not simply a cultural misunderstanding, but involved intergroup dynamics and concerns over identity. These group dynamics and social identity concerns so linked to ethical issues will be considered in a later section, but for the moment I want to focus on the idea behind Fleischacker's (1994) suggestion of negotiation itself, not on the potential outcomes of this specific case.

As noted earlier, too often only the constraints are seen in ethical systems. Such a focus, regardless of one's universal or relativist leanings, discourages dialogue and blinds one to the subtleties of the other culture. Recognizing that norms and values are resources for communication, opens up an awareness of cultural subtleties and allows each system to be treated as a good. Obviously one could approach such a situation from a very closed perspective, "I am right and let me just know enough about you to prove how you are wrong." Such a distortion of the type of dialogue being encouraged here obviously misses the point. Instead, for this type of negotiation to work, one must approach the situation from a perspective which says, "I want to take my good, understand *your* good, and see what good can be built together." Such a move would fit with Casmir's (1997b) third culture building admonition and requires an understanding of the nature of communication and the appropriate forms it takes in particular communities.

For example, Griefat and Katriel (1989) discuss two different recognizable ways of speaking in Israel. One is *dugri* which is spoken by the Israeli Sabra, and the other is *musayara*, which is spoken by many Arabs. Dugri is very straightforward, blunt, simple, and spontaneous, whereas musayara is more indirect, elaborate and planned. When speaking musayara one is going along with the other in the conversation and explicitly showing a high degree of respect for that other person, however, the ability to speak musayara well also reflects well on the speaker. Dugri, on the other hand, is based on a need for the speaker to be true to his or her feelings and thus shows explicitly a greater concern for one's self. However, to speak dugri to another is also to honor them with the assumption that the person can handle it because of a bond deeper than outward appearances. Griefat and Katriel's (1989) work shows how even when Arabs and Sabras begin an interaction with good intent, the very nature and form of the communication may lead to difficulties and frustrated feelings. Particular forms of communication are woven into our conceptions of what is "good." To understand the nature of ethics and to deal with the difficulties that arise when ethical systems are positioned in opposition to each other without understanding the impact and role of communication is like trying to row straight while only using the oar on one side of a boat.

I will draw on a personal experience to illustrate how communication is interwoven with what is good, both in reflective and constitutive ways. When I was very young we moved to a place that was within walking distance of my mother's parents' home. Around the age of 7 or 8 I started helping out around my grandparents' place (probably at the urging of my mother) by mowing, weeding, etc. After one of these early experiences my grandmother gave me some money for my help. Quite excited about this turn of events, I told my mother, who was not as excited as I. "Didn't you tell her no?" she asked. My uncomfortable silence was answer enough. She then tried to explain to me about fixed income and helping out just because we were family, and that I should not be taking my grandparents' money for helping. So, after helping out the next time I told my grandmother, "No thanks, I was just happy to help out." My grandmother insisted on paying me. Finally, after going back and forth a bit she stuffed the money into my pocket and told me to get an ice-cream or something. Worried that my mother would find out (she always seemed to), I explained to her what had happened. Instead of being upset, she explained that as long as I had tried not to take the money that was what counted, because we didn't want Grandma to feel bad. I quickly learned that if I communicated in the right way, said no at first and presented altruistic motives, it was okay to get money (which I wanted), but that if I did not communicate appropriately, the same motion of receiving money was not acceptable. Done in a culturally appropriate manner, my communication both reflected and constituted a good.

One may complain that the "good" in this case could be faked and that I could have manipulated the situation through my use of communication. I would not argue that this is a possibility and that perhaps initially it was somewhat the case in my situation. However, as time went on I found that it *felt* right to help without getting any money, and I managed to do some jobs without my grandma giving me money. At times she would still track me down and I would get some cash recompense, but I would only reluctantly accept it because I *felt* that would help her to feel good. This development of the right "feelings" was an important part of my cultural education. It was part of the development of my cultural competence as well as my communication competence as I learned when to say no. However, cultural competence should not be treated as totally separate from communication competence, because communication competence serves as both a mirror and a lamp for cultural competence.

SOME CONCLUSIONS

This chapter is intended to be heuristic in nature and has not attempted to provide specific guidelines that will solve all of the ethical crises that can occur when members of different cultures come in contact with one another. It has, however, argued that a key element in understanding and dealing with these situations lies in our understanding of communication and its relationship to the norms and values which make up any ethical system. This relationship is one of resource, not cause. Humans are not some form of cultural robot. Norms and values are resources for our communication and the patterns of relationships we develop through our communication. These norms/values may be positioned in opposition to each other. This tension allows us, as humans, agency and it provides a basis for accountability both within and across cultures. Communication allows for both continuity and creativity in dealing with conflicts that arise out of diverse common senses. However, we must avoid focusing only on the constraints of communication, community or culture. It is through our communication choices that we form, maintain and transform our identities (see Weider & Pratt, 1990). Thus, attempts to deal with ethical based conflicts without understanding communication is like trying to hit the swinging pinata while blindfolded. Occasionally we make a hit, but it is hard to know why one swing was better than another, and there is an alarming lack of consistency.

In discussing the incident involving Salman Rushdie, I noted that even if the type of communication or dialogue suggested by Fleischacker (1994), one that treated each culture as good, had been attempted and proven successful in that a common sense was woven from these two cultures which allowed Rushdie to avoid the death sentence, the death sentence may still have been maintained by Khomeini. This was not the case because of anything peculiar to Khomeini, but because of issues related to intergroup dynamics, self interests and identity. Through dialogue a cultural misunderstanding may be resolved in the sense that each side can see and appreciate the reasonableness of the other's common sense and a reasonable way to deal with the potential conflict, but that does not guarantee that people will act on this understanding. Tajfel and Turner (1986) explain how the sheer division into groups and the subsequent social identities that become salient because of that division influence our actions. Khomeini may at one level have been able to see the reasonableness of other options, but, because of a perceived threat to his group and his own personal and social identity, he may not have changed his decree. Thus, ethical conflicts across cultures cannot be reduced to simple conflicts between two different common senses that are devoid of emotion. Such conflicts and the discussions which follow them are complicated by the consequences they have for personal and social identity.

Given the emotional aspect involved in dealing with communication, culture and ethics, I believe it is essential to recognize the importance of one particular "emotion" in all of this, *love*. In some ways I hesitate to bring this issue up, but part of that is due to the academic cultural constraints I feel in writing this chapter. I do not choose to succumb to that constraint and as a result I will end by commenting on what I *feel* is an essential part of dealing with the ethical quandaries that arise from intercultural communication. The details and nuances associated with the concept of love tend to be varied within a given culture, let alone across cultures. However, the form of love that I emphasize here is that which is defined by Peck (1978) as the "will to extend one's self for the purpose of nurturing . . . another's spiritual growth" (p. 81). I use this definition because it is active in nature and implies a type of emotion and communicative action that can be chosen regardless of what others may be choosing. Some may be concerned about the use of terms like "spiritual" and "growth," and the potential cultural baggage that goes along with them. Mistakes may be made as one tries to promote this ideal, but if people accept the definition fully, they will openly acknowledge these mistakes without retreating to the strategies of hate, avoidance and name calling. Love is no guarantee that there won't be problems, only a guarantee that open efforts to deal positively with these problems won't cease. Without this form of love, the best we can hope for is a manipulative form of negotiation in which our only concern for the other is grounded in how it might better serve us. However, when the form of love suggested here exists, many of the perceived threats to and concerns over identity tend to fade away. A person or group who has this love, or feels that "others" have it for them is by definition engaged in a type of communication which produces understanding and finds ways to weave the different common senses together in mutually satisfying, even joyful ways.

REFERENCES

Austin, J. L. (1962). *How to do things with words.* Cambridge, MA: Harvard University Press.
Baker, J., & Gudykunst, W. B. (1990, June). *Privacy regulation in Japan and the United States.* Paper presented at the annual meeting of the International Communication Association, Dublin, Ireland.
Basso, K. (1979). *Joking as a "Whiteman" among the Western Apache.* Cambridge, MA: Cambridge University Press.
Basso, K. (1990). *Western Apache language & culture: Essays in linguistic anthropology.* Tucson: University of Arizona Press.
Bilmes, J. (1976). Rules and rhetoric: Negotiating the social order in a Thai village. *Journal of Anthropological Research, 32,* 44-57.
Bilmes, J. (1986). *Discourse and behavior.* New York: Plenum Publishing.
Brislin, R., Cushner, K., Cherrie, C., & Yong, M. (1986). *Intercultural interactions: A practical guide.* Beverly Hills: Sage.
Burke, E. (1955). *Reflections on the revolution in France.* New York: Liberal Arts Press.
Burke, K. (1969). *A grammar of motives.* Berkeley, CA: University of California Press.
Carbaugh, D. (1988). *Talking American: Cultural discourses on Donahue.* Norwood, NJ: Ablex.
Carbaugh, D. (1990). Toward a perspective on cultural communication and intercultural contact. *Semiotica, 80,* 15-35.
Carroll, L. (1934). *Through the looking-glass.* New York: Grosset-Dunlap.
Casmir, F. L. (1997a). Foreword. In F. Casmir (Ed.), *Ethics in intercultural and international communication.* Mahwah, NJ: Lawrence Erlbaum Associates.
Casmir, F. L. (1996b). Ethics, culture and communication: An application of the third- culture building model to international and intercultural communication. In F. Casmir (Ed.), *Ethics in intercultural and international communication.* Mahwah, NJ: Lawrence Erlbaum Associates.

Cronen, V. E., Chen, V., & Pearce, W. B. (1988). Coordinated management of meaning: A critical theory. In Y. Y. Kim & W. B. Gudykunst (Eds.), *Theories in intercultural communication* (pp. 66-98). Newbury Park, CA: Sage.

Davies, B. & Harré, R. (1990). Positioning: The discursive production of selves. *Journal for the Theory of Social Behavior, 20*, 43-63.

Doi, T. (1973). *The anatomy of dependence* (J. Bester, trans.). Tokyo: Kodansha.

Durkheim, E. (1965). *The elementary forms of the religious life* (J. W. Swain, trans.). New York: Free Press.

Elliot, G. (1977). *Middlemarch*. New York: W. W. Norton.

Fitch, K. (1990/91). A ritual for attempting leave-taking in Colombia. *Research on Language and Social Interaction, 24*, 209-224.

Fleischacker, S. (1994). *The ethics of culture*. Ithaca, NY: Cornell University Press.

Friedrich, G. (1989, December). Make mine a tossed salad. *Spectra, 25*, p. 3.

Geertz, C. (1973). *The interpretation of cultures*. New York: Basic Books.

Griefat, Y., & Katriel, T. (1989). Life demands *musayara*: Communication and culture among Arabs in Israel. In S. Ting-Toomey & F. Korzenny (Eds.), *Language, communication and culture* (pp. 121-138). Newbury Park, CA: Sage.

Hall, B. J., & Noguchi, M. (1993). Intercultural conflict: a case study. *International Journal of Intercultural Relations, 17*, 399-413.

Hall, B. J., & Noguchi, M. (1995). Engaging in *kenson*: An extended case study of one form of "common" sense. *Human Relations, 48*, 1129-1147.

Hall, E. (1983). *Dance of life: The other dimension of time*. Garden City, NY: Anchor Press.

Hatch, E. (1983). *Culture and morality: The relativity of values in anthropology*. New York: Columbia University Press.

Hauerwas, S. (1983). *The peaceable kingdom*. South Bend, IN: University of Notre Dame Press.

Herskovits, M. (1972). *Cultural relativism: Perspectives in cultural pluralism*. New York: Random House.

Howell, W. S. (1982). *The empathic communicator*. Belmont, CA: Wadsworth Publishing.

Kale, D. W. (1991). Ethics in intercultural communication. In L. Samovar & R. Porter (Eds.), *Intercultural communication: A reader* (pp. 421-426). Belmont, CA: Wadsworth.

Katriel, T. (1986). *Talking straight*. Cambridge, MA: Cambridge University Press.

Katriel, T., & Philipsen, G. (1981). "What we need is communication": "Communication" as a cultural category in some American speech. *Communication Monographs, 48*, 302-317.

Kroeber, A., & Kluckhohn, C. (1952). *Culture: A critical review of concepts and definitions*. Cambridge, MA: Peabody Museum.

Martin, J. N., & Nakayama, T. (1996). *Intercultural communication in contexts*. Mountain View, CA: Mayfield Publishing Company.

Nilsen, T. R. (1966). *Ethics of speech communication*. New York: Bobbs-Merrill Company.

Peck, M. S. (1978). *The road less traveled*. New York: Simon and Schuster.

Philipsen, G. (1987). The prospect for cultural communication. In D. L. Kincaid (Ed.), *Communication theory: Eastern and Western perspectives* (pp. 245-254). San Diego: Academic Press.

Plato. (1967). *Gorgias* (W. R. M. Lamb, trans.). Cambridge, MA: Harvard University Press.

Simpson, J. A., & Weiner, E. S. C. (Eds.). (1989). *The Oxford English dictionary* (2nd ed., Vol. 17). Oxford: Clarendon Press.

Sitaram, K. S., & Cogdell, R. T. (1976). *Foundations of intercultural communication*. Columbus, Ohio: Charles E. Merrill.

Steiner, L. (1997). A feminist schema for ethical analyses of intercultural dilemmas. In F. Casmir (Ed.), *Ethics in intercultural and international communication*. Mahwah, NJ: Lawrence Erlbaum Associates.

Swalehe, R., Rogers, E. M., Gilboard, M. J., Alford, K., & Montoya, R. (1995). *A content analysis of the entertainment-education radio soap opera "Twende Na Wakati" (let's go with the times) in Tanzania.* Albuquerque, NM: University of New Mexico, Department of Communication and Journalism; and Arusha, Tanzania, POFLEP Research Report.

Swidler, A. (1986). Culture in action: Symbols and strategies. *American Sociological Review, 51*, 273-286.

Tajfel, H., & Turner, J. C. (1986). The social identity theory of intergroup behavior. In S. Worchel & W. G. Austin (Eds.), *The social psychology of intergroup relations* (pp. 7-17). Chicago: Nelson-Hall.

Tylor, E. B. (1958). *The Origins of Culture.* New York: Harper & Brothers.

Weider, D. L., & Pratt, S. (1990). On being a recognizable Indian among Indians. In D. Carbaugh (Ed.), *Cultural communication and intercultural contact* (pp. 45-64). Hillsdale, NJ: Lawrence Erlbaum Associates.

Case Study

THE GREAT HANSHIN EARTHQUAKE
AND THE ETHICS OF INTERVENTION:
A CASE-STUDY IN INTERNATIONAL AND INTERCULTURAL
COMMUNICATION

Deni Elliott[1]
Director, Practical Ethics Center

INTRODUCTION

January 17, 1995, the Japanese Kansai area south east of Tokyo shook with an earthquake that destroyed lives, homes and businesses. Offers of assistance and gifts of food, clothing, medical supplies and voluntary assistance poured in from around the world as local and central governments in Japan were still assessing the extent of the disaster and only beginning to react to it. The offers and arrival of aid were not accepted by local and national Japanese governments with the gratitude expected by the donors. Thus, Japanese governments had to deal with criticism at home and abroad because of their slow responses to the calamity.

Of major interest to this case study are conflicting cultural interpretations. Responses to foreign offers of help are intended as gestures of assistance within the offering culture may be perceived as condescending or unjustifiably paternalistic by another. On the other hand, what was seen as a well-

---

[1] With thanks to research assistants Erica Nishioka and Gerald Johnson, and to fellow researcher Hideto Mosukowa.

considered, comprehensive response within one culture, can be perceived as negligent bureaucratic inaction by representatives of another cultural value system.

The Great Hanshin Earthquake is the basis for an analysis of the ethics of humanitarian international intervention, because it allows for the consideration of the ethical communication challenges faced in many intercultural situations by focusing on a well known, specific instance.

As technology, media and easier access increasingly move the world toward some type of global community and a multi-cultural town square, it is important to understand acceptable differences among neighbors. Ethical communication interactions require an understanding of such variations rather than quick judgment of another's response based on a projection of one's own cultural norms. Culturally burdened, or unjustified negative moral judgments about how another country is handling its problems may cause harm within the world community by creating further suspicions and tensions based on cultural or ethnic differences. As will be seen, however, some disastrous situations can provide us with an opportunity to learn from a diverse set of responses how we may improve the overall management of crises and global relations, while avoiding intercultural or international communication problems.

This case study begins with a summary of events related to of the Great Hanshin Earthquake. The case is then analyzed through the use of generalizable principles in four areas: the dangers of using one's own cultural norms as a basis for moral approbation, the nature of a gift, paternalism, and the limits of pluralism.

The Great Hanshin Earthquake and U.S. Intervention

A 7.2 earthquake hit in the pre-dawn hours January 17, 1995 in the area surrounding Kobe, Japan. Although the quake lasted less than 30 seconds, 5,500 people were killed and, more than 41,500 were injured. Some 320,000 people were displaced with 230,000 homes and buildings destroyed (Sogo,1995a).

News organizations were essential channels of communication during the crisis. Although some newspapers continued publication, the dislocation of people made radio the primary news source for those in need of survival information. Television told the world of the disaster's magnitude; and the world responded. Nations throughout the world[2], the United States in

---

[2] The United States, Switzerland, Russia, France, Germany, Israel, Italy, Britain, South Korea, China and The Philippines.

particular, offered and organized airlifts of volunteers, medications, money and goods. Of the eleven countries offering or dispatching aid, Japan accepted no aid from seven and only partial aid from four of them (*Asahi Evening News*, 1995b, p. 1).

Markman (1995a) reported one attempted U.S. effort in the Los Angeles Times as follows:

> The Americans had been organized less than a week ago in the belief that Japan needed trauma-care specialists to assist in the treatment of the Kobe earthquake's 50,000 wounded. Upon arrival in the city, however, the gung-ho emergency room doctors and nurses discovered that their Japanese counterparts had a much more narrow view of volunteerism. It is a foreign concept in this stubbornly self-reliant society. Hospitals in one section of town don't even like to accept help from physicians in other sections, much less from other regions of the country or world....Their arrival was a bit clumsy, as Japanese health executives tried to figure out how to accommodate colleagues whom they considered guests more than assistants....[E]mergency room chief Jung Hyo Kim....drew the line of his welcome at the notion of asking the Americans to help out with rounds or in the operating room, saying the differences between the countries' practices were too great (p. B3).

Within hours of the quake, U.S. forces in Japan offered the Japanese Self-Defense Agency personnel, buses, trucks, multipurpose vehicles, aircraft for transport, water, engineering support, road-clearing, electrical generators, tents, blankets and medical advisers. Takahama (1995) noted that of these offers, "The Japanese government accepted only blankets and water from the U.S. forces, three days after the earthquake" (p. 6).

Three weeks after the earthquake, an American offer to fly as many as one million doses of flu vaccine to Kobe within 48 hours, free of charge, was politely declined by the Health and Welfare Ministry. At that point, search teams and undertakers, airlifts of food and clothing, as well as medical help had been, at lest initially, refused. When the aid was accepted, it was accepted only grudgingly. As of February 5, fourteen forklift pallets of Tylenol sent by one American relief organization had been left untouched in a warehouse near Kobe (Kristof, 1995).

While foreign governments and relief agencies wondered what they could do to help, Japanese citizens responded in a culturally appropriate way. During the morning of the earthquake, Japanese workers, after quickly assessing the physical state of their family members, left wives, children and elders dazed and disoriented among the chaos and headed through the rubble to their offices and companies. There, workers organized into cooperative work teams, as they have would have done in a less chaotic time. In each case, any given company took the lead in providing help for those employees who were most severely affected. Companies provided food, water, money, emergency supplies and housing, with less affected employees delivering goods, services and information. While it was acknowledged that the companies were quicker to respond than local or central governments, they were criticized by some for dealing with the situation without regard for those outside their group (Sogo, 1995b, p. 5).

The slowness of response by the central Japanese government and the lack of coordination between local and central governments was criticized as well. Although the quake struck before 6 a.m., the Japanese Self-Defense Force was not officially deployed until 1 p.m. In addition, Prime Minister Tomiichi Murayama was criticized for failing to quickly declare an "Disaster Emergency Status" to control emergency goods allocations (Sogo, 1995c, p. 7). As chairman of the Cabinet, he explained that he lacked the power to enact the order without the consent of the Cabinet, a move that is purposefully designed to take time and thought (Takahama, 1995).

Cultural Expectations and Bias. While acknowledging that criticism occured in Japan as well as externally, the focus here are intercultural, international communication problems that arose, along with their ethical implications. The culturally predictable reaction of U.S. news media to Japanese refusals of aid was disbelief. The conclusions drawn by representatives of mass media in the United States, included suggestions that the Japanese government was not interested in caring for its own people. For example, New York Times reporter Kristof (1995) focused a story on how the Health and Welfare Ministry in Japan refused free flu vaccinations from the U.S., despite the fact that flu viruses were "rippling through the refuge camps where 270,000 people live huddled together in classrooms and tents" (p. B1). He included phrases in his story which are indicative of a culturally biased interpretation, including his impression that that "the biggest losers and complainers have been the Japanese people themselves," quoting a displaced Japanese citizen who complained that the government was "just acting out a diplomatic game." Kristof (1995) quoted another individual who told a visitor to the refugee center that (despite the government's response), "We're so grateful for the foreign help" (pp. B1, B8).

It should not be surprising that any reporter would have been able to find expressions of dissatisfaction. However, it is surprising that no one was quoted in Kristof's (1995) story who could be considered a plausible, authoritative source speaking in defense of the Japanese approach. In other words, Kristof's (1995) story treatment reflected U.S. expectations of how the Japanese ought to respond. In the United States, we tend to prize quick action, decisive government leaders and gratitude when assistance is offered. No wonder that the U.S. news media, products of those national expectations or biases, reported the Great Hanshin Earthquake as they viewed it, namely through U.S. eyes. That view resulted in moral approbation when probing for deeper understanding or examinining cultural differences would have been more appropriate and informative.

An analysis of some of the cultural assumptions behind Japanese action and non-action sheds new light on the events in the aftermath of the Great Hanshin Earthquake.

Governmental Localities. Policies on disaster relief, like many other governmental functions in Japan, are developed locally rather than nationally. "Help from outside a stricken prefecture cannot be mobilized until local authorities request assistance. Under this system, the first step is for the local government to assess the extent of the damage; only after this is completed do they request the dispatch of self-defense forces and other forms of outside help" (Konoe, 1995, p. 3.).

Japan is even more reticent than other countries to rely on national forces when local response will do. The world community, after World War II, built into the Japanese people a fear of where a renewed, Japanese nationalism might lead. At the time of the quake, the Social Democratic Party was the ruling governmental faction in Japan. According to one Japanese news source, "[the SDP], led by Murayama has traditionally been opposed to the dispatch of SDP personnel to disaster sites because they believed it would open the way for a more ambitious deployment of troops to maintain security and order" (*Yomiuri Shimbun*, 1995, p. 1). Thus the slow reaction by the post-war central government to the earthquake can be seen as a result of earlier U.S. intervention, a point not explored in the US mass media. The constitution of Japan, which went into effect May 3, 1947, was the product of General Douglas MacArthur's and the U.S. occupation government's efforts. Article nine of the constitution reads in part, "In order to accomplish the aim [of renouncing war as a way of settling international disagreement] land, sea, and air forces, as well as other war potential, will never be maintained" (Tanaka, 1990, p. 165.).

It seems inconsistent to criticize the Japanese military for not being in the state of readiness that the U.S. forces maintain to cope with such a disaster. After all, the United States is in large part responsible for constitutional constraints which resulted in Japan *not* having the capability to quickly mobilize military forces.

While the SDP was awaiting official deployment, the defense forces were not idle. Although the SDP did not begin official operations until more than six hours after the earthquake, they were unofficially mobilized before that time. Some of the work that the forces accomplished prior to the official call, included aerial inspections of damage, rescue of dozens of people waiting at the Itami train station, rescue of victims from a collapsed house behind Nishinomiya Citizens Hospital, a meeting between SDP liaison officers with Hyogo prefecture government officials, and the assembly of SDP personnel arriving from Himeji, Kisarazu and Zentsuji in stricken areas (Matsuoka, 1995, p. 1). Yet, it was simply and erroneously reported in the U.S. press that the Japanese government had taken six hours to mobilize its forces.

Decision making. A second cultural norm that affected the Japanese response to the emergency is the prevalent decision-making process in that nation. Official decision-making in Japan uses a cooperative method of consensus-building called "nemawashi." Nemawashi, which seeks the approval of all, is not a swift process and is based on the cultural belief that quick action is often quickly regretted. Decision making in Japan happens from the bottom of a hierarchical structure to the top rather than from the top down, as it commonly the case in the United States. Since everyone cooperates in making a decision, everyone shares responsibility for the consequences of the decisions made. As a result, local governments had to first reach the decision to request national assistance in dealing with the earthquake. The resulting determination of how the central government could best offer aid was thus based on reflection by the people's representatives in the country at large, a time consuming process but one which was designed to truly involve all those who would be affected by a final decision.

Self-sufficiency. The Japanese assumption that their disaster policies are adequate, and that the country has necessary supplies for any emergency also needs to be considered. This belief in self-sufficiency meant, in the case of the earthquake, that there was no method or motivation to secure the needed interpreters, lodging and transportation for foreign volunteers. It was the government's judgment that such assistance, though well-intended, would only make the already chaotic situation worse (Konoe, 1995).

Tylenol, which was included in an airlift of medical supplies immediately following the earthquake, was dispatched to a warehouse rather than to victims, because health officials felt that the dosage might be inappropriate for Japanese bodies. Indeed, in Japan over-the-counter pain relievers contain 300 milligrams of acetaminophen rather than the 500 milligrams in equivalent U.S. products (Kristof, 1995). With the number of injured overwhelming available medical assistance, there was no time for those who would make such decisions to reach a carefully reasoned conclusion on how to handle the influx of foreign drugs.

An instance widely covered by the media in the United States involved a team of emergency room doctors and nurses from Southern California, which landed in Kobe within 48 hours of the quake, but was not allowed to treat the injured. This, too reflected the Japanese belief that such intervention was not necessary, as well as the Japanese suspicion of foreign procedures. Cultural assumptions were the foundation for responses on *both* sides; that is, they could be identified in the eager offers of foreign trauma team help, as well as in the Japanese reluctance to accept them. As one of the Southern California team members, a Japanese-American paramedic, noted, "Americans think they're the good guys and we should ride in on a white horse to help grateful people. The Japanese, on the other hand, think saving face is the most important thing, and the effort to control your country and environment tops any individual's welfare" (Markman, 1995b, p. 1). On January 23, the Ministry of Health and Welfare finally allowed foreign doctors to treat victims as an emergency measure, as long as the treatment was limited to the minimum needs (Sogo, 1995a). By that time, the U.S. doctors realized that they were redundant. "By the end of the week...so many Japanese doctors had arrived in drug-stuffed vans to assist in Kobe's care that the Americans' efforts were often in vain" (Markman, 1995c, p. B3).

The Japanese believe that their government knows best how to care for its people. Strict regulations that apply to the quarantine of animals, use of foreign pharmaceuticals and medical assistance resulted in swift refusals when search dogs and medications were offered, or when they simply appeared. While some assistance was accepted after thoughtful consideration, the initial response was based on the cultural or nationalistic value system response that had served Japan well in the past.

Volunteerism. There is also an important cultural difference in how U.S. and Japanese societies view volunteerism. The United States encourages private volunteerism; Japan does not. The "Give Five" campaign launched in the 1980's in the United States by the Independent Sector[3] provides one of many

---

[3]A nonprofit coalition of more than 800 corporate, foundation and voluntary organizations devoted to encouraging giving, volunteering, and not-for-profit initiative.

examples indicating how the notion of "helping out" fits in with the cultural assumptions of American citizens. The campaign successfully played on the notion that every person could and should "give five"—five dollars, or five hours of volunteer service each month—as a contribution to the social good. In Japan, there existes no tradition of volunteerism or private action on behalf of community welfare, based on the cultural consensus, involvement-of-all model discussed above. That tradition changed, however, with the earthquake. The Great Hanshin Earthquake, as an interesting instance of how cultures change and adapt, is credited with creating a volunteer movement in Japan. "It was estimated that a total of 1.4 million volunteers participated in the rescue mission during the three months following the earthquake. According to a later survey, for more than 70% of these volunteers, it was their first volunteer experience" (Sogo, 1995a, p. 4).

Loyalty to Employer. Despite the lack of tradition of *individual* volunteerism, intense loyalty to one's employer created a type of *group* volunteerism demonstrated by the response of businesses during the crisis. Since the Japanese employee can generally expect to be employed by the same company for his entire career, "people can concentrate on their work in the realization that they and their company share a common fate" (Tanaka, 1990, p. 215). Even when disagreements arise between workers and employers, the company is "a communal group first and a functioning group second....the company is the community and home is just where they sleep" (DeMente, 1993, p. 8).

Caring for co-workers is, therefore, as important to Japanese as caring for family members. Getting the company back on its feet after the earthquake was an act of beneficence, self-interest as well as an expression of the fierce competition that exists between businesses. According to a Wall Street Journal article, "Some Japanese executives are bursting with pride at the swiftness of their comebacks. Outside Osaka, the quake toppled machines and parts bins at a Daihatsu Motor Co. auto plant. Production director Takashi Higashi crowed, 'I issued an order to muster by 6 a.m.' (less than 15 minutes after the quake). The very next evening, Mr. Higashi had cars and parts rolling off the assembly lines....Until the quake, Yokohama's longshoreman had Sundays and wee hours off—and were battling a management plan to open the wharves 24 hours a day, seven days a week. Right after the disaster, though, the union volunteered to keep the port running around the clock....."(Williams & Shirouzu, 1995, p. A4).

Gift Giving and Receiving

Although it is easy to interpret foreign aid as only politically motivated, either as an act of reciprocity among allies or as outright coercion, such a cynical interpretation seems less appropriate when aid is offered at times of disaster. The outpouring of care from the world community during one country's crisis seems as simple and lacking in political agenda as the outpouring of care by individuals in a community when a family's home is destroyed by fire. Even if one believes that gift giving and receiving is part of an accepted exchange—my country will respond to yours because I would expect the same from you when my country experiences an emergency—at the moment of offer, assistance, in effect, is a quintessential gift.

The relationship of a waiter's service and a customer's tip, as we practice it in the United States provides a common example of this reciprocal gift exchange. The waiter provides good service without knowing whether the customer will leave a good tip or not, and certainly without having a way of compelling the tip. At the same time, the customer cannot affect the quality of service already received by leaving a tip. Even if tipping is understood as a convention, the giving of good service and the tip can both be seen as gifts at the moment that they occur (Frank, 1992, p. 326).

Offering of assistance in the aftermath of a disaster is appropriately viewed as a gift, at least from the perspective of the giver. But, what is viewed as a gift by the one offering help, may also be legitimately refused by the receiver. That is the case, because a gift may be deemed inappropriate by the recipient, in spite of the best of intentions by the one presenting it. One relevant example in the case of the Great Hanshi earthquake relates to the used clothing and food items which were among the items donated by Americans to the Japanese affected by the earthquake. These gifts were culturally not appropriate.

The Japanese have a cultural aversion to any used items. It can be observed anywhere in the country that consumer goods in Japan are *carefully* sealed and wrapped, and service and sales personnel commonly wear gloves. All that is done in order to assure customers that when they touch an item no one before them will have handled it with their bare hands. The U.S. tradition of shared goods and hand-me-down clothing is seen as unclean and embarrassingly personal in a culture in which touching or embracing is inappropriate, except in the most intimate and sanctioned relationships (Nakamura, 1993). Just as importantly, Japan is a highly developed industrial country with a well-stocked larder. Food was available following the earthquake, although it was not necessarily easy to transport it into the stricken area, and, of course, the transportation problems would have equally applied to food items received from foreign countries. These well-intentioned gifts thus created more chaos for the Japanese. According to a program officer for an international aid coalition, "If you complicate a logistics system that's already overburdened by bringing in inappropriate things from the outside, you are actually hurting rather than helping the situation," (Green, 1995, p. 10).

Technically speaking, a gift has the following characteristics:

    1)   It is something of value,

    2)   that is bestowed intentionally by the giver,

    3)   to someone

        a)   who accepts it knowing it is a gift,

        b)   agrees that it is of benefit,

        c)   who has no right to or claim upon it,

        d)   who is not expected to pay for it, and

        e)   which brings into being a new moral relationship

    4)   between giver and receiver (Camenisch, 1981, p. 2).

The offers and deliveries of aid to Japan were noncontroversial in meeting the first two criteria for being a gift. However, it is not so clear that Japan met the necessary characteristics of the receiver of a gift. While the donated goods and services were meant for the affected citizens of Kobe and surrounding areas, the role of government in Japan as related to the acceptance or rejection of gifts of this magnitude, is much like that of a parent's acts on behalf of a child. Even in the United States, one can easily imagine a situation in which a parent may refuse a gift on behalf of a child, even if the child may substantially benefit from the gift. When we consider those Japanese cultural traditions relating to paternalism and gifts, that comparison becomes especially meaningful to this case-study.

It is quite legitimate for governments to turn down offers on behalf of their citizens if the benefits of those offers are not clear. At the time of this particular crisis, the risks associated with offers such as rescue teams, foreign medical assistance and pharmaceuticals seemed to outweigh their benefits from the Japanese government's point of view. The added chaos created by the need to find interpreters, housing, transportation, and the extension of what the Japanese consider to be required amenities for foreign guests, seemed to be too much of a burden for the amount of assistance likely to be provided. Although the potential benefit may have actually outweighed the risk in this case, this sort of risk/benefit analysis is neither irrational nor foreign. Nor is it unusual to realize later, using hindsight and facing fewer time constraints, that another type of response might have been better.

What appears quite clear then, is the fact that offering a gift does not automatically carry a moral obligation to accept the offer. The moral judgment by Americans and their media that the Japanese had acted ungratefully when turning down offers of aid, or by accepting them only grudgingly, suggests that the relationship created in this intercultural and international exchange is different from the nature of the moral relationship normally created in a gift exchange. Camenish (1981) makes that point when he writes, "Both grateful conduct and grateful use attach to every gift, and only taken together do they show that the recipient is grateful to this donor for this gift....The acceptance of a gift implies that the recipient feels gratitude for what is being offered. Therefore, to avoid misleading others, gifts should not be accepted unless such [gratitude] is felt" (pp. 10-11).

Without true acceptance, the offered gift begins to take on the characteristics of coercive external interference. According to Warwick and Kelman (1973), involvement of the target population in all intervention is the best way to protect against the imposition of foreign values,

> Thus in an ethical evaluation of a social intervention, one would want to consider criteria such as these: To what extent do those who are affected by the intervention participate in the choice of goals? What efforts are being made to have their interests represented in the setting of priorities, and to bring their perspectives to bear on the definition of the problem and the range of choices entertained? (p. 396).

In the case of the Great Hanshin Earthquake, the Japanese government was not invited to assess and then inform others of its needs. Needs were intuited by others and responded to based on foreign intuitions. In this respect, the offerings and dispatch of aid were, or could easily be interpreted as acts of paternalism.

Paternalism

Paternalism is the action of one competent adult (or nation) in spite of the desires of another competent adult's (or nation's) desires or beliefs. Paternalism involves the actor believing the following:

1) That the proposed action will benefit the other,
2) that the action will deny the other the opportunity to act on behalf of itself,
3) that the action does not have the other's past, present or immediately forthcoming consent,

4)   that the other is competent to give consent (Culver & Gert, 1982, p. 130).

According to this definition, the United States, both in the actions by its governmental agencies and by various relief organizations, acted in ways that were paternalistic. The obvious intent of the actions was to benefit Japan. But, in shipping goods, drugs and medical assistance that were not requested, the U.S. actions in effect denied Japan the opportunity to act on its own behalf. The U.S. response assumed that the Japanese victims needed certain actions, regardless of what Janpanese national or local governments might conclude. The fact is that Japanese governments did refuse gifts or protest certain intervention when given the opportunity. Since Japan is a sovereign country, its governments had the authority and assumed competence to make decisions on behalf of their citizens. Paternalistic acts can be justified, but only if the evil likely to be suffered is obviously greater than the evil suffered by the imposition of one's decisions on another. It is not clear that the Japanese would have suffered more evil if the unwelcome assistance had not arrived.

History has shown that a slow, well-coordinated response to a crisis is not necessarily worse than a quick, reactive one. After the earthquakes in Mexico in 1985 and in Armenia in 1988, for example, "huge amounts of unsolicited aid came pouring into the affected areas. While this 'forced' aid was effective in some respects, it also invited confusion and in some cases actually worked against efficient rescue operations" (Konoe, 1995, p. 3).

Limits of Pluralism

If offers of foreign aid are interpreted as gifts, it is legitimate for those offers to be refused. However, governmental refusals to accept assistance for its citizens can also be interpreted as a violation of governmental duty. The special duty of government is to protect its citizens from the suffering of particular types of evils (Gert, 1988). When that concept is violated, that is when intended governmental action or non-action is likely to lead to unnecessary pain, death or suffering of citizens it is reasonable to assume that a government has gone beyond the scope of acceptable action. According to a common standard adopted in 1933 by the International Red Cross and other international aid organizations, "The right to receive humanitarian assistance, and offer it, is a fundamental principle which should be enjoyed by all citizens of all countries." This right served as the basis for assistance given to the Kurds in Iraq, for instance, even though that assistance involved infringement on the sovereignty of the Iraqi state (Konoe, 1995).

In this case study, the question is whether the slowness of action and refusal of foreign assistance by the Japanese government was like the refusal of a gift, or more like an obstacle to the reception of much needed aid. If the Japanese government was creating an obstacle for it citizens who needed aid, then the paternalistic actions of the U.S. government and other nations that sent aid without the permission by of Japanese governments, or who criticized that government for its refusal of such offers would be justified. It is interesting to note in that connection that Japanese citizens asked that question as well. A commentary that appeared four days after the earthquake in Asahi Evening News, an English-language newspaper in Japan, poignantly dealt with the issue, "The earthquake destroyed not just cities in the southern part of Hyogo Prefecture and the lives of hundreds of thousands of victims....It also destroyed the sense of confidence that the government protects citizens in a crisis" (Okamoto, 1995, p. 1). In other words, the solution of such difficult problems, or the discussion of such issues has both intercultural and international dimensions, but it is also an issue in our complex world which engages directly involved media and citizens within the affected cultural environment.

CONCLUSION

Cultures are lasting and important component parts of human survival efforts. But cultures do change as human needs for survival and control of the environment change. Thus it should come as no surprise that Japan is changing in response to what it learned in the Great Hanshin Earthquake. The government has instituted what the Prime Minister calls a total revision of the nation's disaster policies, including some of the following,

> Strengthening equipment to forecast earthquakes and to assess the ability of structures to withstand them. This despite the fact that prior to the earthquake, Japan was thought to have the strictest building regulations on earthquake resilience, the strongest elevated expressways, and a state of the art earthquake prediction system. Local and national governments have drawn up plans to bring about quicker responses in future disasters. Local governments are stockpiling food, water and supplies to be prepared for future disasters. (*Asahi Evening News*, 1995, p. 1).

In the wake of the earthquake, the Japanese government has also allocated billions of dollars to prepare for future disasters, and has recognized a previously unrecognized resource: individual volunteerism. In the opinion of the publisher of *Understanding Japan*, "What Japan needs is more people who have the individual authority, and personal initiative, to respond quickly in disaster situations. I believe that each individual is blessed with a variety of talents, and that what the government should do is create an environment in which such talents can be utilized to the fullest to benefit society whether in routine situations or in emergencies" (Sogo, 1995a, p. 3). An editorial in a major Japanese newspaper concluded, "Rescue operations for people hit by a natural disaster is no longer something to be conducted by a single country." (Asahi Shimbun, 1995, p. 8). This is a big change for a people who believe that accepting help in serious situations is dangerous because of the degree of indebtedness involved (Kiritani, 1995). All that points to the fact that Japan is recognizing that today it exists not only as a separate cultural entity but also as part of a global community.

The very idea of a global community suggests, however, that intercultural and international communication is a part of that system or process. Interaction between representatives of nations or states, as was illustrated in this case study, continue to present human beings with significant interactional, communication challenges. The ethical questions which arise in such situations as the Great Hanshin Earthquake, make it clear that far-reaching solutions require more than changes by any one culture, group, organization or state involved. A mutually beneficial model for the resolution of intercultural and international communication and ethics problems, is probably one of the most immediate needs if we are to truly build some kind of global community.

What this case study has attempted to show is that beyond abstract or theoretical considerations, intercultural and international communication scholars face the challenge to respond meaningful to very real, often very confusing and sometimes very important contemporary challenges. It appears to us as Americans, that as is true in the case of neighbors, in trouble, that we have an obligation to watch for international and intercultural opportunities to assist, or at least offer assistance. What needs to become an integral part of such concerns, however, is an expansion of our effort to understand when such interventions are appropriate. Furthermore, ethical efforts to assist others must include a deep concern for the value systems of others involved in the process. Specifically that means states, countries, nations, media and individuals should grant others the right to make their own, considered, responsible choices as free human beings. It means that we should be concerned about others' dignity, rights, values and concerns as much as we are about our own. Of course, such an attitude can also result in applauding the learning and growth processes of individuals and nations as their intercultural and international communication efforts become more effective, more caring, and their judgments of situations and people more adequate. Japan coped with its crisis under the watchful eye of the world's broadcast media; and we need to remember that it is easy to pass judgment from the sidelines, particularly when those judging have little understanding of the cultural assumptions that underlie seemingly inappropriate decisions.

It is the purpose of this book to address the ethical communication challenges of our day, rather to assume that we can survive on the basis of mottoes which claim that "leopards cannot change their spots" or that we must deal with "business as usual." After all, our focus is on human beings, not leopards or business as abstract concepts. And human beings can and do change in order to survive.

REFERENCES

Asahi Evening News. (1995a, January 21). New quake steps planned. *Asahi Evening News*, p. 1.

Asahi Evening News (1995b, January 21). Aid offers from abroad. *Asahi Evening News*, p. 1.

Asahi Shimbun (1995, January 20). Editorial: We must pool our wisdom to cope with disasters. *Asahi Shimbun*. p. 8.

Camenisch, P. (1981, Spring). Gift and gratitude in ethics. *The Journal of Religious Ethics*. 9, pp. 1-34.

Culver, C. & Gert, B. (1982). *Philosophy in medicine: Conceptual and ethical issues in medicine and psychiatry*. New York: Oxford University Press.

DeMente, B. L. (1993). *Japanese etiquette in ethics & business*. Lincolnwood, IL: NTC.

Frank, R. (1992, July). The differences between gifts and exchange: Comment of Carol Rose. *Florida Law Review*. 44(3), p. 326.

Gert, B. (1988). *Morality: A new justification for the moral rules*. New York: Oxford University Press.

Green, S. (1995, February). Americans donate millions for earthquake victims in Japan. *The Chronicle of Philanthropy*, VII(8), p. 10.

Kiritani, E. (1995, February 9). Thanks and thanks again. *Daily Yomiuri*. p. 14.

Kristof, N. (1995, February 5). Japan reluctant to accept help from abroad. *The New York Times*, p. B1.

Konoe, T. (1995, June). Assistance from abroad. *Look Japan*, p. 3.

Markman, J. (1995a, January 25) Emotional rescue quake: Stymied by Japanese reluctance to let foreigners treat patients, southland medical team provides a grief therapy session—and kitchen help—instead. *The Los Angeles Times*, p. 1.

Markman, J. (1995b, January 24). Frustrated U.S. doctors get ok to treat quake victims. *The Los Angeles Times*, p. 1.

Markman, J. (1995c, January 27). U.S. team allowed to treat quake victims, aid: After frustrating delays, volunteers are permitted to run clinics for those left homeless in Kobe. *The Los Angeles Times*, p. B3.

Matsuoka, I. (1995, January 31). Why SDP didn't charge to the rescue. *The Daily Yomiuri*, II, p. 1.

Nakamura, T. (1993). *Nippon, the land and its people*. Japan: Nippon Steel Human Resources Development Co., Ltd.

Okamoto, Y. (1995, January 21). Leaders fail in quake. *Asahi Evening News*, p. 1.

Sogo, S. (1995a, July). The Kobe earthquake. *Understanding Japan*, 4(4), pp. 2, 4, 6.

Sogo, S. (1995b, July). "Impact on business", *Understanding Japan*, 4(4), pp. 5, 8.

Sogo, S. (1995c, July). "Laws & disaster," *Understanding Japan*, 4(4), pp. 6, 7.

Staff writer, (1995, January 28). Premier recognizes SDP's relief role, *Yomiuri Shimbun*, p. 1.

Takahama, T. (1995, January). "High-handed quake response under fire abroad" *The Daily Yomiuri,*
       p. 6.
Tanaka, Y. (1990). *Japan as it is: A bilingual guide.* Tokyo: Gakkan Publishing.
Warwick, D., & Kelman Cole, H. (1973). Ethical issues in social intervention. *Readings, Institute of
       Society, Ethics and the Life Sciences,* No. 1711, pp. 377-417.
Williams, M., & Shirouzu, N. (1995, March 17). Hopping island, Kobe quake wreckage poses a
       thousand tests for Japanese ingenuity, *The Wall Street Journal,* A4, p. 1.

A Feminist Schema for Analysis of Ethical Dilemmas

Linda Steiner[1]
Rutgers University

This chapter draws on feminist theorizing in order to suggest an ethical schema that may be helpful in intercultural communication. Recent social, political and cultural conflicts illuminate only too dramatically the potential usefulness of an ethical map that citizens could use to track, albeit in fairly broad contours, intercultural dilemmas. Ideally, such a map would not only mark locations of relevant landmarks and landmines, but would also point out the general directions of moral action. The intercultural dimensions of many international and domestic battles—debates over popular culture, jury decisions, public policy (including mass communications policy) and in the workplace—are often invoked to imply that cultural conflict renders ethical analysis, much less ethical action, impossible. That view is both paralyzing and wrong. Feminist theories, and especially the emerging scholarship in feminist ethics, offer criteria by which dilemmas can be understood and ethical constructs evaluated. The commitment of feminists to everyday moral action and to making feminist literature accessible predicts a concern for useful, practical ideas about

---

[1]The author wishes to acknowledge the considerable help of Rutgers colleague Prof. Radha Hegde in conceptualizing issues presented here.

principles and processes. This chapter does not advocate a particular grand theory or a single map. Since there is no single feminist theory, there cannot be a single feminist ethic. Nonetheless, feminist perspectives, with their intellectual heterogeneity and affective breadth, generate principles and methods that promote ethical inquiry.

The perspective outlined below is feminist in several key respects, all of which will be elaborated. First, it follows from feminist political and moral philosophy, including feminist conceptions of moral agency. As such, it rejects ethical schemas that could or would justify acts that increase the oppression of women. A perspective that would apologize for the physical or emotional abuse or misuse of women, or that trivializes or degrades important aspects of women's experiences would likewise be rejected. It also assumes that all people have equal potential as moral agents. The perspective suggested here does not assume that ethical frameworks must necessarily be gendered, that this framework works better in women's hands, or that female moral agents need a distinctive approach exclusively centered on women's lives. Indeed, the view proposed here depends on rejecting gender essentialism as vigorously as it rejects cultural essentialism (see, for example, Spelman, 1988). Mohanty (1991) asserts: "If such concepts [as patriarchy or a sexual division of labor] are assumed to be universally applicable, the resultant homogenization of class, race, religious, and daily material practices of women in the third world can create a false sense of the commonality of oppressions, interests, and struggles between and among women globally. Beyond sisterhood there are still racism, colonialism, and imperialism!" (p. 68). Rejecting notions about women's culture and women's commonality as not merely descriptively false but also misleading and politically damaging means that communication between males and females should not be treated as "inter-cultural." More importantly, no singular life of "women" is available that otherwise might give rise to a distinctly woman-centered approach to morality.

After briefly introducing what is entailed by a feminist approach, this chapter suggests several criteria for a feminist ethic of intercultural communications; it explains what a method for ethical inquiry would need to accomplish to be effectively feminist. Treading more and less successfully a fine line between sounding overly abstract and sounding overly simplistic, the chapter outlines how such a schema for ethical analysis and decision-making might work procedurally. Finally, the chapter illustrates the method with reference to one intercultural dilemma, in this case, drawn from popular culture.

FEMINISM AS A NORMATIVE MOVEMENT

Before launching this schema, a few stipulations must acknowledged. First, regardless of how clever and intellectually seamless a pure ethical theory appears, once applied by people to real situations and dilemmas, no single theory is perfect. Ethics, as Baier (1994) concludes fairly generously, "is a polyphonic art form, in which the echoes of the old voices contribute to the quality of the sound of all the new voices" (p. 312). Therefore, feminist ethicists inevitably draw from many sources. As Held (1993) notes, a moral theory that would result from relying on feminist methods would be highly unlikely to proclaim as transcendent any single principle such as the Categorical Imperative. Indeed, Held concedes that even a feminist ethic may not be useful across all domains and will not resolve all bureaucratic, legal, and market problems. Perhaps the counter-hegemonic and transgressive impulses of feminism subvert any moves toward a monolithic approach. In any case, the goal here is to describe broadly an approach to moral inquiry that takes into account differences and that accommodates as much relevant information as possible. Ideally, moral agents could use it to generate ethically justifiable decisions in domestic and professional life, including the inevitable conflicts between work and family, many of which have intercultural dimensions. Held (1993) points out that moral inquiry involves not merely knowledge attained through cognition and understanding, but also activity and feeling; moral theories themselves must confront lived reality and must be grounded in actual experience. A feminist ethic requires a strong musculature. Precisely because it lacks the arm of the law, it must be hearty enough to be applicable to the issues of people's everyday lives. In this case, flexibility and synthesis secure that strength.

A feminist ethic also postulates that people are essentially sincere and good. Although feminists are often (but wrongly) attacked as being anti-male, a feminist ethic not only is mindful of the need to distinguish structural problems from individual ones but also sees women and men as generally motivated by much more than self-interest, including financial self-interest. Nevertheless, people inevitably, and even often, face thorny situations involving contradictions among values that are legitimate, if perhaps not necessarily equally legitimate. The issue, then, is not individuals' temptation to put self-interest and personal desire before morality. Nor is it the conflict between "good" and "bad" persons. Rather, the question is how to choose among relative goods. Indeed, because at some level they involve contradictions among admirable and legitimate value systems, intercultural dilemmas may be foremost here.

Yet, even the most loving and generous person, that virtuous-minded person who sincerely wants to serve social justice, may not know intuitively or instinctively how to act morally at a given moment. This is the case not merely because social constructionism has radically undermined confidence in academic discourse about instinct and intuition; even the "sense" of intuition may not be adequate to analyze moral impasses. This is not to denigrate the person who seems to respond to a particular context unself-consciously. This is simply to say that troublesome dilemmas emerge in an increasingly complex world—where we confront many situations out of our usual ken and meet up with many different kinds of people of all kinds of backgrounds criss-crossed by religion, class formation, geographic location, sexual orientation and so forth. In such a world, discomfort over our recognition that we do not automatically or immediately know what to do is fairly predictable. That uneasiness can only be ameliorated by working with some set of guidelines for analyzing the dilemma and for evaluating alternative responses.

The question of cultural relativity (whether culturally-bound moral agents ought to challenge the practices condoned in another culture, and under what conditions that challenge might be permissible) eventually becomes irrelevant here, because the issue is not abstract: People literally must confront inter-cultural problems. The framework proposed here does not force any group to accept wholesale the cultural system and values of another; there is no intent to produce what Casmir (this volume) calls an "integration" model. Presumably no moral system proclaims an interest in reifying anyone's value system or mores or in essentializing any category. On the other hand, people must be able to analyze and eventually act in the face of intercultural conflict. Again, even after those few "obviously" unacceptable elements have been rejected (those facets of a cultural apparatus peculiar to a social system that no ethical framework could justify), vexing conflicts among acceptable values and systems will sometimes persist. The fact that no single universal system exists for permanently resolving contradictions does not absolve people of the responsibility for doing their best to act morally in the short-term.

Feminists learned the hard way the pitfalls of ignoring national, racial, ethnic and class differences, as well as those of sexual orientation and religion. As painful as it was to sacrifice the rhetorical purity and political drama of references to a universal womanhood and a global notion of sisterhood, feminists have learned to acknowledge a trinity of gender, race and class, and not always in that order. Benhabib (1987) accuses Western universalistic moral theories of surreptitiously identifying everyone's experiences with those of white men. Having accepted the critique of "substitutionalism," one cannot then allow the issues and experiences of white middle-class U.S. women to be conflated with those of all women. Intercultural sensitivity relies on extending this acknowledgment, without romanticizing or orientalizing certain groups of women. At the same time, as a practical matter, even the most inclusive and flexible approach has its limits, including geographic limits, if it is to avoid vagueness and vacuity and to be useful. At least in the short run, the notion of the transcultural universal is no more likely than that of androgyny to succeed in solving ethical quandaries. At some level, unfortunately, moral conversation and application of moral principles may collapse in the face of confrontation with wholly different cultural universes. The simultaneous fragmentation and global interdependence characteristic of contemporary society produce many moral quandaries that are both intercultural and international. Diaspora and hybridization not withstanding, substantive cultural differences remain. So, when feminists advocate multiculturalism, this refers to appreciation and acknowledgement of cultural difference, not the notion that there exists a single, albeit synthetic or cross-cultural identity. To avoid defending claims about a trans-national scope, then, the examples in this chapter have a United States context. One certainly can hope that ethicists will provide further guidance on how to investigate and address a wider variety of international dilemmas. Perhaps the principles outlined here can be useful in that larger project.

CRITERIA FOR A FEMINIST ETHIC

Just as feminism is inherently normative, so feminist ethics is normative. It affirms particular values per se, and calls for ethical decision-making in light of those values. While assuming, as noted above, a conception of human nature as essentially (i.e., in the long run) committed to moral outcomes, feminist ethics allows for the possibility, indeed the probability, that transformation is necessary. As a framework derived from feminist philosophy, feminist ethics expects that intervention is necessary, at least at the level of organizations and institutions. It is activist, not passive. Feminist theorizing focusses on structural, institutional, and fairly obdurate historical patterns (which themselves may be social-cultural or economic) and it calls attention to the reasons for change at those levels. Nonetheless, a feminist ethic both acknowledges and encourages the possibilities for moral action at the level of the individual. Bartky (1995) and others have even discovered "a good Foucault" who understands the prospects, albeit limited ones, for political agency and thus for meaningful projects of social amelioration (i.e., as opposed to the dystopian "bad" Foucault who refutes the notion of the "free subject"). Stated in even stronger terms, feminism may even be said to insist on moral action: Not merely producing structures or relationships that systematically dehumanize, trivialize, or disempower women but even accepting them or giving them additional currency is morally repugnant and needs to be challenged on ethical grounds, across a variety of realms, whether work sites, media representations or personal relations.

Specifically, feminist ethics holds to its ultimate goal of undoing the oppression of all marginalized peoples. The feminist movement opposes imperialism and colonialism, as well as racism and sexism. Not every ethical dilemma involves marginalization on the grounds of identity defined categorically. Nonetheless, a global star respecting the fundamental humanness of all people must light feminist ethics. Furthermore, even applied to what seem to be relatively minor questions, application of feminist ethics must not result in actions or ideologies that further the oppression of women. Moreover, it must consider not only gender but also and no less centrally geography, class, age, physical ability, religion and sexual orientation. All these are crucial to feminist analysis, at least as conceptualized here, because undoing categorical oppression in one respect cannot be used to justify increasing oppression in another respect. These aspects of self and experience are structurally and philosophically interrelated in ways that potentially always can—and in actuality often do—divide women. Furthermore, and as importantly, these intersecting axes of identity enter into the calculus of power and authority, rendering casual, unidimensional assertions about oppression and liberation naive, if not ridiculous. Incorporating dynamic inequalities in apparatus of knowledge, organizations and institutions, Smith's (1987) concept of "relations of ruling" highlights the powerful unevenness in the operations of patriarchy. Put bluntly, structural inequities hang more heavily on some women than others, rendering a Utilitarian approach to ethics abhorrent.

Differing versions of feminist ethics usually also involve some secondary goals. The knowledge that these intersect with historically- and materially-specific practices and are intensely informed by cultural differences that come in and out of view does not necessarily invalidate them as values. These goals may at times come to be at odds with one another or with values embedded within other value systems. One example of this is free expression, long regarded as a hallmark of U.S. values. Continuing debates over political correctness in speech betray how the goal of encouraging free expression, while not itself antithetical to feminism, carries the seeds of an moral dilemma: Can promoting free expression for a particular group or particular position have the result of silencing another group or position? Put in the reverse, when, if ever, is it ethically permissible to protect the voices of one group by silencing another? If everyone's voice cannot be heard, whose will be? Feminist theorizing goes beyond providing explanations for distorted and distorting images of women; it suggests that to accept such images, much less to produce them, is ethically problematic. Although her key point concerns the status of women of color in white theorizing, Bhavnani (1993) notes how feminism has challenged the "EDITing" of women; the processes she discusses—Erasure, Denial, Invisibility and Tokenism—all occur in mass media. Systematic distortions, symbolic marginalization and trivialization are abhorrent, at the level of women's role as professional media communicators, as consumers/audiences and as subjects/content. Yet, the notion of free expression offers no corrective here.

Having stated this fairly stridently, it is also worth indicating that feminist ethics are typically couched in terms of what one generally aims for, rather than what everyone must always do. Feminist ethicists speak the language of principles rather than the language of rules. As Grimshaw (1986) points out, principles invite reflection, while rules exclude it. Without entering into philosophical debates over any specific rule-based ethical theory, a feminist ethic is unlikely to be sympathetic to Kantian imperatives or call for reverence of imposed duty. Even as general statements—perhaps because they are only abstract statements—ethical universals per se do not articulate moral solutions. Therefore, at the level of actual analysis and prescription, feminist ethics avoids the language of "must always." More specifically, a feminist ethic that works specifically in mediating or ameliorating intercultural conflict inevitably must meet the test of acknowledging cultural difference. Thus from the start, a feminist ethic refuses to essentialize particular ways of being or to "naturalize" assumptions. A feminist ethic acknowledges different moral voices. As events around the world have recently dramatized, a feminist ethical schema recognizes the utility of compromise, tolerance, and flexibility. It aims for seeing issues and interests through another's eyes and adopts a language of moderation rather than extremism.

Having acknowledged not merely the existence of difference but also the value of difference, feminist ethics celebrates differences in people's ways of thinking, judging, acting. Thus, feminist ethics refuses to conflate the experiences of one group into those of another. One consequence of this is that feminist ethics takes women's experience into account. As Jagger (1991) insists, feminism is "incompatible with any form of moral relativism that condones the subordination of women or the devaluation of their moral experience" (p. 95). Disputing the canard that women are morally inferior to men, feminist ethicists affirm that women are potentially as capable of moral reasoning as men. On the other hand, feminist ethics would not assume that all women share the same experiences or behave in identical ways. Although popular conceptions of gender posit dichotomous categories, men and women do not live in mutually exclusive worlds. As powerful as gender appears as an explanation for cultural phenomena, gender difference cannot be taken as the only meaningful difference among people or as the explanation for all conflicts. One major outcome of this is that feminist ethics (in contradistinction to an explicitly woman-centered ethic) cannot assume that women necessarily operate with moral principles distinct from men's, much less opposed in a polar way. Rather, it takes into account all sorts of differences, issues, and variations in perspectives.

The perspective suggested here does not assume that—either because or despite a grounding in oppression—women's ways per se, including their ethical schemas, are moral. Referring specifically to the reach of intellectual ability, feminist standpoint theory suggests that dominated peoples develop special analytic capabilities given their need to study their oppressors. Nonetheless, at least in its socialist version, feminist theorizing allows for the possibility that oppression can distort intellectual processes and structural relationships as well as workplace or personal relationships and loyalties. Borrowing from socialist feminism, then, feminist ethics acknowledges that not only do structural and material conditions present decision-makers with ethical dilemmas, but historical conditions, most centrally economic constraints, can distort people's interests and their sense of values. Indeed, these constraints not only challenge people's ability to analyze ethical dilemmas and to act morally, but they also can produce anti-ethical and anti-feminist actions and motives. Women are not categorically exempt in this context. In any case, the ethical schema proposed here neither pretends that structural constraints and personal relationships do not exist, nor pretends that one particular relationship or particular structure can be taken out of context and alone relied upon to resolve ethical problems. Instead, among several factors, these relationships and constraints are to be openly acknowledged and taken into account.

Another corollary assumption is that women and men do not face different ethical dilemmas. Spheres of moral action are not dichotomously gendered. As Jagger (1991) argues, to posit that "women's issues," which often amount to family and domestic responsibilities, are distinct from men's excludes women's voices on many important issues. Furthermore, such "sexual apartheid" absolves men of the responsibility for being concerned with these issues and for cultivating empathy and altruism.

Finally, feminist ethics will not automatically rule out emotions or (dis)regard intuitions as illegitimate. Indeed, among the several characteristics that distinguish feminist ethics from most other ethical proposals is its willingness to take into account emotions, sentiments, and intuitions, as well as individual decision-makers' experiences (Nussbaum, 1985). Crucial to a feminist ethic is the insistence that formal justice and rationality are not the sole tests of morality. Jagger (1989) underscores the importance of emotions, including love and anger, within feminist epistemology; emotions are intentional and are logically connected to knowledge. This point that "outlaw emotions," specifically feminist emotions, may be politically subversive has relevance for epistemology and for ethics.

But while a feminist ethic may begin with individual experiences, emotions, and intuitions, it does not end there (in contrast, see Manning, 1992). On an even more explicitly methodological note, this feminist perspective is openly analytic and works primarily through cognitive inquiry, rather than intuition. Again, just as values and behaviors may be systematically distorted by economic conditions and other structural problems, so intuitions may be misguided. Jagger (1989) wants to argue that just as the cognitive perspective available from the standpoint of the oppressed is less partial and more reliable than the dominant standpoint and thus enjoys epistemological privilege, so "the emotional responses of oppressed people in general, and often of women in particular, are more likely to be appropriate than the emotional responses of the dominant class" (p. 146). In contrast, no special epistemological or moral status is here claimed for women, even oppressed women or, for that matter, feminists (Steiner, 1989). One implication of the sophisticated feminist theorizing now emerging is that nothing, including emotions, can be naturalized as "authentic." While they may be "personal," emotions are socially constructed, as Jagger (1989) herself concedes with reference to their use in the production of knowledge. Thus, while useful in moral reasoning, emotions cannot be the sole basis of moral choice.

The approach proposed here is notably different from the anti-theoretical and ultimately anti-intellectual "speaking from the heart" perspectives of feminist ethicists such as Manning (1992). Nonetheless, the desiderata here are very much in line with those of Manning, who says an adequate feminist ethic should offer a picture of the self that grants the connected nature of humans; a model of reasoning that is contextual, with rules of thumb grounded in experience; a further blurring of the division between theory and practice; an understanding of beliefs grounded in experience, and guidance about practical life; a rejection of dichotomies between reason and emotion or between mind and body; a concern with problematics from the private as well as public spheres; and an explicit discussion of the ethic's moral conceptions.

Alternative Ethical Proposals: Caring and Dialogue

These criteria can be made more explicit by noting the continuing and heated debate over Gilligan's (1982) refutation of Kohlberg's (1981) research. Perhaps merely echoing Kant's view that "the fair sex" knows "Nothing of duty, nothing of compulsion, nothing of obligation" (quoted in Spelman, 1988, p. 6), Kohlberg (1981) had concluded that women rarely achieved the same level of moral reasoning as men. Gilligan (1982) suggests that women speak in a different voice, not a deficient one. Borrowing from Chodorow's (1978) object-relations account of gender development, Gilligan's (1982) *In A Different Voice* finds that whereas males tend to refer to justice and to abstract principles, women tend to use a language of relationship, affection, sense of responsibility. The debate cannot be fully elaborated here. Gilligan herself attributes the resistance to her work to fears about "the dangers of stereotyping, the intimations of biological determinism, and the fact that in recent discussions of sex differences there is no disinterested position" (Gilligan & Wiggins, 1987, p. 278). Indeed, several philosophers and social scientists offer wide-ranging critiques of the methodological and philosophical problems plaguing Gilligan's work (see, e.g., Benhabib, 1987; Flanagan & Jackson, 1987; Nails, 1983; see also, Steiner, 1989). Some scholars criticize Gilligan for providing too little data—which itself is at best anecdotal and narrowly-conceptualized—that actually supported her claims about gender-related differences (see, e.g., Walker, 1984). Wood (1992) dismisses Gilligan's conception of caring as regressive: "The view of women that Gilligan and those working from her ideas appear to hold resonates with entrenched conservative, patriarchal identities prescribed for women" (p. 5). Cortese (1990) criticizes the universalizing of Anglo-American culture, although he accepts Kohlberg and Piaget's notion of developmental stages and he defends both Gilligan's formulation of an ethic grounded in relationship and her view that gender matters. As opposed to Kohlberg's individualistic, objective, and rational conception, Cortese substitutes a view of morality as socially and culturally determined not only by demands of gender roles but also class interests, national policies, and ethnic antagonisms.

Yet, others find Gilligan plausible in the light of gendered role socialization (Donenberg & Hoffman, 1988). Although few people explicitly state that women's ways are superior to the masculine approach, some scholars, especially in education, have celebrated women's way of thinking (Belenky et al., 1986). In any case, Gilligan provides warrants for an epistemology and style of moral reasoning based on caring and relationship (Stewart, forthcoming) or, put more broadly, trust (Baier, 1994), as distinguished from the conventional emphases on rights and reciprocity.

Indeed, this claim has been extended to the advocacy of motherhood per se as an ethical model (Nodding, 1984; Ruddick, 1980; Trebilcot, 1984). Feminists correctly reject impartiality as the dominant moral virtue and reject moral theories that either categorically disparage or ignore family relationships. They are acutely sensitive to how parents, as such, engage in ongoing moral deliberation and moral teaching. The position argued here, however, is that women's biological capacity to give birth does not itself "engender" significant commonalities among women, including morality. Over-emphasizing the celebrated bonds between mothers and children may wrongly encourage parents to regard the material well-being of their own already-comfortable children as more important than the minimal well-being of very needy non-relatives. Indeed, mothering can be irrational and selfish, if not for oneself, then on behalf of one's own children. Even its self-sacrificial mode can be patronizing and downright racist.

Furthermore, as the history of how white women (mis)treated slaves and domestic servants all too poignantly evidences (Lerner, 1972; Rollins, 1985), the question of who, and in what ways, deserves to be treated as appropriate beneficiaries of caring and nurturing has significant intercultural implications worth noting. In contrast to presumably impartial, rule-based ethicists, some feminist ethicists defend the spouse or parent who puts the life of a mate or child above the lives of others, when presumably only one can be saved. But the question of which one individual should literally be rescued does not exhaust the range of moral dilemmas that U.S. families typically face. The more relevant question concerns at what point family members can and ought to stop investing time and energy in luxuries, in order to provide for those non-family members less fortunate. At the least, if parenting is to be prescribed as a moral framework, it needs to cast off its nuclear focus in favor of a more global embrace.

Again, there surely are different ways of engaging in moral reasoning. Thus, no person or group should be regarded as morally suspect simply on account of gender, class, race, or nationality. On the other hand, empirical (and perhaps romanticized) descriptions of how groups have appeared to approach moral issues should not be elevated into normative prescriptions. Moreover, even those attempts to provide social scientific investigation into gendered (or, in Cortese's case, ethnic) approaches not only admit some vagueness about what justification schemes people use, but do not even begin to suggest what justification schemes might be embedded in the description. More crucially, they do not reveal what analytic and justificatory schemes *could* be applied to a given dilemma. Even if, for example, caring takes on a properly complex and social conceptualization and thus can be defended as a moral bedrock, the question is how people, recognizing a sticky situation, can operationalize caring to arrive at a response they feel ethically comfortable with and can defend.

In response to the dogmatism and individualism of rule-bound ethical theories generated in philosophy, feminist philosophers have increasingly emphasized the importance of voice, conversation and hearing. They suggest that consensus is more likely when grounded in "actual dialogue between actual persons" (Held, 1993, p. 41). Acknowledging the impossibility of being totally detached and impartial, Young (1987) asks people to enter into dialogue in which conflicting perspectives would be heard and taken into account. Young's (1987) "dialogic conception of normative reason" is quite different from Rawls' (1971) "theory of justice," for example, which requires that moral agents abandon their own perspective and adopt that of another. Held's (1993) notion of a very broad "reflective equilibrium" likewise both echoes and repudiates Rawls, since his notion of reflective equilibrium is that it deliberately excludes judgments based on feelings or partiality. Such proposals may be helpful, at least as long as one does not take descriptions of experience as necessarily morally prescriptive and as long as one tries to distinguish appropriate from inappropriate feelings. Indeed, Buber's notion of the I-Thou or dialogic relationship has been largely accepted as moral grounds in interpersonal communication (see, for example, Johannesen, 1990; Stewart, forthcoming).

Others have suggested that women's differences—especially by color and class—be transformed from source of conflict into grounds for mutual dialogue and appreciation for multiple voices. Criticizing the imperialist distortions implicit in feminism, Lugones and Spelman (1990) call upon Anglo women to work harder at understanding women of color by hearing them out and engaging in egalitarian conversation. Typically, the notion of "voice" assumes that only/all women listen to "the other," that is, women's voices are never heard and men never listen. Held's (1993) feminist moral theory is useful because it requires dialogue that is cognizant of differences among women. Conceding the irony of Gilligan's attention to a gender-specific voice, Moody-Adams (1991) accuses Gilligan of neglecting the plurality of women's voices that would logically follow from their diverse cultural experiences. Applying to organizational communication the musical term "harmonic discourse" (this refers to the importance of hearing the single voices in the whole ensemble), Fine (1991) advocates interculturally-sensitive dialogue "in which all voices retain their individual integrity yet combine to form a whole discourse that is orderly and congruous" (p. 266).

This emphasis on dialogue and mutuality also marks the drive to ethical codes in intercultural communication. Sitaram and Cogdell (1976) propose 35 imperatives for the intercultural communicator; these range from the fairly general (try to understand the cultural bases of others's values, recognizing that each culture has something to offer the world; and do not impose one's own values on others) to the specific (respect the way other people speak, dress, pray, and eat). A recent definition of the ideal intercultural communicator is broader and more economical (Kale, 1991). Kale's principles take the form of four descriptive statements about ethical communicators: They address people of other cultures with the same respect that they would like to receive themselves; seek to describe the world as they perceive it as accurately as possible; encourage people of other cultures to express themselves in their uniqueness; and strive for identification with people of other cultures. These are admirable qualities. Nevertheless, these four principles may not answer the questions of someone who is unsure of which course of action is ethical. Likewise, metaphors of dialogue may not be sufficiently helpful to someone who needs to make a decision, whether in the corporate world, in personal relationships or in policy-making arenas. Questions remain: How do persons facing dilemmas decide what to do? What happens when dialogue does not resolve agonizing conflict? Are there ways to resolve the dilemmas that emerge despite people's beliefs that they are respectfully listening to others, are accurately describing the situation, and are even trying to identify with others? Are all positions are equally defensible, or even equally worth hearing? Do all claims warrant equal accreditation? How can students learn to distinguish between cultural pluralism, which is defensible, and ethical relativism, which is not (Rosen, 1980)? Given that so many debates about ethics alternate wildly between highly abstract pleas for toleration and highly unfocussed debates about specific cases, can one define an ethics that is neither a warm cozy nest of mutual appreciation nor a boggy swampland oozing eerie mists of ambiguity and personal speculation?

A Schema for Ethical Decision-making

In its abstract form, the schema proposed here borrows heavily from the so-called Potter Box (after Harvard Divinity School professor Ralph Potter) as Christians, Rotzell and Fackler (1991) have thoughtfully elaborated it. They articulate a four-celled model in such a way as to be consistent with their general concern for social responsibility. Most discussions of applied ethics, however, refuse to commit to any particular philosophical, political, or value position; this is the case whether the model refers to a profession or discipline such as mass media (see Bivins, 1993) or is more general (see Edel, Flower, & O'Connor, 1994). Therefore, as will become evident, the interest in feminism requires several significant, substantive departures from the Potter Box. Essentially the schema involves subjecting a dilemma to sequential investigation of several major points. The aim is not to provide some simple-minded, six-step Dale Carnegie course on moral problem-solving, or even a 12-step moral recovery program; for moral diagnosis involves much more than a skill learned through programmed training. Again, this schema cannot resolve every long-standing intercultural conflict. Nonetheless, asking certain questions may point toward a morally defensible answer.

The schema requires taking seriously several elements, including several that Western philosophers have traditionally disregarded or even repudiated as irrelevant. Key here is committing to the notion that, just as morality does not rest on a single motive, no single question is determinative. The ethical analyst (referring here and elsewhere not to the professional philosopher or the academic ethicist but rather the "ordinary" decision-maker) can settle on no solution, even tentatively, until all the issues are addressed. Even when responses point in mutually inconsistent directions, or the information seems to predict contradictory decisions, the analyst should not try to force the answers in anticipation of a particular decision. The questions concern:

1. Definition of the Situation: As Christians, Rotzell, and Fackler (1991) point out, the decision-maker begins by analyzing the circumstances of the particular problem or dilemma to be resolved. Presumably any situation can be defined in terms of a near-infinite number of particularities. Therefore, the analyst must determine which elements ought to be taken seriously and which should not. The would-be ethical analyst must sort out aspects of the situation that are most relevant from those that are irrelevant, must separate those aspects of the case with the most bearing from those with the least. Edel, Flower and O'Connor (1994) underscore the significance of "how we identify, classify, and recognize a problem, and *how we come to see that it is a problem*" (p. 102). Edel, Flower and O'Connor (1994) specifically highlight the necessity of being acutely sensitive to language: Just as the choice of descriptive terms unavoidably has direct and major consequences for politics (as the debate over abortion, to take one example, demonstrates), this has major implications for ethical analysis.

Rigorous and purist-minded philosophers, especially Kantians, of course, assert that local details are precisely what should be ignored in ethical analysis. In contrast, feminist ethicists' serious commitment to contextualism suggests that not only internal factors (what fundamentally seems to be going on, in the narrowest sense) but also external factors, including economic, political and social histories and material conditions, should be addressed. This is certainly not to apologize for or defend profit motives or political self-interest, but to recognize their explanatory value. The issue may involve conflicts between corporate and/or university cultures, national and/or local cultures, and between alternative or sub-cultures.

Edel, Flower and O'Connor (1994) add that one initial component of inquiry reduces to whose problem it is. Feminist analysts pay particular attention to the possibility of power struggles, particularly those between dominant and oppressed peoples or cultures. Gender conflicts often loom large here, that is, attempts by men to marginalize women and attempts by women to resist that marginalization. What initially appear to be intercultural problems may turn out more fundamentally to involve issues of gender, with questions of local or national culture either applied as false "covers" for sexism or at best relatively trivial concerns. This possibility must be seriously investigated. That is, one examines what happens when one asks whether gender is an issue. What evidence turns up when one asks whether women are being significantly debased in or by a specific media representation or whether a woman is being silenced or disempowered in an organization? On the other hand, gender is not the only issue. Notions of gender that ignore intersections with class, race and sexuality (i.e., that conflate gender with the concerns of white, middle-class heterosexual women) or that treat gender independently of other identity features are particularly problematic.

2. *Values and Ideals*: Secondly, the analyist stipulates the relevant values and operant ideals. The context of any dilemma implies some relatively specific values, although these vary by medium, by time, by geography. Within a particular place and time, these may be not only ideological, or communal, but also aesthetic (clean lines, for example), professional (in the case of journalism, timeliness and accuracy are often cited as values), or analytic. But again, the ethical analyst must be alert to the possibility that aesthetic and professional values vary across cultures. Furthermore, even one's personal catalog of operant ideals will contain conflicts, thus forcing judgments about the relative importance of the ideals. If they cannot be all equally honored, then the analyst may consider the order in which standards should be honored, given the costs of honoring them, or failing to do so. Again, while the assumption here is that no single issue is determinative, the analyst may legitimately aver that no circumstances could justify compromising a particular value.

Most importantly, a feminist approach to ethical analysis is likely here to put a set of feminist values front and center. Different feminist theories as such inevitably not only have embedded within them different explanations for women's oppression and different understandings of how this should be redressed, but they also imply different values (Jagger, 1983). Therefore, no laundry list of feminist values will perfectly fit every feminist position. Furthermore, articulating such values will merely appear to parody politically correct bedtime stories. But, for the sake of completeness, one might include as a feminist value caring for the family at both its most local levels and at larger social and global levels, including caring for the community and for the environment. Feminists also advocate preserving communities and a sense of communal responsibility (that is, in contradistinction to more individualistic or competitive definitions of the self); and encouraging social and cultural processes that listen and give voice to a range of expressions. Other ideals potentially relevant here include human goodness, social justice, cooperation and other methods of non-violent collaboration, mutual respect for differences and promoting a sense of integrity.

3. *Ethical Principle*: The Potter Box involves reference to an over-arching ethical principle such as Mill's Principle of Utility, Kant's Categorical Imperative, the Aristotelian notion of the Golden Mean, or another virtue-based approach. Rather than committing to one, Edel, Flower and O'Connor (1994) suggest "building up an inventory of resources from the theoretical reservoir" (p. 139). Since feminist philosophers have produced a large and helpful body of literature critiquing various philosophical traditions, that corpus will not be repeated here. Suffice it to say that feminist inquiry is generally unsympathetic to rule-based ethical theories or theories that—as they usually do—exclude consideration of emotion. As noted previously, these ethical theories have historically resulted in dismissing what turn out to be, descriptively, women's ethical analyses. Instead of applying one single rule—even one so amiable and flexible as the golden mean—a feminist ethic, then, suggests returning to the emancipatory and empowering values mentioned above and the more general ambition of feminism: ameliorating and undoing oppression of all kinds.

4. *Loyalties:* In ways notably analogous to Rawls' (1971) theory of justice, feminist ethics entails some consideration of the potential claimants on one's sense of responsibility. Rawls proposes that the moral agent don the so-called Veil of Ignorance in an attempt to bury one's own interests and to adopt the perspective of another. Feminist ethicists, in contrast, underscore the impossibility of impartiality and the distorting effects of this attempt to be unbiased and neutral (see Jagger, 1989, 1991). That is, a feminist approach to decision-making suggests that open analysis of loyalties is a vital component,

not merely a reluctant concession. As already noted, many feminists are uncomfortable with the presumption that women's only or even primary sense of responsibility is to their immediate loved ones. Therefore, the list of potential claimants can be broad and often should be broader than first appearances might suggest.

The culturally-bound issue of loyalty presents thorny complications, as with the larger issue of agency. Indeed, allegations about women's subordinate status and passivity would seem to contradict feminism's call for assertive activity. Nelson-Kuna and Riger (1995) propose to resolve this tension with the construct of communion but admit that race, ethnicity and social class structure the environment within which women live. For example, assumptions about agency and loyalty are severely challenged by instances of women who, socialized to be loyal and subordinate to men in the context of very specific cultures, including immigrant cultures, obediently return to their abusive husbands (Hegde, 1996). Culturally-specific gender implications resonate through both political-personal spheres and the moral domain.

Even with respect to a single situation, the claims of those to whom we owe responsibility or have a sense of duty will come into conflict. Certainly women are likely to be injured by immoral actions the most often, and to the greatest extent. Thus, moral agents must not only consider the range of people potentially injured or helped by a particular act, but set priorities for protecting their interests. Rawls' call for a concern with justice is consistent with the feminist goal of seeking to protect those most vulnerable, which may be women of color, lesbians, disabled or poor women. Analogously to the proviso mentioned with respect to ideals and values, ultimately the analyst may vigorously express unwillingness to allow injury to certain claimants, when not all claimants are equally entitled to immunity.

5. *Options*: In light of the definition of the situation, the short-term values and long-term ideals, and a sense of those to whom one owes loyalties, the moral analyst then proceeds to consider her options, the potential routes to addressing the problem. Kant's notion of the Categorical Imperative suggests that only one action is ethically correct (i.e., the action which the moral agent is willing to have universalized). The feminist analyst, however, may imagine several. Indeed, imagining and identifying alternatives is at the heart of the third-culture building model Casmir (this volume) suggests.

Since alternatives will be more and less appropriate, however, the issue is not merely imagining solutions but evaluating them. Furthermore, any particular option is unlikely to please everyone equally, especially with respect to short-term consequences and especially given the types of problems that intercultural conflicts produce. Indeed, if there were a resolution that would hurt no one and please everyone, one might speculate that the dilemma was not very tough in the first place. On the other hand, feminists do not necessarily authorize the Aristotelian preference for the middle position between two extremes, given its avoidance of strong-minded commitments as well as its assumption of dichotomy. Instead, the moral agent must consider what harms to which people are likely to result from any of these potential solutions. Borrowing from Rawls (1971), the central principle is that good resolutions entail the least harm to those who can least afford to be harmed. Again, feminist theorizing justifies discarding polarized notions of alternatives and it favors multiple alternatives.

6. *Harms*: Bivens (1993) urges application of conjunctive rules to winnow down the options. Presumably, any options resulting in serious harms to important beneficiaries or directly violating of principles can be eliminated as untenable. Conversely, if this first consideration does not lead to the exclusion of some options, the student may reanalyze the dilemma. This reformulation of the "facts," beginning with the definition of the situation, occurs not tabula rasa but in light of previous inquiry and accounts. Such reanalysis is quite likely to be required, since not every response to these questions will point in the same direction. Not all statements produced to define the situation and to clarify ideals, principles and loyalties will be mutually accommodating and consistent. In the end, the best case is a solution that, while it may not please everyone, those most likely to be put in jeopardy can understand, if not defend it themselves. As Casmir (this volume) shows, decisions that are mutually agreed upon and mutually enacted are more valuable than those unilaterally imposed. Asking for response and discussion maximizes the likelihood of consensus.

Debates in the Popular Culture Domain: The Case of Gangsta Rap

Feminist theorizing takes popular culture seriously, if not literally. The minimalist and "negative" structure of media law (stemming as it does from the First Amendment, which protects speech and the press, and by extension, other media, from governmental intervention or abridgement of their freedom without requiring any particular actions in return) makes moral responsibility vital.

From an ethical perspective, concerns about the moral implications of popular music, film, television, comic books, cable and television programming, Internet sites and so forth need not derive from assertions about effects. First, causal arguments that popular cultural forms "drive" people to commit anti-social acts or destroy the self-images of consumers may be wrong. At the least, although expressions of increasing support for censorship in courts and in public opinion commonly invoke such effects, these are impossible to prove scientifically. Indeed, responses to particular cultural products become suspect when couched in wholesale condemnation of popular genres, especially when they vehemently accuse all popular culture of undermining social norms. Moral debates about popular culture should not ride on whether or not they appear directly to result in oppressive acts, or, for that matter, in resistant or subversive acts. Nor is the issue merely capitalism, although there certainly is much money to be made, spent or potentially lost in popular culture; this fact may be one of those "external factors" that could be taken into account in articulating a "definition of the situation."

On the other hand, analysts can legitimately make judgments about, for example, whether (or not, hypothetically) particular forms of popular culture rely on debasing and dehumanized representations, depicting women as no more than mindless sexual playthings. So, at one level, it is quite simple and straightforward to repudiate as morally repugnant those popular cultural representations that "symbolically annihilate" (the term is Gaye Tuchman's) particular groups of women, that silence women and consign them to oblivion, or that portray women as deserving to be sexually assaulted. At another level, as the debates over pornography show, the issues are complicated by a host of political and cultural questions of greater and lesser legitimacy. They become even more tortuous given a set of intercultural clashes. They raise ethical questions about whose decisions about repugnance and vulgarity "count." Moreover, the judgment that particular images are horrid does not itself answer the question of what, if anything, ought to be done about those images. If the answer to crude media representations of women as sexualized object is not a sanitized, romanticized and desexualized version of femininity, what are the alternatives? What kind of interventions are ethically required or permissible?

What should be the response, then, to the descriptions about and references to black women in, for example, rap music? Let's make this specific and difficult, through a relatively realistic, but hypothetical situation: I book the music for a variety entertainment show that is aired late on Saturday nights on a major cable television channel. I can consult with anyone I wish, but typically the decision is mine. Iam now considering a new "gangsta" rap group which is not quite as popular as Snoop Doggy Dogg, but is working its way up the charts. To my mind, Dead Meet's lyrics are clever and rhythmically slick, but also sexist and demeaning, as are the visuals on their music videos, which essentially dramatize sexual assault. For the purposes of this book, Dead Meet's most nearly quotable description of women refers to "hoes" and "bitches." My friends protest that my repugnance reflects little more than reactionary Victorian prudery that misses the alternative cultural and intercultural questions raised by rap. First, they quote Grossberg's (1989) sarcastic dismissal of the moral panics aroused by music television: "Whether coming from the 'moral' Right, the 'moral' Left, or from rock and roll fans (usually baby boomers), the criticisms echo the fears that have greeted many other popular cultural forms: music television is *another* example (surprise!) of sexist, violent, hedonistic, commodified, and alienating discourse" (p. 254). Similarly, McClary (1994) connects recent diatribes against the music of the young to Plato's worries that unsanctioned music would encourage listeners to value their own judgments and to resist authority (of the church and state) and would arouse sensuality. Since, according to McClary (1994), contemporary Leftists echo Plato, Saint Augustine, and Calvin, she concludes that the "anxieties over masculinity and mind-body dilemmas are not the exclusive preserve of conservatives" (p. 31).

Second, my friends and colleagues cite Ross's (1994) interpretation of gangsta rap as "a highly visible forum for debating the limited roles and opportunities available to working poor African-American youth" (p. 5). Rose (1994) insists that rap, as the music of hip hop culture, represents an Afro-diasporic form operating on the margins of post-industrial urban America; it is a form of black urban renewal. This reasoning is intended to show that the group's attitude is acceptable because rap reports on vital issues, especially underclass "street life." In fact, many rap fans argue that sheer racism precipitates the complaints about gangsta rap's honest, if angry, reflection of contemporary urban life. Celebrating rap's tenth birthday, one cultural critic applauded rap for crystallizing "a post-civil rights, ultra-urban, unromantic, hyperrealistic, neonationalistic, antiassimilationist, aggressive Afrocentric impulse" (George, 1994, p. 93). Indeed, the history of popular and rock music, from the very roots of rock to the commodification of disco and the subsequent anti-disco movement, is replete with racism (Garafolo, 1993; McClary, 1994). Mainstream music labels were no less indifferent to rap's caustic edge (George, 1994).

While troubled by the racist possibilities of my discomfort, however, I cannot be wholly intimidated by this charge. Notably, in a 1985 *Village Voice* column, after quoting a rap producer vehemently rejecting the insinuation that rappers "bust out" young girls (in George, 1994, p. 56), one black cultural critic fairly mildly commented on rap's characteristic "machismo" (p. 55). I am reminded of McRobbie's (1990) remark, directed at Dick Hebdige's otherwise-sophisticated analysis of working-class culture: "Despite his emphasis on the neglect of race and racism in youth and subcultural work, he seems oblivious to the equal neglect of sexuality and sexism" (pp. 71-72). Even male critics who are relatively critical of rap's misogyny avoid the moral implications and avoid calls for intervention. Lipsitz (1994), for example, merely concedes, "One ugly aspect of the popularity enjoyed by hip hop among suburban youth has been its symbolic value to them as a franchise on an imagined male power created through the degradation of women" (p. 24). Known for his sensitivity to the ethical consequences of scholarship, Dyson (1996) goes further than other public intellectuals, black or white, in bemoaning the sexism and homophobia of gangsta rap; yet, he sees the condemnation of rappers as scapegoating: "The demonization of gangsta rappers is often a convenient excuse for cultural and political elites to pounce on a group of artists who are easy prey" (p. xiii). Moreover, black culture is too broad and intricate for blacks to be obsessed with how whites view it (Dyson, 1996).

The question is, should I book Dead Meet? Let's say I accept Grossberg's (1989) argument that music television is produced in a complex and contradictory articulation of economic, textual and communicative practices. Let's grant that much of the public responses to the "cock-iest" of rock and roll and of MTV betrays both the knee-jerk reactivity of moral panic and ignorance of the interpretive creativity of fans. Does this close off all entry points for ethical and critical readings of particular forms of rap? If a feminist ethic is activist, pretending never to have heard of the band is inadequate. Legally I am probably on safe ground, whatever I choose. Quietly bypassing Dead Meet in favor of less controversial groups is hypocritical. Instead, I must consider the ethical rationale for booking the band or for refusing to do so. Here is how I apply the criteria from above to this dilemma:

1. In defining the situation, I begin with the notion that "representation" is important, not despite but because of its symbolic weight. The politics of representation are significant now as ever. Thus, the brutal sexism of Dead Meet lyrics is a major "fact." They significantly demean all women, regardless of color. If the rappers were to appear on my show, the relatively simple concert form would not reproduce the technical theatrics of their music video. Nonetheless, the audiences in the studio and at home will clearly hear the words, which are the primary signifiers in rap. And they will witness the "actions," which, for all the theorizing about audiences' multiple interpretations, are fairly crude. Without question, the studio audience (which includes the women and men who help produce the show itself) and the television audience are adult and sophisticated; they will have heard similar— or even more objectionable—lyrics outside the show. One practical issue for me, however, is whether they have heard similar—or more objectionable—

sentiments expressed on this particular show. I would like to think not, and believe that I can say this consistently about the music groups I have booked in my three years working for the show. The skits and the comic openings performed by some guest stars enact sentiments that often run to the gross and sophomoric, I admit with some regret, but they have avoided the levels of obscenity "achieved" by Dead Meet.

I take the fact that both the main rapper and the four members of his Dead Meet posse are black to be somewhat significant, since, overall, people of color are not sufficiently seen on broadcast and cable television; this includes music video channels (with the obvious exception of channels like Black Entertainment Television), which historically have been helpful to white groups (domestic and foreign) while hostile to black musicians. Yet, this is not hugely significant, since, in my mind, *how* people are seen—whether complex diversity replaces a constricted set of caricatures, and whether and how black women are represented—is more important than quantity. Historically and contemporaneously, rap music is already associated with African Americans males—who write, produce, perform, and otherwise earn money from rap, and who also, for the most part, control it. Therefore, the fact that this group is African American is not pioneering.

I worry that the celebration of misogyny slurs creates an environment which seems itself to glorify and sanction sexism. I worry about how younger teenagers, particularly girls and even more particularly African American girls, respond to the hyper-masculinized messages they hear in gangsta rap, messages that surpass even the sexual and sexist messages of most rock. The public responses to other controversial rap lyrics, as well as to news events such as the rape conviction of Mike Tyson and the confirmation hearings of Judge Clarence Thomas, speak to the tortured relations, including regarding sexual relations, of African American women and men. These distorted relations are celebrated, not challenged, in the lyrics of Dead Meet and other gangsta rappers. Indeed, that exaggerated and essentially anti-woman notion of masculine camaraderie and loyalty to the "homeboys" pervades the very culture and style of gangsta rappers more generally, even apart from their music (Hirschberg, 1996). At least in the late 1980s, criticism of rap groups like 2 Live Crew invoked notions of causality. Nonetheless, the rioting that broke out at a few rap concerts and even the arrests of certain rappers—Tupac Shakur was convicted of sexual assault and Dr. Dre bragged about throwing a black woman through a door—are disregarded here. I am attributing the fighting to the individual fighters, not the music. At least hypothetically, no particular kind of musician is categorically exempt from accusations of criminal behavior.

Although I do not know the precise financial status of Dead Meet, it seems to be doing well. Both the fact that the rappers won't starve without the appearance and the fact that Dead Meet will profit from an appearance on my show, which would not only potentially bring them additional bookings but also promote their forthcoming CDs, are of little significance to me. I am not opposed to musicians becoming wealthy. Besides, my cable network show profits from musicians. On the other hand, I regard as highly relevant that many gangsta rap groups have consciously inserted misogynist lyrics to enhance their marketability. The gangsta rapper Too Short, well-known for lyrics that denigrate women, told a CBS *48-Hours* interviewer, "I know I'm doing something bad. It might be tasteless to you. And even me. I'm targeting a certain market. A major market...multimillions!" (quoted in Gooch, 1995, p. 47).

2. The position of the cable network's producers is that musical groups must be hip, current, and popular. Beyond that, and the ability of the guests and the show to withstand the scrutiny of the network censors, they do not much care. I share the values of media workers, thus preferring minimal restrictions on content in the name of freedom of expression. Nonetheless, I understand the manifold constraints on media freedom—primarily ones of economics, although this is also an issue of the inherent limits of time and space. Furthermore, I want to entertain people. I like discovering new bands with something to say, especially with messages that otherwise are rarely heard.

3. My job is not to change the world, the network or the recording industry. But the corollary understanding that this job is perhaps not the best venue for political or personal transformation does not change my feminist commitments: I will not conduct my work in a way that promotes oppression as a means or end. As a feminist, I "dis-value" virulently sexist messages and I want to de-value them.

The relevance of feminists' general commitment to respecting and preserving distinct cultural identities, to the extent that cultural practices do not conflict with larger ethical goals, is unclear in the present instance; thus, as a white middle-class woman I must procede carefully. Nonetheless, even those who emphasize gangsta rap's truth-telling, however crudely put, about ghetto life do not defend its misogyny (see Dyson, 1996). I certainly would argue that sexism is not intrinsic to black culture.

4. Typically, musicians would be among the claimants on my sense of moral responsibility. I want to help struggling artists, particularly ones with

counter-hegemonic commitments and particularly women. Yet, conceding that Dead Meet rappers do present an artistic form with political overtones, I regard myself as having no particular responsibility to rap musicians. In any case, Dead Meet are doing fine without my help. And I have loyalties to my employers, all the way to the top, to corporate management, not merely because my colleagues and I owe them our employment, but also because management allows that irreverent spirit, albeit within clear (and sometimes not-so-clear) for-profit business limits. I have no particular concern either about earning money or saving face for management.

At the forefront are the responsibilities to audiences. That sense of obligation does not entail sanitizing, much less censoring, the show in order to protect the audience. Yet, even if professional responsibility is maximally a matter of presenting material audiences will find entertaining, a central assumption here is that audiences will be alienated by materials they find demeaning. In particular, African American women are radically under-served as a popular culture audience. Granted, for the purposes of this debate, this is a problem that can cut both ways. I believe I can legitimately put loyalties to otherwise under-served women ahead of those to men, on the theory that most of popular culture is sexist and aimed at the masculinized gaze. I would also speculate that gangsta rap (as opposed to other hip hop music genres) first and foremost titillates white adolescent males, who are already very well served by popular culture. Yet, many black women might enjoy Dead Meet. "There are alternative ways of viewing African American women as rap fans other than as objectified, self-degrading, video-dancing, sex-crazed, 'gold diggers' or 'skeezers'" (Gaunt, 1995, pp. 277-78). Noting how African American girls' jump-rope songs also tend toward vulgarity and allude to sexuality, Gaunt (1995) speculates that African American women's attraction to rap and hip-hop is connected to the rhythmic rapping style of their childhood games. Gaunt's (1995) explanation, it should be said, focusses on non-gangsta hip hop, especially as performed by women.

Of course, multiple audiences produce multiply-varied interpretations. Even for a highly particular cultural product, audiences' interests and tastes may be mutually contradictory. Gilroy (1987) emphasizes how, on one hand, the compounded intersections of race, gender, class and locality are shaped by subjective interpretations of a shared identity. On the other hand, no "community" can ensure that every member will accept even those meanings ascribed to the group (Gilroy, 1987).

One can note that some black women, in concert with Jewish and Baptist leaders, publically condemned the misogyny and violence in rap lyrics. Having purchased a few shares of Time Warner stock, the chairwoman of the National

Political Congress of Black Women attended the May 1995 shareholders' meeting in order to attack Time Warner, as parent owner of a major gangsta rapper label Death Row, as "a conspirator in the denigration and destruction of the black community" (Hirschberg, 1996, p. 30). As it turns out, her comments apparently precipitated a firestorm of protest, such that the Warner Music Group distanced itself from Death Row. Unfortunately (that is, immorally), Warner did not withdraw from the business arrangement by which the company, since it still owns the rights to the songs, continues to profit from the lyrics. Moreover, when these publishing rights to the lyrics came to light, the chairman of the Warner Music Group denied any hypocrisy: "In a volatile atmosphere we made a decision. Owning the publishing was about Time Warner making money, not about what we put in front of our children" (Hirschberg, 1996, p. 30).

5. Several options are open. One, of course, is booking the band—under the logic that audiences who quickly decide they dislike the band can turn off the music, or the program. Another option is refusing to book the band. After all, those who were most likely to enjoy the band will find other ways to discover the group, if they have not already done so. Hypothetically, I could also explicitly ask Dead Meet to temper its sexist lyrics, although I suspect this would backfire. Either such a request would be condemned as Puritanical interference with artistic license, or it would provoke sneers and even more virulently sexist lyrics and visual behaviors, or both. In any case, although I am unwilling to define the hypothetical request as an act of prior restraint, others are likely to construe it as such. If the healthy sales and profits of 2 Live Crew's album "As Nasty as They Wanna Be" are any predictor (not despite, but because of publicity over attempts to censor the rappers), accusations about censorship are nearly guaranteed to increase Dead Meet's sales.

Another possibility is to book Dead Meet as well as another group, perhaps a woman rapper such as Queen Latifah, self-proclaimed "Queen of Royal Badness." The problem here is that despite the success of innumerable "answer records" in vigorously returning insults and boasts (Gaar, 1992), even female rappers, who take on names like Hoes Wit Attitude and Bytches With Problems, do not publicly condemn the sexism of male rappers. This probably represents market constraints more than deference to racial solidarity. The example of BO$$ "demonstrates that women *can* access the male 'gangsta' pose" (Gaunt, 1995, 302). Yet, several rap producers reportedly did not sign Lichelle "Boss" Law because she did not curse enough, and Def Jam gave her a recording contract only after she inserted explicitly profane references to street life and cop killing (Pulley, 1994). Even if female rappers engaged in public criticism, one action does not cancel out the other. Incorporating feminist commentary by an academic popular culture critic would likewise be "lame," in the eyes and lingo of the audience. Turning the show over to overt political education would not be equally ineffective and would unfairly provoke the cliched canard that feminists are humorless and overly-literal.

Could a skit, either preceding or following the music, critique, albeit entertainingly, cruelty against black women? Even if a skit incorporated into an upcoming episode of the show challenged the gangsta message, this would not resolve the ethics of disseminating misogynist messages in the first place. Furthermore, parodies inevitably risk trivializing (making laughable) a non-trivial issue; or they can be misunderstood and thus seem to celebrate rather than subvert sexism.

6. No decision is perfect. No action harms no one. The weight of all the above leads me to decide that, since only a few groups can be booked and despite the negative connotations of "gatekeeper," inviting Dead Meet would be complicit in an illegitimate and indefensible posture of misogyny. Given the "value" of time on the show and the time of its audiences, I see the decision to make choices based in part on the content and political direction of the lyrics as no less legitimate than to select bands based on surface musicality and technical sophistication. Since someone must make a decision based on some criteria, Dead Meet can be judged in the context of its poisonous view of African American women. I am certainly not arguing that such lyrics cause male audiences to assault women, or even that such lyrics fatally undermine women's sense of self. Indeed, critics point to a long, complex, and tortured history of domestic and sexual relationships in the African American community. In the wake of the Clarence Thomas hearings, Patterson (1995) suggested that the consequences of slavery produced more psychological damage on black men than on women. But the fact that these lyrics do not cause rape (or the fact that this refusal "looks like" no more than yet another instance of moral panic) does not ethically justify disseminating and thus celebrating these messages.

While I can ethically defend not booking the band, it should be noted, this "negative" act is at best a band-aid. Refusal to book Dead Meet will not end the problem. It does not itself actively challenge the misogyny and racism of gangsta rap as a cultural product, nor does it clarify how those views are illegitimate. Refusing to book the rappers produces no critical thinking. Perhaps my corporate employers, colleagues and I could learn from some formal and informal discussions of racism and misogyny.

CONCLUSION

Because feminist ethics aims for consistent moral behavior, the very complexity of this entire analytic scheme is admittedly problematic. The analysis presented here required extensive research into feminist theory and ethics, the history and economics of rap music, and the racist and racial history of popular culture, as well as some hypothetical consideration, if not formal historical research, of the show's economics and content. Applying this moral schema to every decision we face in everyday life, or even not-so-ordinary life, is inconvenient, if not impossible.

Moreover, possession of an ethical framework certainly does not ensure that one will always apply it. First, knowing how to analyze a problem does not itself guarantee that a moral dilemma will be diagnosed as such in the first place. No less crucially, some virtuous-minded people who generally try to act ethically will not always be able (or willing) to do so. Given daunting self-interests—profit, job stability, promotions—individuals may on occasion be unwilling to sacrifice, whether in professional or domestic contexts. On the other hand, self-interest is not always at stake. Nor does one always suffer from making moral choices. In the debate about gangsta rap, for example, although the context was capitalism and the hypothetical employer's interest was maximizing profit, neither booking nor not booking a particular rap group had significant impact on the employer's or employee's financial statements.

More importantly, feminist ethics is aspirationalist. It urges people to stretch themselves morally, without condemning them outright when they engage in particular actions that are morally questionable. The goal is that we try to anticipate and recognize moral traps, and then practice applying analytic frameworks that serve social justice. Perhaps repeated practice makes ethical analysis easier, more efficient, even quicker. Furthermore, at least for those who want to enhance their sensitivity as moral agents, engaging in analysis will cultivate commitments to moral actions and relationships, most especially in the intercultural context.

REFERENCES

Baier, A. C. (1994). *Moral prejudices: Essays on ethics*. Cambridge, MA: Harvard University Press.

Bartky, S. L. (1995). Agency: What's the problem? In J. K. Gardiner (Ed.), *Provoking agents: gender and agency in theory and practice* (pp.178-93). Urbana: University of Illinois Press.

Belenky, M., Clinchy, B., Goldberger, N., & Tarule, J. (1986). *Women's ways of knowing: The development of self, voice, and mind*. New York: Basic Books.

Benhabib, S. (1987). The generalized and the concrete other: The Kohlberg-Gilligan controversy and feminist theory. In S. Benhabib & D. Cornell (Eds.), *Feminism as critique* (pp. 77-95). Minneapolis: University of Minnesota Press.

Bhavnani, K. (1993). Talking racism and the editing of women's studies. In D. Richardson & V. Robinson (Eds.), *Thinking feminist: Key concepts in women's studies* (pp. 27-48). New York: Guilford.

Bivens, T. H. (1993). A worksheet for ethics instruction and exercises in reason. *Journalism Educator*, *48:2*, 4-16.

Chodorow, N. (1978). *The reproduction of mothering: Psychoanalysis and the sociology of gender*. Berkeley: University of California Press.

Christians, C., Rotzoll, K. B., & Fackler, M. (1991). *Media ethics: Cases & moral reasoning* (3rd ed.). New York: Longman.

Cortese, A. J. (1990). *Ethnic ethics: The restructuring of moral theory*. Albany: State University of New York Press.

Donenberg, G. R., & Hoffman, L. W. (1988). Gender differences in moral development. *Sex Roles*, 18, 701-717.

Dyson, M. E. (1996). *Between God and gangsta rap: Bearing witness to black culture*. New York: Oxford University Press.

Edel, A., Flower, E., & O'Connor, F. W. (1994). *Critique of applied ethics: Reflections and recommendations*. Philadelphia: Temple University Press.

Fine, M. (1991). New voices in the workplace: Research directions in multicultural communication. *Journal of Business Communication*, *23*, 259-275.

Flanagan, O., & Jackson, K. (1987). Justice, care, and gender: The Kohlberg-Gilligan debate revisited. *Ethics*, *97*, 622-39.

Gaar, G. G. (1992). *She's a rebel: The history of women in rock & roll*. Seattle: Seal Press.

Garafolo, R. (1993). Crossing over: 1939-1992. In J. L. Dates & W. Barlow (Eds.), *Split image: African Americans in the mass media* (pp. 57-127). Washington, DC: Howard University Press.

Gaunt. K. D. (1995). African American women between hopscotch and hip-hop: "Must be the music (That's turnin' me on)." In A. N. Valdivia (Ed.), *Feminism, multiculturalism and the media: Global diversities* (pp. 277-308). Thousand Oaks, CA: Sage.

George, N. (1994). *Buppies, B-boys, Baps & Bohos: Notes on post-soul black culture*. New York: HarperPerennial.

Gilligan, C. (1982). *In a different voice*. Cambridge, MA: Harvard University Press.

Gilligan, C., & Wiggins, G. (1987). The origins of morality in early childhood relationships. In J. Kagan & S. Lamb (Eds.), *The emergence of morality in young children* (pp. 277-305). Chicago: University of Chicago Press.

Gilroy, P. (1987). *"There ain't no black in the Union Jack": The cultural politics of race and nation*. Chicago: University of Chicago Press.

Gooch, C. R. (1995). Gangster rap: message music or mayhem for profit? *Media Development*, *3*, 46-49.

Grimshaw, J. (1986). *Philosophy and feminist thinking*. Minneapolis: University of Minnesota Press.

Grossberg, L. (1989). MTV: Swinging on the (postmodern) star. In I. Angus & S. Jhally (Eds.), *Cultural politics in contemporary America* (pp. 254-270). New York: Routledge.

Hegde, R. (1995). Personal communication.

Held, V. (1993). *Feminist morality: Transforming culture, society, and politics.* Chicago: University of Chicago Press.

Hirschberg, L. (1996, Jan. 14). Does a sugar bear bite? *New York Times Magazine,* pp. 24-31+.

Jagger, A. (1983). *Feminist politics and human nature.* Totowa, NJ: Rowman & Allanheld.

Jagger, A. (1989). Love and knowledge: Emotion in feminist epistemology. In A. Garry & M. Pearsall (Eds.), *Women, knowledge, and reality: Explorations in feminist philosophy* (pp. 129-56). Boston: Unwin Hyman.

Jagger, A. (1991). Feminist ethics: projects, problems, prospects. In C. Card (Ed.), *Feminist Ethics* (pp. 78-104). Lawrence: University Press of Kansas.

Johannesen, R. L. (1990). *Ethics in human communication* (3rd ed.). Prospect Heights, IL: Waveland Press.

Kale, D. (1991). Ethics in intercultural communication. In L. Samovar & R. Porter (Eds.), *Intercultural communication: A reader* (pp. 421-26). Belmont, CA: Wadsworth.

Kohlberg, L. (1981). *The philosophy of moral development.* New York: Harper & Row.

Lerner, G. (Ed.). (1972). *Black women in white America.* New York: Vintage.

Lipsitz, G. (1994). We know what time it is: Race, class and youth culture in the nineties. In A. Ross & T. Rose (Eds.), *Microphone fiends: Youth music & youth culture* (pp. 17-28). New York: Routledge.

Lugones, M.C. & Spelman, E.V. (1990). Have we got a theory for you! Feminist theory, cultural imperialism and the demand for 'the woman's voice. In A. Y. al-Hibri & M. A. Simons (Eds.), *Hypatia reborn: Essays in feminist philosophy* (pp. 18-33). Bloomington: Indiana University Press.

McClary, S. (1994). Same as it ever was: Youth culture and music. In A. Ross & T. Rose (Eds.), *Microphone fiends: Youth music & youth culture* (pp. 29-40). New York: Routledge.

McRobbie, A. (1990). Settling accounts with subcultures: A feminist critique. In S. Frith & A. Goodwin (Eds.), *On record: Rock, pop, and the written word* (pp. 66-80). New York: Pantheon.

Manning, R. C. (1992). *Speaking from the heart: A feminist perspective on ethics.* Lanham, MD: Rowman & Littlefield.

Mohanty, C.T. (1991). Under western eyes: Feminist scholarship and colonial discourses. In C. T. Mohanty, A. Russo & L. Torres (Eds.), *Third World women and the politics of feminism* (pp. 51-80). Bloomington: Indiana University Press.

Moody-Adams, M. M. (1991). Gender and the complexity of moral voices. In C. Card (Ed.), *Feminist Ethics* (pp. 195-212). Lawrence: University Press of Kansas.

Nails, D. (1983). Social scientific sexism: Gilligan's mismeasure of man. *Social Research, 50,* 643-666.

Nelson-Kuna, J., & Riger, S. (1995). Women's agency in psychological contexts. In J. K. Gardiner (Ed.), *Provoking agents: gender and agency in theory and practice* (169-177). Urbana: University of Illinois Press.

Noddings, N. (1984). *Caring: A feminine approach to ethics and moral education.* Berkeley: University of California Press.

Nussbaum, M. C. (1985). Finely aware and richly responsible: Literature and the moral imagination. *The Journal of Philosophy, 82,* 516-529.

Patterson, O. (1995). The crisis of gender relations among African Americans. In A. F. Hill & E. Jordan (Eds.), *Race, gender, and power in America: The legacy of the Hill-Thomas hearings* (pp. 56-104). New York: Oxford University Press.

Pulley, B. (1994, Feb. 3). How a 'nice girl' evolved into Boss, the gangster rapper. *Wall Street Journal,* p. A1, 16.

Rawls, J. (1971). *A theory of justice.* Cambridge, MA: Harvard University Press.

Rollins, J. (1985). *Between Women: Domestics and their employers*. Philadelphia: Temple University Press.

Rose, T. (1994). *Black noise: Rap music and black culture in contemporary America*. Hanover, NH: Wesleyan Press.

Rosen, B. (1980). The teaching of undergraduate ethics. In D. Callahan & S. Bok (Eds.), *Ethics teaching in higher education*. New York: Plenum Press.

Ross, A. (1994). Introduction. In A. Ross & T. Rose (Eds.), *Microphone fiends: Youth music & youth culture* (pp. 1-13). New York: Routledge.

Ruddick, S. (1980). Maternal Thinking. *Feminist Studies, 6*, 342-367.

Sitaram, K.S., & Cogdell, R. T. (1976). *Foundations of intercultural communication*. Columbus, OH: Charles E. Merrill.

Smith, D. (1987). *The everyday world as problematic: A feminist sociology*. Boston: Northeastern University Press.

Spelman, E. V. (1988). *Inessential woman: Problems of exclusion in feminist thought*. Boston: Beacon Press.

Steiner, L. (1989). Feminist theorizing and communication ethics. *Communication, 12*, 157-173.

Stewart, L. P. (forthcoming). Facilitating connections: Issues of gender, culture, and diversity. In J. M. Makau & R. C. Arnett (Eds.), *Communication ethics in an age of diversity*. Urbana: University of Illinois Press.

Trebilcot, J., (Ed.). (1984). *Mothering: Essays in feminist theory*. Totowa, NJ: Rowman & Allanheld.

Walker, L. J. (1984). Sex differences in the development of moral reasoning: A critical review. *Child Development, 55*, 677-691.

Wood, J. (1992). Gender and moral voice: Moving from woman's nature to standpoint epistemology. *Women's Studies in Communication, 15*, 1-24.

Young, I. M. (1987). Impartiality and the civic public. In S. Benhabib & D. Cornell (Eds.), *Feminism as critique* (pp. 56-76). Minneapolis: University of Minnesota Press.

Ethics, Culture, and Communication: An Application of the Third-Culture Building Model to International and Intercultural Communication

Fred L. Casmir
Pepperdine University

SOME INTRODUCTORY THOUGHTS AND DEFINITIONS

Any ethic or ethical system is, quite obviously, the result of human actions in response to a felt need. In other words, ethics building or organizing is an attempt to bring order, structure or organization to human interactions so that some perceived challenge to the survival of a culture or society can be overcome or managed. Ethics, cultures, and communities are closely related because, as Schoening and Anderson (1995) point out: "Everyone who enters a community—through birth or joining—necessarily enters into a historical sphere of tacit agreements about what can and cannot constitute the 'known.' One does not merely accept ideas about the world; one also agrees to act accordingly, to 'do things as we do them'" (104). Both the communicative aspects and the environment in which the actual process of creating or organizing of an ethic develops thus are impacted to various degrees by the culture and cultural values of participants involved in such processes of organizing or building. The more varied the expectations and the nature of the generally accepted agreements which we face in intercultural and international communication processes, the more important becomes the need for building acceptable, mutually beneficial agreements for future actions or interactions *together*.

What is not quite as obvious, however, is the fact that most commonly we have concerned ourselves merely with the outcome, the end-product, the identifiable, existing ethic or ethical system, with little or no attention paid to the processes which were involved in its creation. In this chapter I will discuss, from the standpoint of a communication scholar, those factors which are involved in the ongoing cultural and intercultural interactions of human beings as they strive to organize and codify the value-systems of their cultures or societies. The third-culture *building* model is one means of doing more than identifying outcomes or endstates, it suggests that positive, one might say *ethical or desirable* communication strategies are available to produce mutually beneficial results for all participants in a process of building third-cultures and mutually empowering ethics or ethical systems (Casmir, 1978). That process would enable participating individuals to make meaningful contributions to societies or cultures, which are needed to sustain and secure common efforts over time. Schoening and Anderson (1995) remind us that "without the mutual work between two or more actors to limit the range of meaning possibilities generated by signification, the interpreter of an expression is left to deal with a great range of indeterminacy as to which 'reality' should be fashioned from an expression and how this fashioned 'reality' is to be understood. The interpreter would, therefore, be engaged in guesswork, not communication." (105) An important challenge to both the student and practitioner of international and intercultural communication is encapsulated in this brief statement. Humans communicating are most effective when their efforts are discursive, dialogueic "building" processes that do not merely end up with descriptions of differences or similarities, or even with "sensitive" interpretative guesswork as far as the meanings are concerned which others may or may not hold. Thus Schoening and Anderson (1995) and this chapter stress the need for discursive action to "determine" meaning and reality. Any common understanding, any common value system thus requires people to work together to produce, maintain and even destroy it. The development of any system of ethics, indeed the development of mutually beneficial intercultural or international communication, is a "sensible" way of linking together two or more "signifying behaviors" by human beings. (Schoening & Anderson, 1995, p. 107)

I would define ethics as codified or organized perceptions, and usually formal statements, which are built on and responsive to cultural and social value systems resulting from and undergirding long-term human interactions.

As is true of all human endeavors, ethical systems, while relatively stable, are modifiable in keeping with the perceived needs of human beings, but within certain limits related to generally accepted social or cultural value norms. The purpose of ethics or ethical systems can be identified as an attempt to control or direct human interactions for the benefit of a group or segment of society.

Throughout this volume, my colleagues have explored many of the philosophical, historical, cultural and moral issues related to ethics. Probably the most telling comment by one of them, in a private conversation, was how little those of us interested in intercultural and international communication studies have done when it comes to reacting in a scholarly or even concentrated fashion to the challenges in today's world which are related to ethics. If publications are any indication of our interest, their paucity could certainly be interpreted as lacking concern.

In this chapter I hope to take us a step beyond understanding and reacting to ethical problems we face in what have been called "multicultural societies" and a "shrinking world." My question is: What would be a workable theoretical model and approach to actually building our value- and ethics-bases for the world which is to rapidly developing around *together* us? That world, in which almost daily interactions with those from other countries and from other cultures are becoming the norm rather than the exception, requires different solutions from those which dominant powers in the past forced on the less powerful.

I believe that Deetz (1983) has been among those who have been aware of the challenge, and who have dealt with it in numerous publications, though he did not necessarily focus on international and intercultural aspects as is the case in the chapter contributed by him and his colleagues to this volume. He and I share the conviction that "All communication, whether interpersonal or mass, conversational or argumentative, social or scientific, has implications for the continuing formation of the human character. Responsible communication in this process of formation is a central ethical consideration." (Deetz, 1983, p. 270) It is the juxtaposition of factors in this statement which intrigues me. Serious consideration, as it is suggested in Deetz' (1983) statement, would require more than description or reaction, it would require the development of some bases in theory and practice which have long-term impact on human interactions. It certainly must be acknowledged that in the process of human character formation, as in the process of value- and ethic-building, communication plays a central role. Going far beyond earlier sender-receiver orientations, relationship and a recognition of the importance of the "other" are central to the emphasis in this chapter. White (1990) summarized my point when he stated that in applying postmodern analyses there is a "...need to be attentive to that which lies beyond the margins of our identity, our concepts, our projects—that which is 'other' to me or us. Especially important here is the appreciation of how the very process of constructing, developing concepts, and conceiving projects necessarily generates 'others'" (White, 1990, p. 81). To me, as a communication scholar, what such a statement requires is not merely awareness of the "generation of others," but the necessity to face the process of how, when and why such generations take place when we build, when we construct and when we organize. Both White (1990) and I are concerned that *moderns* have neglected the moral dimension, the dimension of otherness.

Even more significantly, we have probably lacked the will or means to build such a concern into our "scientific" communication models. Gibbons (1991) writes of the modernist action-oriented ethic and its action-coordinating language, which he sees as being in stark contrast with the postmodernist "world-disclosing account of language and its responsibility to otherness." (p. 96). Citing White, Gibbons (1991) summarizes his own perception of the need for a language (and I would add, of a communication process) concreteness, which he believes is necessary "for an ethic of responsibility toward otherness." (p. 99) In that insistence Gibbons (1991) relies on Foucault's insights about dialogue with others, reminding us that "The dialogue setting is absolutely essential, he [Foucault, ED.] claims, for 'whole morality' is at stake, the morality that concerns the search for truth and the relation to the other." (p. 100) The third-culture BUILDING model discussed later in this chapter is an attempt to directly respond to that dialogueic setting and the challenges which result.

The insights provided by some feminist scholars have taken us one step further in our search for developing a dialogueic theory or model of communication which does take into consideration the "other." Nodding (1984) wrote of "Ethical caring, the relation in which we do meet the other morally...that relation in which we respond as one—caring out of love or natural inclination." (p. 5) Similarly, Dietz (1989) pointed to the "Ethics of care [which] revolves more around responsibility and relationships than rights." (p. 11) As will be shown in this chapter, however, even the foundations for caring, for commonality, for building and organizing *together*, probably should not merely be considered as something brought by participants to the process, but as something developed together by all who have a stake in the future of the process. Only if every phase of the development of the process is directed by those who hope to benefit from it, can we achieve what Deetz (1983) suggested, "Every act should have as its ethical dimension an attempt to keep the conversation going—that is communicative action and communication research should have as a normative aim an attempt to establish the conditions for further less restrained communication" (p. 279). That is the reason why my third-culture building model is not, and should not be seen as an endstate model, but part of an ongoing process of personal and cultural change and growth. Johnstone (1981) underlined Deetz' and my central concern when he wrote "And from the very concept of duty it seems deducible that it is my duty never to deprive another of the capacity to perform *his* duties. I must allow him, therefore, to be resolute and open—to take a stand and to listen" (p. 312). Indeed, the theoretical foundation for the model proposed in this chapter is not communication-centered, is not primarily effects-centered in the traditional sense—it is, ultimately centered on enabling *all* those who engage in the building of third-cultures and their ethics systems. Such an enablement would produce the foundation for making individuals both resolute and open, both able to take a stand and to listen, while keeping in mind the need for being part of the future *together*.

What undergirds my considerations in this chapter is the fact, as Kale (1991) put it, that "Ethics are based on values and values are culturally determined. Thus, there cannot be such a thing as an entirely individual system of ethics" (p. 422). Like Kale (1991) I would also have to confess my own belief in the human spirit which everywhere has made possible the development of "...some universal values on which we can build a universal code of ethics in intercultural communication" (Kale, 1991, p. 423). Even if a "universal" code may seem either undesirable or too far-fetched, the principle that foundations exist for building third-culture ethics *together*, certainly points to more immediate tasks which require our attention. Not doing violence to the concept of self which we or others hold, not doing violence to the dignity of other human beings or our own, and not crushing the human spirit, are some convictions both Kale (1991) and I share. That requires more than a theory, of course, it requires translating the "doable" into the "done."

In this chapter I explore the relationship of work dealing with organizing and transforming by Weick (1979, 1984), insights on the socio-cultural enactment of environments provided by Jacobson (1993), contributions to our understanding of human relationships and relational cultures by Wood (1982), Baxter (1987; 1992), Bell and Healy (1992) and others, as well as discussion of the interrelationship of communication and communication theory by Krippendorf (1993) to the theoretical underpinnings of my own third-culture *building* model-in-progress, with a focus on the development of intercultural and international value- or ethics-systems for mutually beneficial interactions (Casmir, 1978; Casmir & Asuncion Lande, 1988; Casmir, 1992). The term *building* is used throughout this chapter to indicate a cooperative, mutually beneficial process in contrast to a superimposed or coercive approach. My agenda includes an attempt to overcome what I consider to be a central problem. Sampson (1993), similar to may other authors, identifies the problem or challenge as follows, "For too long our major cultural and scientific views have been monologic and self-celebratory—focusing more on the leading protagonist and the supporting cast *he* has assembled for his performance than on others as viable people in their own right" (p.IX). The question thus becomes, how do we develop value systems, including ethics, which are not merely monologic or self-celebrating?

CULTURE AND COMMUNICATION

Culture is a focal point, not a peripheral or minor contributing factor in my paradigm (see also: Shuter, 1990), as is true of my process-orientation—thus my choice of the term third-*culture* building model. Because we have employed certain expressions so frequently in our past, I find it useful to employ them here. However, in an attempt to assist me and my readers in re-focusing our attention on what I consider to be fundamental concerns with *com*-munication, rather than other components of cultural studies, I will employ the rather simplistic method of using italics or underlining to emphasize certain words or prefixes. Hopefully, that will cause at least a momentary consideration of my interest in overcoming the shortcomings of common usage. This device should be seen as a means to negotiate meanings rather than as an expression of intensity of feeling on my part.

Theoretical Foundations.

Intercultural communication theorists face no greater challenge than addressing the implications of the simple prefixes or word-components such as *com*- in words like *com*-munication and *com*-munity, *inter*- in such terms as *inter*-cultural, *inter*-national or *inter*-active, and *co*- as found in the word *co*-operation. These language-components are mentioned here to indicate my emphasis on their important relationships to human beings who seek to achieve outcomes or fulfill needs based on mutually beneficial *inter*-actions *between* those of differing backgrounds, using *com*-munication as the means for working *together*. For the purposes of this chapter I will focus on the "*com*" aspect, which emphasizes emic concerns related to those things which happen as individual human beings or groups, together *build* third-cultures, which require new value- or ethics-systems for their continued existence and growth. I will use the term *emic* to refer to specific, mutual, often dialogueic communication efforts, which are here associated with the word *together*. On the other hand, the term *etic* will be used in this chapter to identify approaches to communication which do not include mutuality as a prerequisite. The latter, in the following pages, will often be associated with the concept *between*. While common practice causes me to also use the term intercultural, I recognize it as frequently much more related to the etic idea of what happens between people as we deal with such events from the *outside* or from a standpoint *above* the involved members of cultures. I would argue that much of our past emphasis on intercultural communication was based on that kind of observation of between-actions of individuals within one or more cultures. As a result, our methodologies and theoretical assumptions often caused us to deal only with those instances where human beings appeared to support and use our own, readily identifiable and well-established cultural norms, including those ethics we brought to our investigations. Berry, Poortinga, Segall & Dasen (1992) trace some of the resulting problems both of our initial approaches and the eventual interpretation processes we use, when they state, "Many cross-culturalists make a distinction between culture-specific and culture-general (or universal) aspects of behavior. The danger of an etic approach is that the concepts and notions of researchers are rooted in and influenced by their cultural background....The researcher begins with a construct which appears to be *etic* and then develops *emic* [emphasis mine, Ed.] ways of measuring it. This implies that instruments are constructed locally in each cultural setting. It is claimed that with such an instrument an emically defined etic construct is obtained that can be used for comparisons. However, it is not entirely clear how the validity of such claims can be established unambiguously if instruments differ in content from culture to culture" (pp. 232-235). The supposedly almost absolute power or authority of culture and its "enforcers" was, furthermore, often stipulated to be a central factor when it came to reporting intercultural interactions intended to accomplish the purposes of the humans involved, and that absolute control was also often assumed to be central in the consideration of all ethical issues.

My concern with developing an adequate communication theory responsive to the process stipulated in the following pages, is based on our more recent insight that the negotiation of meaning, or dialogueic nature of human *com*-munication can be seen as a central feature of all *com*-munication-processes involving those who consider themselves to be part of the same culture, or part of emerging international, global or similar third-cultures. That is the case because dialogue and negotiation deal with the study of those things we do *together* in any given setting, a feature of every culture with which I am familiar, although the components of the process, including the resulting value-

or ethics-systems, usually differ between cultures, and probably differ within cultures under different circumstances and at different times. It is also one of my basic assumptions that the more apparent or stipulated differences between individuals from *different* cultures increase the complexity and challenges of that process.

Redefinition

Before a more general, conceptual re-orientation or re-focusing can become successful, it appears necessary to re-define or at least re-focus our usage of related terms and concepts. The study of culture or cultures is of great importance. However, from the standpoint of communication scholars, simple additive models or statistical manipulations based on observed cultural similarities and differences have virtually nothing to do with a process orientation. It has been relatively easy, though often time-consuming, to identify, define and describe the common or different aspects of a given culture, including existing ethics, as they relate to groups or individuals. Academic studies associated with this subject matter were usually done in an attempt to identify *emic*, culture-specific, or *etic*, culture-general data. In order to develop a theory of third-culture and ethics *building* as a *com*-municative effort, it would appear to be necessary to redefine these terms on the basis of communication-, rather than philosophical and sociological or anthropological concerns. My own orientation is succinctly echoed by Saville-Troike (1982) who points out that, "The traditional focus of anthropology and sociology on the abstract patterns of cultural and social organization to the neglect of details of their enactment, has left us largely ignorant of the role of language and other modes of communication in the realization of social life" (p. 249). Of course, there have been what one might call good reasons for such a neglect, as Geertz (1990) explains, "The main reason anthropologists have shied away from cultural particularities and taken refuge in universals is that, faced with an enormous variation in human behavior, they are haunted by fear of historicism, of becoming lost in a whirl of cultural relativism" (p. 48). My chapter is based on the belief that the time has come to abandon both the fears and the clearly inadequate theoretical foundations (not merely the research methodologies) which have provided us with often distorted views of ethics, culture and certainly of human beings in culture. Sampson (1993) shares my determination when he argues "...against any unitary view of human nature and in support of its inherent multiplicity....We are fundamentally many, never just one—not many in the sense of many thoroughly organized and coherent personalities; for that is the error of our current way of thinking about human nature. Rather, we are many because we are members of diverse conversational communities...."(p. 125) What would seem apparent if one accepts such a premise, is the need to try and make sense of the processes in the diverse conversational communities which result when diverse humans, even within one culture, play their *com*-municative roles in all cultural *building* process *together*. That would cause us to change our emphasis from considering organizations, cultures, existing ethical systems or other endstates and focus on *organizing* or building, and the dialogueic, conversational *com*-municative approaches we use to do so.

The Mystery of the Other

Burke's (1969) use of the term "mystery" can provide us with a starting point for making our search distinct. He points out that human *inter*-actions must take into consideration the mystery of the "other." (see also my discussion of "other" above and in Sampson, 1993) As a result, we must begin with an understanding of the fact that we need to create or develop understanding through the process of negotiating meanings, rather than by merely discovering it in an objectivist fashion. Mystery arises at "that point where different kinds of beings are in communication" (p. 115). We should, therefore, come to deal with "other" as basically unknown or different, but also as a welcome partner in a meaningful discovery and building process. Here we can clearly identify the need for considering emic aspects. Such explorations, understanding and eventual *mutual* negotiation of meanings can become beneficial to all those participating, specifically because of an emic focus on *com*munication as a basic, required process between members within one or between several cultures, as they build the value- and ethics-systems needed for future, mutually beneficial and ongoing interactions.

THIRD-CULTURE BUILDING AND ETHICS

Responding to my perceived need for a more adequate explanatory model is a necessary part of my third-culture *building* paradigm, in fact it is the driving or central issue in the development of the theoretical work discussed in the following pages. More than a theoretical stipulation, however, my emphasis results from the common or natural survival- and adaptation-needs of those belonging to one, two, or more different cultures in the same environment, which require me to focus on their *com*-munication processes rather than merely on existing cultural norms or problems. At best, descriptive studies or models can only inform us about the observer's attempts to classify similarities or differences on the basis of his or her assumptions, in order to fit them into a preconceived framework. Focusing on the *com*-munication process, on the other hand, helps us to understand the reasons behind observable results of intercultural or international processes.

Culture as an Endstate

Let us consider what happens when we focus our attention in traditional ways on certain readily identifiable endstates, such as cultural institutions, norms, values, ethics or rules related to the relationships of majorities and *sub*-cultures.

Sub- and Co-Cultures. It becomes almost a self-fulfilling prophecy when we "discover" the presence of these cultural factors in specific *inter*-active events between majority- and *sub*-cultures. Our underlying assumptions, for instance, may very well lead us to develop acculturation models which are only able to identify positive relationships as a result of the dominance or greater power of a majority culture. Those belonging to a *sub*-culture are not only assumed to be powerless but may be easily categorized as relatively unimportant to cultural-development and maintenance. In response to built-in expectations, acculturation is thus easily interpreted as the willing submission of sub-cultures and their total absorption into the majority culture. An ethic, under those circumstances, can also become a means of control, a tool used by the majority for purposes of dominating minorities or less powerful segments of a society or culture. In other words, a melting pot model thus can be seen not only as functional but as desirable. There is probably some value in such efforts, but only if one is primarily concerned with a description of outcomes or endstates in keeping with the pre-conceived value system of a powerful majority. History teaches us, however, that "melting pots" may lead to quite unexpected results. I am certain that when Rome conquered Greece it had no idea how resilient and influential Greek culture would remain, eventually changing many of the conquerors' perceptions and value systems.

If we consider the less threatening term *co*-cultures, once again it becomes apparent that our models may deal more with etic *inter*-actions, that is with the mere description of those things we observe happening between people. However, as we may notice in certain applications of the term multiculturalism, *co*-cultures can continue to exist side-by-side, professing a certain amount of tolerance or acceptance for one another, but without necessarily ever seeing a need for *com*-munity or *com*-munication. That is, they may be unable to identify a need for developing mutually beneficial ends *together*. *Co*-culture identifications do not necessarily help us to understand that a desirable basis for *com*-munication is the attempt to negotiate meanings which eventually are accepted and found useful by all the participants in such a process, something which would appear to be the initial basis or concern in the building of all cultural value systems which are considered to be meaningful in a shared environment. The concept of *co*-cultures is certainly indicative of respect and side-by-side existence, but not necessarily descriptive of the attempt to build a third-culture or a common new ethic. A focus on *com*-munication, however, requires that we primarily pay attention to those processes between people that result in continued efforts to *build* mutually beneficial ethics and third-cultures *together*.

Culture and Change

It needs to be stressed here that we may have hindered progress by overly simplified models of cultures as much more static, much more fixed than they are. Cultures, like all human attempts at organizing our experiences while striving to meet simple or complex survival needs, are always in a state of adaptation, flux or change as a direct response to the need for making adaptation fit changing environments. Culture is created by and exists within people, and it is represented by those institutions, artifacts, and norms such as ethics, which become influential cultural icons and which in turn, influence their creators. Adaptation thus refers not merely to our using existing cultural artifacts to deal effectively with our environment or with each other, but rather may be most meaningfully seen as a result of the needs of individuals to survive emotionally, intellectually or even physically. The development and adaptation of culture itself is a kind of supreme example of those concerns. Culture results, after all, from the combined efforts of human beings, over time, to assure as much as possible that our survival needs are met. Thus it can be argued that rather than being totally dominated by a culture, its members frequently negotiate and re-negotiate together the meanings of the culture's concepts and value-systems, including ethics.

Negotiating Meaning. Quite obviously, if they are forced to leave one environment, humans have again and again demonstrated that they can adapt to almost any new situation by re-negotiating meanings. In that process they may make use of escape-routes provided by culture, or rather built into the culture by human beings, to avoid onerous rules. Two examples would be a law which permits paying someone else to "serve the fatherland" as a soldier in our stead, or providing "cities of refuge" for those under the harsh Old Testament law, who otherwise would have had to be killed after accidentally killing someone else. We are, in other words able to work out solutions to difficult problems which were created by cultural rules, through the use of negotiated, mutually acceptable compromises. Contemporary struggles in the United States to maintain the perceived cultural value of the term "family," while changing the nature of the traditional relationships described by it, come to mind in that connection. Such negotiations of meaning apply to cultural change within any country where emerging or new sexual mores, as well changing perceptions of the roles and relationships of men and women have to be dealt with in order for the society to survive. Of course, my proposed focus on *com*-munication or on how we accomplish negotiations and outcomes *together*, also helps us to identify significant aspects of third-culture *building* which involve human beings from more widely differing cultural backgrounds who must achieve their adaptation-tasks *together*. Our insistence on the primacy of established institutions, organizations or states, both of the latter defined by some lawyers as legal "fictions" which ignore the centrality of human actions to their existence and maintenance, has frequently caused us to short-circuit processes leading to deeper more complex insights as we are building the bases for our future existence together.

Culture and Continuity

All that I have said so far should not be interpreted to mean that continuity and frequently mentioned lasting qualities associated with culture, like ethics, do not form a vital part of our *belief* system, as we strive to provide balance, security and stability for our experiences. However, these values which we associate with culture may be more indicative of a society's rhetorical and psychological needs than of the motivations of individuals or groups *com*-municating both within and between cultures, as they strive to achieve mutually beneficial ends or outcomes. In such situations the need for change may be greater than a need for continuity, in order to assure social, physical or emotional survival of individuals and groups. In other words, culture does not change itself by some sort of abstract "culture-imposed-decree," but rather because of the needs of the human members of that culture. Thus, in our emerging world, we need to focus on the same reason for which all cultures were originally created or developed, which is human survival. Of course, culture-leaders may resist or try to ignore such efforts because they represent a threat to the assumed or real cultural authority undergirding their positions.

Categorizing Cultures. Our earlier attempts at categorizing and cataloging have been marginally helpful, but they have not automatically led to any valid conclusions about the third-cultures which result from *com-municative processes*. My description of such cataloging attempts is *academic museum construction*. Cultural artifacts, under those circumstances, are separated from their actual living, changing environment, put on display as representative of much more than they signify in and of themselves, and arranged according to patterns which make sense to the curator/researcher, or which are pleasing and meaningful to the observer. As I stated above, the only *inter-*or *cross-*cultural emphasis in such studies may have resulted from the inter-relating of observed cultural features by a researcher. To be sure, scholars like Durkheim (1938) reminded us, that if sociological studies are to be meaningful, a comparison of all aspects is necessary (see also: Edelstein, Ito, Kepplinger, & McCombs, 1989). But such comparisons do not necessarily include an intensive concern with processes or *com-*munication as a creative, interactive, symbolic activity. In fact, demands made on earlier social scientists to stay "scientifically" objective and "uninvolved" made a process-oriented basis for our studies virtually impossible. Very little of past insights into so-called intercultural communication prepared us to adequately deal with what happens when people have to *negotiate meanings* across or between cultures, including those related to ethical systems, rather than being able to assume meanings as a constant or given. In recent years Triandis (see among others: Triandis, Brislin, & Hui, 1991) has been among those who have worked to overcome simplistic, traditional dichotomies, based on the concepts of individual *versus* society. His allocentric and idiocentric categories have gone a long way towards achieving that goal.

I need to cite also a less positive example of our attempts to identify differences and similarities within and between cultures. We have been able to demonstrate repeatedly that individuals from low-context cultures deal with each other differently than do people from high-context cultures. (Hofstede 1980; 1986) What we do need to explain more adequately, however, by means of a theoretical model or paradigm, are the processes which are involved when individuals from two such culturally divergent groups have to mutually work out answers to various challenges *together*. The answer can obviously not be found in simplistic problem-resolution models, as those provided in our society by individuals who embrace the well-meaning concept that we simply need to accept one another for who and what we are. The other extreme is exemplified by those who favor the continuation of *integration* models which require one group to accept and use the cultural system of another. As mentioned earlier, the application of the latter paradigm even appears to make acceptable the right of a stronger, more powerful culture to *impose* its cultural model on another. That is especially the case when that assumed right is combined with the claim that such domination is in the "best" interest of those being subjugated. Decades perhaps, or centuries, of colonial domination which were based on the "rights" of supposedly superior cultures come to mind. The moral, ethical or religious value systems of the colonialists, in that framework, were considered to be more correct, adequate or valuable than those of the indigenous people they had conquered.

In between those extremes can be located various, often poorly defined and politically- or idealistically-motivated approaches. Very seldom, if ever, do any of them use a well-developed generative, creative, cooperative *com*-munication, relationship- or culture-*building* model or theory, comparable to or based on anything which can be demonstrated to have developed naturally in the human environment during past centuries or at the present time. That may not preclude, by the way, the repeated mention of the *term* process when speaking of the study of human communication. It is of concern to many contemporary communication scholars, and especially some in the area of international and intercultural communication, that the significant implications of the term *process* have not been adequately translated into theoretical foundations or the development of models which help us to understand not merely the term *communication*, but to understand humans as they communicate.

Intercultural Communication

In many cases, the dichotomous, linear, cause-effect thinking and models of our Western/Northern cultures have been so pervasive, that they became the dominant basis for our academic efforts to understand and explain intercultural communication.

Cultural Studies. That has been the case even in so-called cultural studies, which were supposed to overcome the limitations of such thinking. In media studies, Hall's (1982) insistence on differentiating between basic mediating processes as en- and de-coding, for instance, left no room for an innovative concept like *co*-coding. The very power of the technological system with which such media studies dealt, and still deal, makes dichotomies of this type (as old as Greco-Roman philosophical assumptions) an easy preconception. Later efforts by scholars like Brunsdon (1991) and Morley (1986), overcame some of these problems by including structures such as the family- environment, which have a direct impact on en- and de-coding. However, they still did little to help us understand the *co*- or *com*-munication aspects of such settings. It seemed as if the mere presence of so-called mass media provided the basis for an assumption that *com*-munication had taken place, a problem which can only increase as our world becomes more and more interconnected electronically and mass-media impacted.

Feminist Studies. Early feminist studies also contributed to a dichotomization which provided little insight into what we identified as interactional or intercultural processes. Considering the uses of soap operas within different cultures is only one example of how it was assumed that the identification of feminist concerns and insights would lead to valid cross- or intercultural conclusions (Katz & Liebes, 1987; Seiter, 1981; Seiter, 1982; Lee, 1990; Abernathy-Lear, 1994). Perhaps most interesting in that connection was the fact that many of the earlier feminist studies were based on the preconception that the concerns of white, middle class women were automatically representative of the experiences of all women, including those of color (see the critical reactions of Bobo & Seiter, 1991, among others). No model has yet emerged out of these efforts which adequately deals with the *com*-municative or *dialogueic* aspects. These aspects of interaction need to be understood if intercultural communication between women, as well as between men and women, is to be seen as more than a necessary conflict or a problem which has to be removed on the basis of an observer's preconceived value categories. If we are concerned, as *com*-munication scholars, and especially as intercultural communication scholars, with an effort to build *com*-munity or relationships, rather than with merely describing or identifying conflicts, divergence or even agreement, our paradigms and theories need to become more responsive to such concerns.

Speech Communication Studies. Communication studies of many types, including those dealing with media, feminism and certainly with intercultural communication, have repeated the inadequate approaches of earlier speech- and communication-studies, almost condemning themselves to "inventing the wheel over and over again." In most of these instances, the preconceptions of scholars and frequently the unidentified assumptions brought to the study of human beings communicating rather than what was available for *discovery in the field*, appear to have been the driving forces. Anderson and Goodall (1994) emphasize that point as they suggest a conceptual move from an anatomy of inquiry to a poetics of expression. Among their re-focusing attempts is a concern with the fact that "communicative dimensions of experience are socially construct*ing* as well as socially construct*ed* (Anderson and Goodall, 1994, p. 111). Their conclusion is that we face multiple co-present realities which cannot be, quite obviously, encompassed by averaging out their existence in the form of limited descriptive data or simplistic additive procedures initiated and carried out by so-called objective observers. Baxter (1992), even as she confesses that observed aspects of interpersonal communication shook her faith in the objective verification of how individually situated variables causally affect one another, moves on to the insight that "Social reality is polysemous and fluid with meaning constructed in the ongoing negotiated interaction between persons," (pp. 330, 331) a conceptualization which is very closely related to the focus of my third-culture *building* model and its relationship to the building of ethical systems.

Building the Third-Culture Model

There are a number of scholars whose work has helped me over the years in constructing my third-culture *building* paradigm. Their work has indicated to me again and again that it is not necessary to focus intercultural communication research on the predominant Western or Northern concern with failures, confrontations, or pre-established categories, rather than on studies of what takes place or took place in third-cultures which have been successfully built by people who needed them to survive. More recently studies are being reported which indeed seem to be concerned with changing the negative focus on failure or confrontation to one of investigating what has been called communication satisfaction, in one case dealing specifically with interethnic communication (Martin, Hecht & Larkey, 1994).

The Impact of Related Studies

Let me briefly indicate at this point the impact other than specific intercultural studies have had on my work.

Area - Studies. Approaching third-culture *building* from a very practical standpoint, Bird, Heinbuch, Dunbar and McNulty (1993), studied the effects area-studies have on trainees who are about to enter another, usually overseas culture. They found that information (facts, data, examples, categories) provided in teaching sessions which did not include interactions with representatives of the cultures studied, was not readily transferred to or usable in the new intercultural situations which participants had to face. Interpretation of information using only preconceived meanings as a starting point, is primarily based on already existing culturally, socially and historically determined pictures in our heads. It results from our socially based preconceptions, as well as the models and methods we *bring* to an intercultural setting rather than on any meaning negotiated together with those with whom we must interact to achieve desired outcomes. (Mirandé & Tanno, 1993)

None of this should be taken to indicate that information about cultures, institutions, history, or the knowledge of other languages is unimportant as we develop theories of intercultural communication and the development of value- or ethical systems. Shuter (1990) was right when he criticized his colleagues for frequently being culturally-uninformed. However, no amount of cultural information will automatically or significantly contribute to our understanding of how human beings *build* relationships *together* and *negotiate* meanings together. That requires emic involvement in such processes.

The Concepts of Building and Braiding. Of course, both social and individual components of this *building* process need to be dealt with if we are to develop adequate theories of intercultural communication. In other words, we need to be concerned with what Krippendorf (1993) calls the *braiding* or *dance*. Such a process involves a number of human beings who are engaged in sense-making. It includes attempts to interrelate individuals in an effort to coordinate individual behavior. The work of Useem, Donoghue and Useem (1963) needs to be mentioned because they used the term third-culture in their work. However, they provided me primarily with the description of an endstate, of something they observed as a result of interactions between people in their environment, without developing their perceptions into a theoretical model related to the *building* or *braiding* of such third-cultures.

Acting, Organizing Systems. Seagraves (1974) took me a step further when he summarized his own insights into socio-cultural systems by describing them as "...open, acting systems which engage in information and energy exchange with their respective environments" (p. 531). While mechanistic in its paradigmatic foundations, nevertheless that author's points could be related to some of the important contributions Weick (1979, 1984) has made to my own thinking. Everett (1994) explores some aspects of the sociocultural evolution of organizing and organizing populations, based on Weick's work. My own interests and concerns cause me to build on that analysis, by pointing out that Weick's (1979) paradigmatic focus on *organizing* rather than the organization, has its roots in thinking which directly relates to concepts of *building* both theories and relationships as a result of *com*-munication processes rather than a mere mixing or combination of existing cultural factors. It is significant to my own model to mention that Weick (1979) wrote of an "....enacted environment which is constituted by the actions of interdependent human actors." (p. 27) Such an environment frequently includes the process of constructing value- or ethics-systems.

The *building* or *enactment* of any culture is the result of interdependent human beings existing in an environment, with limited resources as well as other constraints, which has to be dealt with in such a way that all participants can survive and develop or grow. Culture, ultimately, is about *organizing*-to-relate, relate to other people and to the environment. That *organizing* is carried out in an enacted environment, including institutions and organizations whenever their existence or development are considered to be useful by human actors. Thus, as Anderson and Goodall (1994) point out, both that which has been constructed and that which is being constructed should be considered. It can be stipulated that the communication of what remains significant about one's culture represents an *ongoing* dialogue, a communication process intended to both transmit concepts and negotiate new meanings, which will cease only with the disappearance of that culture, only to be transformed into a new process, as another culture emerges.

Symbols, Systems and Artifacts. To a *com*-munication scholar concerned with processes, the inspection, identification and listing of cultural symbols, systems and artifacts, outside of the actual living communication process, is hardly ever sufficient (Cooley, 1983). Thus I also had to deal with the implications of the early work by Hofstede (1980) and Hall (1969; 1973) which was of that type. It was based on the assumption that there were specific, measurable and seemingly invariable aspects of culture which could be used to identify, for instance, a prototypical Arab, German, or American. Both individual-, sub-cultural and situational- differences were largely overlooked in their work, and the actual process of *com*-municatively *constructing* meaning never was a significant part of their considerations. As a result, meaning in such models appears to me to be culturally-*fixed*. Culture, not individuals, was ultimately stipulated to be meaning-creating in an almost absolute sense, and so-called communication served merely as a means for transmitting that established meaning.

The Problem of Change. Weick's insight (see Everett's discussion, 1994, pp. 100-104) that all organizations tend to have problems with change if they have done something well over time, was one explanation which helped me understand the frequent insistence on studying the results or endstates of cultural norms, values and processes. Cultures are commonly perceived as stabilizing forces in the lives of individuals. Because it also tends to be assumed that one's own culture has done or explained things well, any transformation which is required in intercultural communication processes and which calls for the adaptation of all those who are involved, becomes difficult. Transformation or change, after all, is easily identified as disruptive. It creates feelings of insecurity because the necessary bases or skills to accomplish change-tasks may not be part of the original repertoire available to those who are involved. A discussion by Casmir and Asuncion-Lande (1988) of the necessary preparation to adapt successfully to one's birth-family, while at the same time pointing towards the day when a child will have to be a partner in a new marriage relationship, a kind of third-culture, can be instructive in that connection. The challenge thus is in part cultural, but it is also, to a significant extent, related to an individual's willingness to take chances, to *welcome* change and to perceive benefits from the *building* of new relationships and cultures, including the willingness to build a new conceptual- and skills-repertoire. For all these reasons the third-culture *building* model proposed here is representative of an ongoing process which does not seek total closure but rather the means for "keeping the dialogue going." Nothing less serves adequately in dealing with the need for adaptation to changing environments.

What Everett (1994) referred to as ecological change in such situations, is a factor which by now is well known to all of us who have dealt with the enormous restructuring of contemporary societies. Many of them have been literally invaded by unprecedented numbers of refugees, and the economic confrontations resulting from shrinking resources, consumerism and pollution are readily identifiable across our globe (Nelson, 1993; Hufbauer & Schott, 1993-1994; Lilley, 1994). I accept Everett's (1994) insight that "culture lies between what could be and what is" (p. 101), but I here relate that statement to intercultural communication in general, not just to organizations. Indeed, the reason many of us have invested time and effort in the study of intercultural communication is because we are concerned with the role of culture in accomplishing what could be, not just in maintaining or submitting to what is. Culture is involved in the mediating of human adaptation, because it is significantly connected with *organizing-*, or *building*-processes. These two activities are almost inherently cultural, as those who dealt with organizations as cultures discovered (Ott, 1989; Schein, 1992). In effect, it could be easily argued that if the concept of culture helped us to understand some of the aspects of contemporary organizations, then concepts related to organizing can help us to understand, better the *building* of cultures through symbolic activities, i.e., *com*-munication.

Interactive Participation. Mead (1934) and other symbolic-interactionists helped me decades ago to first consider the implications of a model which made human beings not merely respondents but interactive participants. Equally important was the work of scholars like Wittgenstein (1969) who laid more foundations for my dealing with human beings as active, insightful participants in communication processes. Malinowski's (1959) insistence that language creates as well as names events and objects, was significant. More recently, the work by Giddens (1976, 1977) has expanded views of constructivists for me who have dealt with the active role of human beings in the processes of defining, understanding and communicating, by stressing the interactive relationships of individuals and institutions or systems they develop. The obvious impact of related work on the thinking of individuals like Anderson and Goodall (1994) further determined its importance to my own efforts.

Models of Sense-Making. My third-culture *building* model thus resulted in consideration of the work by scholars and researchers who have attempted to consider human beings as more than respondents to stimuli or objects. Jacobson (1993), for instance, pointed out that the development of *building-* or sense-making models and theories often has not involved the very individuals we have traditionally observed or studied and on whom we based our professional reports. Now it appears obvious to me that the insights and reactions of those "subjects" which are related to our work are very important, since these individuals are actually engaged in the communication activities we try to define and describe as part of their daily lives, not merely as a part of our scientific experiments (Krippendorf, 1993; Mirandé & Tanno, 1993; Delgado, 1994).

In his recent article, Krippendorf (1993), developed this concept of an interrelationship of both human communication and theory *building*. His central proposition suggests a "recursive frame or a generative grammar for relational explanations that can become a predictive theory of communication only after the communication theories held by the participants....are entered." (p. 257) Much of the theory *building* and the construction of paradigms dealing with intercultural communication has suffered, in keeping with my emphasis on third-culture *building*, from a lack of theorizing carried out while we are mutually engaged with those from other cultures. In the past, sense-making function of theorizing thus became, inevitably, a Western/Northern product as did our concerns with ethics. What Krippendorf (1993) suggests in his article, is a requirement widely ignored even by those who claim to study communication as a process—or the process of humans communicating, as I prefer to identify it (see in this connection: Dervin, 1993). That basis for our understanding requires consideration of both the "simultaneous construction of theories about themselves and each other," as well as an "unfolding of these theories into intertwined practices, and in mutual participation in communication" (Krippendorf, 1993, p. 257). I would add that such a process does not require a terminal condition as long as people from different cultures feel a need to continue being *com*-municatively engaged with each other. As a result of all the foregoing considerations, my own concern with a third-culture *building* model has included a focus on the approaches we use in *both* studying and reporting intercultural and international communication processes.

Private Systems of Understanding. A variety of studies dealing with marriage, self disclosure and intimacy have helped me to identify common concerns as I strive to deal with humans communicating (Cozby, 1972; Gilbert, 1976; Chelune, 1979; Powers & Hutchinson, 1979; Wood, 1982; Derlega, 1984; Rosenfeld & Kendrick, 1984; Tyler, 1987). Most informative to my own work have been the insights by Bell and Healy (1992) who discussed dyadic relationships as mini-cultures which are built on social prototypes, a conceptualization closely related to my own use of the term third-culture, though I would stress the possibility of meaningful change of such social-prototypes in the *building* process, as well. Wood's (1982) conclusion that a relational culture is something which is "unique-to-the-relationship" (p. 76), one which was created, built or negotiated by the participants, points to that vital aspect of relationship- *building* or -*organizing* in my third-culture model, which is involved also in the construction or organization of ethics systems. Wood (1982) refers to this as a "privately transacted system of understandings" (obviously *com*-municated or negotiated in the *togetherness* of an emic setting) for the purpose of what Weick and I would call *co*-ordinating or *organizing*. Overcoming confrontational or dominating approaches to relationship-*building* requires, of course, what Baxter (1987) calls a "creative compromise" (p. 474). Again, the concept of a *mutually built* and negotiated third-culture or ethic comes to the foreground.

A Graphic Representation. The process suggested in most of the studies I have considered here is one of deliberately developing, *together*, an extended process, during which participants gain an understanding of and appreciation for others while negotiating purposes, standards, methods, goals and eventual satisfaction in a dialogueic, conversational setting (Alberts & Driscoll, 1992; Simon & Baxter, 1993). A *third-culture*, or new interactive relationship, which thus *evolves*, would represent an expression of mutuality which can be understood, supported and defended by all who shared in its development. Not only that, a system of values or ethics could result whose very emergence-process could be identified as being *ethical*. It's purpose would be to achieve lasting, not merely momentary, maximum adaptation and survival in a framework designed and used by its participants.

At this point it should be helpful to attempt a graphic representation of some aspects related to my third-culture *building* model. I use the word attempt advisedly, since I really do not know of any way to adequately represent processes in static graphics. The model presented here should be seen only as an aid, as one additional way of using symbolic representations to negotiate meanings.

The components of the third-culture *building* process, as indicated in Fig. 3.1, include natural, or common (as illustrated above through the use of a variety of studies from a variety of areas dealing with human communication) processes of *com*-municating and relating. Involved are the initial contacts with a person, object or event in a given, cultural, social, historical existing need,

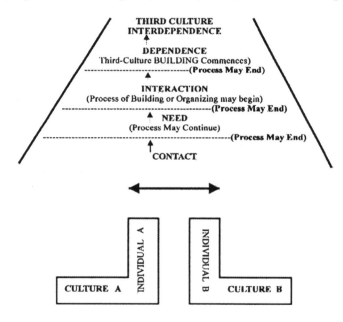

FIG. 3.1. A Dialogic Communication Model of Third-Culture Building.

or may result in the emergence of a need. It is at this point that the process of *building* and *organizing* begins—it is the point where mere awareness of the presence of someone or something in our lives turns into active processing. A need (or needs) may lead us to *inter*-act or to *com*-municate with others. We may decide that we want to simply rely on the established and generally accepted cultural values, rules, norms or interactional patters of the etic, *between*, environment, basically acquiescing to them because that seems the safest and most appropriate route to take. The point is still, however, that that decision should not be assumed to be automatic, robot-like, or culturally-imposed, but that, from a *com*-municative standpoint, it requires understanding of how such a decision is reached. On the other hand we may decide that what we need is to develop a response in an emic, *together*, *com*-municative third-culture *building* process. As the model attempts to show, even the *com*-munication of people building third-cultures takes place within the existing environment. As I mentioned earlier, and some would stress, culture is in people, not merely in some vague contact with an environment existing around them. What is important to the third-culture building model, however, is the fact that culture does not create an overbearing influence resulting in simple stimulus-response situations. Culture itself is seen here as a process not as a static object. In that culture-as-process environment human beings decide, frequently, how to respond and adapt, and one such adaptation process is the building or organizing of value- and ethics-systems. Between two or more human beings from different backgrounds, within one culture or between more than one, it must frequently be decided how to approach that adaptation, whether or not and how to use change or discard existing cultural models or systems. Over time and between those whose physical, emotional or intellectual survival is seen as being at stake, that process continues.

CULTURES AND ETHICS: BUILDING AND ORGANIZING FOR INTERDEPENDENCE

The proposed third-culture *building* model clearly incorporates a cooperative, mutual, ongoing process for the purpose of *building* and *organizing* a relationship which is considered beneficial to all those who had a part in developing it. Thus it *requires com*-munication. Only then, after becoming *dependent* on one another for the development of the process, can the final phase of resulting *interdependence* include a minimum of stress, fear or domination. In effect, the beneficial outcome of the process depends on relationship- and trust-*building* both prior to and during organizing an ongoing relationship. In many ways, third-culture *building* and thus the building of supportive value- and ethics-systems, represents a continuous process of required change, adaptation and transformation on the basis of the changing needs of those involved, as well as on the basis of changes in the environment. At the same time, the vital role of culture as both a starting point and as the fulcrum for change is not denied. Cultural change, can be identified as the result of a multitude of such third-culture *building* events, as individuals *together* respond to their needs in changing environments. It is not culture which produces change, but people as the creators of culture who require change to survive.

Building Over Time

My third-culture *building* model is thus, in the truest sense of the word, representative of a *co*-operative, *com*-munication, *com*-munity *building* process which does not include the need for coercion by anyone, including outsiders, nor is it a process which seeks a predetermined, culturally imposed, finalized, predictable endstate (Casmir, 1978; 1992). Without the involvement of the concept of culture in the *organizing* and *building*-process, however, any lasting, transmitted-over-time aspects of organizing, as I discussed them earlier, would become less relevant. The model would then be able to serve only the function of *describing* interpersonal-communication or interpersonal-relationships at a given point in time. The development of a third-*culture* model, on the other hand, allows us to consider the factors involved in *building, maintaining* and even *terminating* any intercultural or international communication process over time, in naturally (culturally) occurring situations, rather than in laboratory-constructed settings or as the result of preconceived categories in the mind of an observer. My third-culture *building* model is based on the concept that *com*-munication is an ongoing process which will continue to require change or adjustments both to each other and to the environment, for the benefit of those involved. Thus no *endstate* or ultimate outcome is stipulated, while the model indicates that both the processes involved in such *com*-municative efforts and their outcomes, will eventually exert some influence on the etic, cultural, social, historical environment (see also Casmir, 1978, 1992).

A major component of the process is *time*. It is impossible to build third-*cultures, lasting* relationships or value systems in relatively short periods of time. In fact, the establishment and maintenance of meaningful relationships and truly dialogueic, interactive communication will probably be severely limited in short-term interactions. That needs to be understood lest we expect change in communication habits and *outcomes* to result from short term-efforts in *all* intercultural or organizational efforts (Pheysey, 1993).

Communicating and Change

It is to be expected that all participants in an interactive process will bring their own schemata, or *retained enactments* to any given *com*-munication process. However, it is equally expected that transformation or change can be and is brought about by *talk* or dialogue (Burgoon, Dillman, & Stern, 1993; Everett, 1994). While one cannot automatically assume that some positive progress will be made as a result of such talk, it does provide a different environment from socio-political or economic *confrontational, coercive* settings which impose the value system of the stronger on the weaker. Creative, adaptive evolution is the goal of third-culture *building* processes, as it is in Weick's (1979, 1984) model of organizing and socio-cultural adaptation. One can couple that with the insight, long-held, that decisions *mutually agreed upon and mutually enacted* are seen as having greater value, and that they are adhered to more consistently over time by those who participated in their creation, than those which have *imposed* (Kelman, 1961; Shaver, 1977).

Briefly consider with me the possibilities which a third-culture, *com*-municatively based, *building* model provides for the study of acculturation. It makes it possible to determine not only how and when, but also why a variety of adaptations, which impact one another, occur at the same time: Adjustments to a new majority culture, to the old culture, to various sub-cultures, to relationships between old and young within families, and any number of other possibilities which occur in the actual acculturation process. Changes in economic, historical and psychological settings can thus be dealt with not as the result of established categories but through the involvement of those who devise them to deal with their new environment. Nor is it necessary to approach such a study with the assumption that any one way of adapting to or dealing with the environment is best. Rather, it would be more beneficial to focus on what happens as human beings identify or experience needs which can be met only as they find ways to deal with them *together* with other human beings in a *com*-municative process. The only thing required is that we get as close as possible to the process itself, rather than merely reporting its outcomes and endstates on the basis of our own explanatory models. In effect, judging an existing ethic as an endstate or product, will most likely involve the application of assumptions that the ethics- or value-system of the observer is the ultimate or most adequate standard for comparison, which could lead to some serious misinterpretations. The possibilities, defined in action, of multiple ways of dealing with varied, complex environmental challenges comes to the fore when we use a third-culture *building* model. Just as importantly, those involved in the process should be given the opportunity to evaluate our findings to make as certain as possible that our observations, records, data and our explanations make sense to those who developed the process and related value system. That may still not assure total accuracy, especially if we also consider possible distortions in the minds of those to whom we report our findings, because of their preconceptions. However, it goes a long ways towards breaking out of the lock-step procedures and findings of descriptive, so-called objective, numerically-based category systems applied to rather than evaluated by the very processes with which we deal.

Schoening and Anderson (1995) remind us that "science is not so much a program of revelation as a reviewable and recoupable program of constructing platforms of action...If our science is hidden in arcane journals or serves only disciplinary ends, it is clearly parasitical. Science must act in society as an emancipatory force..." (p. 110). Such an emphasis does not denigrate or discourage scientific work, rather it encourages us, as the third-culture building model attempts to do as well, to consider science as a part of human sense-making efforts which require discursive, dialogueic interactions and efforts that empower all human beings for on-going actions.

Culture, History, Change and Dialogue

I hope to have made clear some of the reasons for embracing a third-culture *building* model as proposed in this chapter, especially the need I perceive to go beyond identification and description. At the same time, I very much believe that there is a need to encourage a renewed scholarly interest in the roles history and culture have played, and are playing in intercultural communication processes, but with an emphasis on their discursive, dialogueic, *com-municative* implications for the process of third-culture and ethic-systems *building* (Casmir, 1992; see also the entire issue of *Communication Theory*, 1993, May; Casmir, 1995).

One additional, central point has been made throughout this chapter. Sampson's (1993) volume in celebration of the "other," is an insightful effort to overcome the dominance of "self" in Western cultures. At the same time it is still driven by the traditional dichotomies resulting from those two identifications. Notwithstanding his emphasis on the desirable nature of dialogueic human communication, that particular emphasis appears to me to define a limited, though desirable outcome. Sampson (1993) emphasizes his view that "We learn how many possibilities there are, how open we must be to this diverse range, and how no one voice can be quieted without losing the greatest opportunity of all: to converse with others and to learn about our own otherness in and through those conversations." (1993, p. 186) Rather than denying the importance of these insights, I would like to re-emphasize that my third-culture *building* model deals with a celebration of the *"together"* as the outcome of dialogue and conversation. That insight suggests to me an even greater opportunity than the one suggested by Sampson (1993). *Together* implies, rather than merely considering the relationship between self OR (or even *AND*) other, that we can *build* something that eventually is "ours." Something which sooner or later becomes part of the changes which help all cultures and their societal structures, including value- and ethics-systems, to emerge from it. To put it in other words, such changes can help assure our survival as humans.

REFERENCES

Abernathy-Lear, G. (1994). Soap operas and the African-American audience. In S. Torres (Ed.) *Race, sexuality and American television.* Durham, NC: Duke University Press (in print). See the reference in: Spigel, L. (1994). U.S. feminist criticism: The next generation? *Medien Journal, 1*, pp. 10-18.

Alberts, J. K., & Driscoll, G. (1992, Fall). Containment versus escalation: The trajectory of couples' conversation complaints. *Western Journal of Communication, 56*(4), 394-412.

Anderson, J. A., & Goodall, H. L. Jr. (1994). Probing the body ethnographic: From an anatomy of inquiry to a poetics of expression. In F. L. Casmir (Ed.), *Building communication theories,* (pp. 87-129). Hillsdale, NJ.: Lawrence Erlbaum.

Baxter, L. A. (1987). Symbols of relationship identity in relationship cultures. *Journal of Social and Personal Relationships, 4*, 261-280.

Baxter, L. A. (1992, November). Interpersonal communication as dialogue: A response to the "social approaches" forum. *Communication Theory, 2*(4), 330-347.

Bell, R. A. & Healy, J. G. (1992, March). Idiomatic communication and interpersonal solidarity in friends' relational cultures. *Human Communication Research, 18*(3), 307-335.

Berry, J. W., Poortinga, Y. H., Segall, M. H., & Dasen, P. R. (1992) *Cross-cultural psychology: Research and applications.* Cambridge: Cambridge University Press.

Bird, A., Heinbuch, S., Dunbar, R., & McNulty, M. (1993, Fall). A conceptual model of effects of area studies training programs and preliminary investigation of the model's hypothesized relationships. *International Journal of Intercultural Relations, 17*(4), 415-435.

Bobo, J., & Seiter, E. (1991). Black feminism and media criticism: The women of Brewster Place. *Screen, 32*(3), 286-302.

Brunsdon, C. (1991). Text and audience. In E. Seiter, et al. (Eds.), *Remote control* (pp. 116-129). London: Routledge.

Burgoon, J. K., Dillman, L. E., & Stern, L. A. (1993, November). Adaptation in dyadic interaction: Defining and operationalizing patterns of reciprocity and compensation. *Communication Theory, 3*(4), 295-316.

Burke, K. (1969). *A rhetoric of motives.* Berkeley, CA: University of California Press.

Casmir, F. L. (Ed.) (1978). *Intercultural and international communication.* Washington, DC: University Press of America.

Casmir, F. L., & Asuncion-Lande, N. (1988). Intercultural communication revisited: Conceptualizations, paradigm building and methodological approaches. In J. A. Anderson (Ed.), *Communication Yearbook, 12* (pp. 278-335). Beverly Hills, CA.: Sage.

Casmir, F. L. (1992). Third-culture-*building*: A paradigm shift for international and intercultural communication. In S. Deetz (Ed.), *Communication Yearbook, 16* (pp. 407-436). Beverly Hills, CA.: Sage.

Casmir, F. L. (Ed.). (1995). *Communication in Eastern Europe: The role of history, culture and media in contemporary conflicts.* Hillsdale, NJ: Lawrence Erlbaum (In Print).

Chelune, G. J. (1979). Measuring openness in interpersonal communication. In G. J. Chelune (Ed.), *Self-disclosure* (pp. 1-27). San Francisco, CA: Jossey-Bass.

Cooley, R. E. (1983). Codes and contexts: An argument for their description. In W. B. Gudykunst (Ed.), *Intercultural Communication Theory* (pp. 241-251). International and Intercultural Communication Annual, (VII). Beverly Hills, CA.: Sage.

Cozby, P. C. (1972). Self-disclosure: A literature review. *Psychological Bulletin, 79*, 73-91.

Deetz, S. (1983) The principle of dialectic ethics. *Communication, 7*, 263-288.

Delgado, F. P. (1994, Winter). The complexity of Mexican American Identity. A reply to Hecht, Sedano and Mirandé and Tanno. *International Journal of Intercultural Relations, 18*(1), 77-84.

Derlega, V. J. (1984). Self-disclosure and intimate relationships. In V. J. Derlega (Ed.), *Communication: Intimacy, and close relationships* (pp. 1-9). Orlando, FL: Academic Press.

Dervin, B. (1993). Verbing communication: Mandate for disciplinary invention. *Journal of Communication, 43*(3), 45-52.

Dietz, M. (1989). Context is all: Feminism and theories of citizenship. In J. Comway, S. Bourque, & J. Scott (Eds.), *Learning about Women: Gender, politics, & power* (pp. 1-24). Ann Arbor, MI: The University of Michigan Press.

Durkheim, I. E. (1938). *The rules of sociological method.* Glencoe, IL: Free Press.

Edelstein, A. S., Ito, Y., Kepplinger, H. M., & McCombs, M. (1989). *Communication and Culture.* New York: Longman.

Everett, J. L. (1994, May). Communication and sociocultural evolution in organizations and organizational populations. *Communication Theory, 4*(2), 93-110.

Geertz, C. (1990). The impact of the concept of culture on the concept of man. In H. Caton (Ed.), *The Samoan reader* (pp. 45-55). Lanham, MD: University Press of America.

Gibbons, M. T. (1991). The ethic of postmodernism. *Political Theory, 19*(1), 96-102.

Giddens, A. (1976). *New rules of sociological method.* New York: Basic Books.

Giddens, A. (1977). *Studies in social and political theory.* New York: Basic Books.

Gilbert, S. J. (1976). Empirical and theoretical extensions of self-disclosure. In G. R. Miller (Ed.), *Explorations in interpersonal communication* (pp. 197-216). Beverly Hills, CA.: Sage.

Hall, E. T. (1969). *The hidden dimension.* New York: Anchor Books.

Hall, E. T. (1973). *The silent language.* New York: Anchor Books.

Hall, S. (1982). Encoding/decoding. In S. Hall, et al. (Eds.), *Culture, media, language.* (pp. 128-138). London: Hutchinson.

Hofstede, G. (1980). *Culture's consequences: International differences in work-related values.* Beverly Hills, CA: Sage

Hofstede, G. (1986). Cultural differences in teaching and learning. *International Journal of Intercultural Relations, 10*(3), 301-320.

Hufbauer, G. C., & Schott, J. J. (1993-1994, Winter). Prescription for growth. *Foreign Policy, 93*, 104-115.

Jacobson, T. L. (1993, August). A pragmatist account of participatory communication research for development. *Communication Theory, 3*(3), 214-230.

Johnstone, H. W. (1981). Toward an ethics for rhetoric. *Communication, 6*, 305-314.

Katz, E., & Liebes, T. (1987). Decoding Dallas: Notes from a cross-cultural study. In E. H. Newcomb (Ed.), *Television: The critical view.* New York: Oxford.

Kale, D. (1991). Ethics in intercultural communication. In L. Samovar & R. Porter (Eds.), *Intercultural communication: A reader* (pp. 420-425). Belmont, CA: Wadsworth Publishing.

Kelman, H. C. (1961). Process of opinion change. *Public Opinion Quarterly, 25,* 57-78.

Krippendorf, K. (1993, August). Conversation or intellectual imperialism in comparing communication (theories). *Communication Theory, 3*(3), 252-266.

Lee, M. (1990). Women watching together: An ethnographic study of Korean women soap opera fans in the US. *Cultural Studies, 4*(1), pp. 3-44.

Lilley, J. (1994, Spring). Freedom through trade. *Foreign Policy, 94,* 37-42.

Malinowski, B. (1959). The problem of meaning in primitive languages. In C. K. Ogden, & I. A. Richards (Eds.), *The meaning of meaning.* New York: Harcourt and Brace.

Martin, J. N., Hecht, M. L., & Larkey, L. (1994, September). Conversational improvement strategies for interethnic communication: African American and European American perspectives. *Communication Monographs, 61*(3), pp. 236-255.

Mead, G. H. (1934). *Mind, self and society.* Chicago, IL.: University of Chicago Press.

Mirandé, A., & Tanno, D. V. (1993, Spring). Labels, researcher perspective, and contextual validation: A commentary. *International Journal of Intercultural Relations, 17*(2), 149-155.

Mirandé, A., & Tanno, D. V. (1993, Summer). Understanding interethnic communication and research: "A rose by any other name would smell as sweet." *International Journal of Intercultural Relations, 17*(3), 381-388.

Morley, D. (1986). *Family television: Cultural power and domestic leisure.* London: Comedia.

Nelson, M. M. (1993, Fall). Transatlantic travails. *Foreign Policy, 92,* 75-91.

Noddings, N. (1984). *Caring: A feminine approach to ethics and moral education.* Berkeley, CA: University of California Press.

Ott, J. S. (1989). *The organizational culture perspective.* Chicago, IL: Dorsey Press.

Pheysey, D. C. (1993). *Organizational cultures: Types and transformation.* London: Routledge.

Powers, W. G., & Hutchinson, K. (1979). The measurement of communication apprehension in the marriage relationship. *Journal of Marriage, and the Family, 41,* 89-95.

Rosenfeld, L. B., & Kendrick, W. L. (1984). Choosing to be open: An empirical investigation of subjective reasons for self-disclosing. *Western Journal of Speech Communication, 48,* 326-343.

Sampson, E. E. (1993). *Celebrating the other: A dialogueic account of human nature.* Boulder, CO: Westview Press.

Saville-Troike, M. (1982). *Ethnography of communication: An introduction.* Baltimore, MD: University Park Press.

Schein, E. H. (1992). *Organizational culture and leadership* (2nd. ed.). San Francisco, CA: Jossey-Bass.

Schoenberg, G. T., & Anderson, J. A. (1995, May). Social action studies: Foundational arguments and common premises. *Communication Theory, 5*(2), 93-116.

Seiter, E. (1981). The soaps. *Tabloid, 6,* 36-43.

Seiter, E. (1982). Promise and contradiction: The daytime television serials. *Screen, 23,* 150-163.

Segraves, B. A. (1974). Ecological generalization and structural transformation of socioculture systems. *American Anthropologist, 76,* 530-522.

Shaver, K. G. (1977). *Principles of social psychology.* Cambridge, MA: Winthrop Publishers.

Shuter, R. (1990). The centrality of culture. *The Southern Communication Journal, LV*(3), 237-249.

Simon, E. P., & Baxter L. A. (1993, Fall). Attachment style differences in relationship maintenance strategies. *Western Journal of Communication, 57*(4), 399-415.

Triandis, H. C., Brislin, R. W., & Hui, C. H. (1991). Cross-cultural training across the individualism-collectivism divide. In L. A. Samovar & R. E. Porter (Eds.), *Intercultural communication: A reader.* Belmont, CA: Wadsworth.

Tyler, S. A. (1987). *The unspeakable: Discourse, dialogue, and rhetoric in the postmodern world.* Madison, WI: University of Wisconsin Press.

Useem, J., Donoghue, J. D., & Useem, R. H. (1963). Men in the middle of the third-culture. *Human Organization, 22*(33), 129-144.

Weick, K. E. (1979). *The social psychology of organizing* (2nd ed.). New York: Random House.

Weick, K. E. (1984). Toward a model of organizations as interpretation systems. *Academy of Management Review, 9,* 284-295.

White, S. K. (1990). Heidegger and the difficulties of postmodern ethics and politics. *Political Theory, 18,* 80-103.

Wittgenstein, L. (1969). *Preliminary studies for the 'philosophical investigation.'* Oxford: Blackwell.

Wood, J. T. (1982). Communication and relational culture: Bases for the study of human relationships. *Communication Quarterly, 30*(2), 75-83.

SECTION II

ETHICS AND INTERNATIONAL COMMUNICATION

Fred L. Casmir

Three areas come to mind immediately when we think about international communication. They are related to communication aspects of international mass media, international business and international diplomacy. All three include intercultural factors, as previously mentioned, but each one also incorporates the concept of representation or communication on behalf of larger-than-individual entities.

Just as important is the fact that all three areas have become increasingly interrelated and interactive. Technology and the resulting relative ease with which large numbers of people around the world can at least feel involved in all kinds of international affairs, is the main reason for the increased likelihood that greater numbers of individuals can become directly involved in international-intercultural interactions. However, the mass media, without a question, were responsible for the initial information-sharing climate, and the offering of culturally significant or even culture-changing contributions.

It can be argued that the mass media, especially radio and television, only created an illusion of direct involvement or significant understanding for their audiences. Nevertheless, that illusion has influenced the perceptions and actions of many people around the world. Even policy makers, including economic and political leaders, have had to take that influence into consideration in their own decision-making processes. The ethical and practical implications of the role mass media, and those who control them, thus are the focus of Olson's chapter. Encountering others in our contemporary world is often a direct, face-to-face experience. More frequently, and for more individuals everywhere, such encounters are electronically- or print-mediated. The very complexity of situations in which people respond to pictures and words produced and presented by human beings they have never met, whom in most instances, they will never even see appear on their television screens, have created legitimate ethical concerns. If one adds the fact that internationally sender and receiver may not only be separated geographically but by important cultural differences, it becomes obvious that the systems adopted and used in one culture, even a dominant one, may be totally inadequate or unjustified in international mass mediated communication.

Following Olson's basic introduction to the challenges faced, and the background of the opportunities and problems significant to those using mass mediated communication, it is instructive to translate basic concepts into specific situations. Pratt and Ogundimo make that possible for us by considering in some depth the impact ethical norms have and have had on international reporting in Africa. The authors are uniquely positioned to consider ethical issues from more than one perspective. Their personal and professional backgrounds make it possible for them to enter the existing scene both from the standpoint of Africans and those who have used mass media internationally to reach Africans with their messages. Once more, however, it is important to note that the authors not only identify problems and challenges which may be familiar to many of our readers, but that they begin a dialogue which is intended to create a more positive, ethical response to future international mass media use everywhere.

If mass media provided the initial impetus for international involvement by large numbers of people around the world, international business and industry, especially American and Western companies, have dramatically impacted economic expectations, trade and foundational philosophies related to production, consumption and commerce. As has been the case with the impact of dominant largely Western media systems on other cultures and societies, Deetz, Edley and Cohen help us to see that "doing business" is not a culture-free enterprise. Norms, values, ethics (or their lack) are based on the value systems of societies which initiate international trade and business. In all societal settings organizations, including business and industrial corporations, attempt to turn their own concepts of significant cultural values into control-systems for the purpose of influencing their members. Deetz and his colleagues clearly identify the problems they see, from an ethical standpoint, with such control efforts. When they become part of international trade and business, in attempts to exert influence over other people in different cultural settings, those problems may become even more significant because they frequently lead to serious confrontations. While Deetz and his colleagues see little evidence in the past performance of Western corporations to encourage them to believe in the possibility of significant changes in their approach, nevertheless they clearly identify practices which could improve authoritarian, control-oriented practices.

Belay's subject of diplomacy has been traditionally identified as the most significant international effort in which representatives of states and nations have engaged over thousands of years. Significantly, the impact of international mass media and international business and industry is now so much part of political efforts and agreements across national frontiers that Belay makes them one of his central considerations. The very ideal of public diplomacy, the involvement of masses of people in the decision processes of diplomats because of the information provided them by mass media, is one of the most startling changes in contemporary international diplomatic efforts. That involvement of both media and citizens has transformed once secret negotiation processes between representatives of various states. Belay's detailed tracing of foundational issues should help the reader to understand both the contemporary complexities and the historical foundations of international diplomacy.

Belay, as is true of other authors in this volume, in not content with merely presenting an historical account or a narrative of resulting difficulties. More significant for the purposes of this volume is his effort to provide a basis for building a different, more adequate kind of international diplomacy in the future. In this chapter, as in the preceding ones, it is the unique perspective of communication scholars which helps us to focus on the interactional, dialogue processes which technology is increasingly making possible. But beyond technological solutions which may help us to overcome problems of time and space, there is clearly an overriding need for the development of meaningful, mutually acceptable, non-threatening value and ethical systems. Only then do we have some reason to hope that we will be able to avoid future international communication disasters which, at least in the past, resulted from our almost blind faith in the life-changing, life-improving capabilities of new technologies without building ethical systems to guide us in their use.

Encountering the Other: Ethics and the Role of Media in International and Intercultural Communication

Scott R. Olson
Central Connecticut State University

When told that I was taking an intellectual journey into the ethics of international and intercultural media, a few colleagues responded, "that trip shouldn't take very long: there isn't any." There is some truth to the assertion that ethical behavior is the road not taken in the global media marketplace, but it is no more true there than for the media in general, or for communication in general for that matter. Besides, essays on ethics are rarely just descriptive documentation of normative practices within a profession (Cronen, 1991); where we are is only a part of a map which includes where we have been and where we are going.

Past, present, and future are still inadequate, though, in discussing the ethical considerations which need to be taken into account to examine a terrain as complex as the global media, a domain where hundreds of cultures and subcultures try to communicate with each other using thousands of texts whose meanings defy quickening or consensus, where some are profiteers, some politicians, some terrorists, some terrified, some transfixed. It is a landscape where rules and a road map are increasingly useless because, apparently, there is more than one map to it. Attempts to illuminate moral trajectories are thwarted by a continually shifting surface in this site where media and the stranger, the Other, meet in unpredicted, serendipitous, and frightening ways. The moral person is himself or herself a stranger in this strange land, and the possibility for any pilgrim's safe progress seems dim. Encountering the Other is unavoidable in the international media.

One of the main problems in trying to develop an ethics of international media arises from the interaction of film and television producers, distributors, regulators, and audiences, especially when these may be from different cultures, different nationalities: Whose moral compass is to be used? This essay will argue that depending on which ethical orientation is chosen, a single media text, or its utterer or audience, may be judged fundamentally ethical, fundamentally unethical, or outside the realm of ethical judgment. How to find passage when none of the guideposts are anchored in the ground?

In order to examine the complexities of ethical evaluation in the global media marketplace, this chapter will examine the two primary competing ethical frameworks, at least from a Western perspective; investigate how these frameworks manifest themselves in the realms of international journalism and global film and television narrative production, distribution, and consumption; explore the ethics of various strategic and tactical responses available to the subaltern confronted with extensive media imports; and consider the possibility of a contemporary rule deontology of global media. As is often the case with the consideration of ethics, more questions are raised than answered. On this underexplored moral terrain, however, it is time for explorers, if not yet cartographers.

FIRST STEPS

The word "ethics" certainly has different meanings in the literature, and even inconsistent meanings within particular essays. For the purposes of this chapter, the word will be used to mean a deliberate, internally consistent, organized, humanistic, and purposeful system of behavioral rules designed to make human interaction as fair, orderly, and equitable as possible. Often, these take the form of normative codes, such as the journalistic code of ethics. Ethical systems are not the only way to encourage better behavior, however. One alternative would be a moral system. Systems of morals, as the term "moral" is used here, may consist of rules, but may not necessarily be humanistic in origin (in other words, the rules may come from God or the gods), nor internally consistent (for example, the numerous "exceptions" that seem to apply to the Commandment "Thou shalt not kill," such as wartime, pregnancy termination, or capital punishment). Consequently, systems of morals are not necessarily systems of ethics, at least not as used here. A second alternative to systematic ethics is difficult to name, but Bauman (1993) has conceived of a system which has no rules. This will be discussed later in the chapter.

It has been said many times, but system of ethics or morality do not necessarily have any implications for legal systems. This is particularly easy to see in the international and intercultural context, where different systems of morality, of ethics, and of law are frequently in conflict. Of course, there is often extensive interaction between ethical codes and legal systems, but given the confusion of the two within the United States ("it's legal, so it must be ethical"), it is easy to see how developing effective international laws to monitor the mass media is a doomed project from an ethical standpoint. Ethical behavior can't be legislated at home, so what prospects can such legislation have abroad? The cultural conflicts which underlie this problematic will be discussed in detail below.

Perhaps the most fundamental question about ethics, although one not explored here at length, is the question of human nature. Such an inquiry begs a related question: Is ethics resident in a person or a culture, or both, or neither? This has been a controversial point for ethicists, a controversy which stems from the old question of whether we are personally responsible for our own behavior, or whether social conditioning or biology predisposes us to particular activities and therefore reduces or eliminates personal agency. This fundamental dialogue cannot hope to be resolved here, but this chapter assumes that from a communication standpoint, any substantive discussion of ethical judgment inevitably involves consideration of personal agency.

Such contemplations inevitably lead to the classic dichotomy between what is and what ought to be. Clearly, the export and import of global media is a realm scarcely governed by law, let alone ethics. The prevailing attitude of the exporters and importers seems to be analogous to Nike's ad slogan: Just do it. The ethics of audience engagement with these texts are almost unobservable because they find themselves overwhelmed. There is a lot of room for "ought" in this formula, but given the different cultures which operate in making, delivering, and watching global media, it is difficult to see how to formulate consensus about what ought to be.

It is hoped that the reader will come away from this chapter with an understanding of the basic issues in global media ethics, of the different standards which can be applied to judging behavior in these instances, and of how these standards can be in conflict. Also, it is hoped the reader will consider the ethical responsibilities and conflicts which confront the major players in this international media race: program producers and exporters, international distributors, importers, regulators, and audiences, particularly the non-elite, subordinate audiences. Finally, the reader may see a light at the end of the tunnel, a glimmer of possibility for developing a new standard befitting the complexities of the global media environment. The first step on this journey is the consideration of competing standards for ethical judgment.

Divergent Ethical Maps

The conception of what should be meant by the study and application of ethics has been in a great state of flux for several years, largely because of the ontological and epistemological shifts implicit in a Postmodern perspective. The concept of ethics itself can be said to have begun with Modernism, which had as its project the systemization and universalization of knowledge; prior to Modernism, one doesn't speak so much of ethics as of morality, more of a grab-bag, culturally particular approach to what is right and wrong (see Thayer, 1980). Postmodernism comes after Modernism, at least chronologically, but raises questions about whether ethics per se is still possible, or whether a return to morality is underway. Both Modern and Postmodern approaches to ethics need to be used in the international media environment; Modern ethics because they still constitute the moral language of the primary agents in international media production and distribution, and Postmodern ethics because global media have been the primary harbinger of Postmodernity. What is frequently missing in the literature on communication ethics is the extent to which starting on different paths leads to vastly different judgments.

Postmodernism. Given the relative newness of Postmodernism to the discussion of ethics, its definition is in order. Its semantic definition is comprised of many elements which can be crudely summarized in both positive and negative terms. Its "positive" attributes include a sense of incoherence, indeterminacy, chaos, and disorientation (Jameson, 1991; Lyotard, 1984); related to this, a lack of certitude and a sense of ontological provisionality (Hutcheon, 1987); consequently, a belief in multiple yet mutually exclusive truths (Hutcheon, 1987); a refusal to see the Other as the same (During, 1987, 1993); and a textuality which looks like nostalgia but is in fact a metafictional and critical reworking. Its "negative" attributes are a byproduct of its inherent contradictions and incoherence: the commodification of all cultural products (Grossberg, 1992); extensive use of the narrative apparatus of pastiche and of affectless superficiality (Jameson, 1991); the progressive replacing of representation with simulation and hyperreality (Baudrillard, 1985, 1993); the mutation of Mies van der Rowe's aphorism "less is more" into MTV's trademark "too much is never enough"; a sense that the use of language is futile

(Derrida, 1974); and, perhaps above all, the abandonment of the Modernist belief in a universal project (Lyotard, 1984).

Ethical systems both inform and proceed from the cultural paradigms in which they operate. It is not materialist reductionism to observe that the differences in the normative moral codes found in Judaism, Roman Catholicism, Islam, and Protestantism can at least in part be accounted for by the economies and technologies prevalent at the time of their genesis. In the case of Protestantism, the effect of media technology became important for the first time in the form of the Gutenberg Bible, whose effect on Northern European values and beliefs has been extensively documented. What, then, might be the effect of Modernism and Postmodernism on values and beliefs and on the ethical and moral codes they give rise to?

This question becomes more urgent as media technology and programming become increasingly transnational. Do contemporary media technologies and programming transform cultures, and if so, is our notion of what constitutes important ethical questions and appropriate moral solutions transforming as well? Perhaps more problematically, can we come to any agreement on what constitutes ethical behavior in the global media when the ontological basis for any discussion is in such flux?

Modern and Postmodern approaches each suggest their own guidelines for ethical communication. Modernist ethics are animated by a "belief in the possibility of a non-ambivalent, non-aporetic ethical code" (Bauman, 1993, p. 9)—an ethic defined by universality, objectivity, and certitude. The presumptions that Modernists make about human nature naturally lead them to these conclusions; for them, men and women are naturally rational, discerning, and archetypal (which is to say, connected to universal truths about the human condition). Modernist ethics are constructed so as to capitalize on this nature, and possess a "will-to-purity" (Taylor, 1992), a belief in simplicity and universality and an urge to simplify and universalize.

Communication guidelines. From Johannesen (1990) can be deduced a fairly simple set of communication guidelines which operate within a Modernist perspective, which is to say that they exhibit an implicit humanism, positivism, rationalism, universalism and optimism. These are, roughly, that ethical communication: 1) respects the listener; 2) is honest; 3) uses the best language; 4) addresses genuine needs of its listener; and 5) uses appropriate techniques and appeals. Applied to transnational media, a specific type of communication, these maxims might be adapted as follows: The ethical use of transnational media is one which respects the audience; communicates honestly; uses the highest quality of film/television form and content; addresses genuine needs of its diverse audiences; and uses culturally appropriate techniques and appeals. Clearly, Modernist communication ethics proceeds from the presumption that meanings can be controlled and possessed, that utterances mean what they are intended to mean (Bauman, 1993).

If the Modernist ethics is defined by universality, objectivity, and certitude, then its Postmodern progeny is defined by particularity, ambivalence, subjectivity, and aporetics. Postmodernists see human nature in stark contrast to that seen by Modernists; for the former, the human condition is one of irrationality, ambivalence, doubt, and the impossibility of universals (Bauman, 1993). Postmodern ethics must proceed from this less mechanistic, more organic view of human behavior.

Since Postmodern ethics eschews universals, it chafes at the possibility of a rule deontology, but this is deceptive since there seems to be one consistent Postmodern universal: Ethical behavior is "etre-pour-l'autre" or "being for the Other" (Bauman, 1993, p. 50). From a Postmodern ethical standpoint, my being-for-the-Other has no relationship to whether the Other is for me, and in this sense is different from the Modernist admonition to address real needs of the listener, since in that circumstance each has a similar obligation. For the Postmodernist there is not, and for the most part cannot be, ethical quid-pro-quo. Applied to communication, this standard would be: Ethical communication is always for the Other; or applied to transnational media: The meanings intended and derived from the ethical use of global media are always for the Other.

The most interesting aspect of the Postmodern ethical perspective is ontological: "Being for the Other" is concerned not with essence but with reflection. As such, it has two senses, "being *for*" in the sense of caring about, and "*being* for" in the sense of an existence which is defined by. This is well suited toward trying to define ethicality in a world dominated by global media: As Spivak (1995) has argued, cultures themselves lack a defining essence, always existing in relation to other cultures, always making do with an ontology of reflection. For Spivak, language itself is a part of this reflection, leading her to question whether the subaltern can speak for themselves.

Both the Modern and Postmodern approaches to ethics contain pitfalls. Because it is "ostensibly universal, but by necessity homegrown" (Bauman, 1993, p. 41), Modernism tends toward intolerance. Because it is never universalized and always subjectivized, Postmodernism tends towards having no ethical standards whatsoever. Another pitfall is to assume that the Modern and Postmodern are the only operative ethical modes which can be applied to international media; to presume so would be to engage in a kind of imperialist ethics. "Borrowed ethical systems have severe limits" (Cronen, 1991, p. 36).

These two approaches have their genesis in and are best applied to the West, but some of the most pressing ethical issues concerning the distribution and consumption of media involve the interaction between the West and non-European countries and cultures. It is not within the scope of this chapter to survey non-Western ethical approaches to international media, if that were even possible; Post-colonial theory (Bhabha, 1994; Said, 1993) indicates, if nothing else, that every site of contestation between text and audience is unique. Even within the West, significantly different ethical systems exist (see for example Grant, 1992).

For the purposes of this chapter, then, ethical problematics will be considered using the two ethical systems implied by Modernism and Postmodernism, superimposing them on the two predominant domains of international media and on the four modes of agency. The two domains to be examined are international journalism and international narrative programming. The four modes of agency to be considered are the international production, international distribution, domestic regulation and domestic audience modes. The fundamental problematics can then be summarized as: What are the moral responsibilities of those who produce media to be exported? of those who export media? of regulators who control what is and is not seen? of the audiences who watch the media?

Encountering the International Press

Perhaps the most commonly discussed aspect of the ethics of transnational media concerns journalistic practices across cultures and states. The extent to which this has been important, and has been taken seriously, is measurable in the MacBride Commission report to the United Nations and its aftermath: What is often called the "NWIO" or "New World Information Order" was an attempt to balance and mitigate (some might say ethicize) international practices. The ethic of transnational journalism is often just a variation of the same issues of domestic ethical concern.

This chapter will not offer a full consideration of journalistic ethics, which has been done well and extensively elsewhere, but rather will illuminate those particular ethical problematics which are unique to international journalism. There are two main areas of ethical concern which distinguish the international press from its domestic sibling: national sovereignty and international concentration of ownership. Additionally, there are issues of domestic concern which have unique aspects in the international press, including bias, gatekeeping, emotional appeals, and privacy.

Sovereignty. Perhaps the primary ethical consideration which distinguishes international media from domestic media is the question of sovereignty. To what extent do states have a right to sovereignty, and to what extent is this right mitigated by human rights and commercial considerations which encourage freer flow of information globally? Rupert Murdoch, CEO of the News Corporation, tried to circumvent Chinese sovereignty by establishing a direct broadcast satellite system, but Chinese officials made owning the receiver dish illegal, thwarting his plan (Auletta, 1995). Whether individuals or companies should have a right to circumvent national sovereignty is debatable; Murdoch certainly couches his arguments in ethical terms, claiming that the media represent a freedom against totalitarianism; but some have accused him of disingenuity (Auletta, 1995).

Faith that the state-system is a suitable source of moral authority in international press disputes belies a Modernist confidence in structural solutions, rationality, and, in a sense, the utopian possibility of a "project." On the other hand, faith in the ethicality of unfettered international corporate news organizations like CNN or News Corporation is neither Modern nor Postmodern. But what alternative is there? From a Postmodern perspective, the state is clearly in political and economic decline (Stavrianos, 1976), and "has no more capacity, need nor want of spiritual (and this includes moral) leadership" (Bauman, 1993, p. 138). The state has been replaced by extraterritoriality, pan-national movements, ethnic movements and tribalism, and the omnipresent multinational corporation. All of these undermine the NWIO, which essentially intended to use the state as the determinant of sovereignty and social norms. In light of the diminishing presence of the state, the ethics of international journalism (and indeed of global media themselves) need to thoroughly reconsidered. State ability to influence journalistic practices is ebbing, but no other force external to the journalism industry is stepping up to fill the void.

Concentration. Related to the issue of sovereignty is the issue of media concentration, an ongoing process which is consolidating the control over more and more media outlets into fewer and fewer hands. Whereas some of the ethical issues concerning the global press have been considered for some time, the issue of concentration is relatively new, and one of the more pressing ethical issues facing the transnational media world today. For the most part, it has not been confronted; the transnational press is better characterized by expediency than thoughtfulness. CNN and Ted Turner's acquiescence to the Chinese government which he had criticized a moment before, and *The International Herald Tribune*'s change in editorial position based on a request from the Singapore Prime Minister (Auletta, 1995), are examples of how global business deals compromise ethical media behavior to suit the bottom line.

An example of expediency over ethics and media concentration is Rupert Murdoch, CEO of the News Corporation, one of the most powerful media moguls in the world. Auletta (1995) has characterized Murdoch as "a pirate; he will cunningly circumvent rules, and sometimes principles, to get his way" (p. 84). Murdoch has massive newspaper, broadcasting, and film production holdings in Australia, Great Britain, and the United States under his personal control. In addition, the mergers of Turner with Time-Warner and of Disney with ABC Cap Cities reinforce the suspicion that the global media are coming under the control of fewer and fewer players, and that soon there may be only one or two. It is ironic that the same media moguls who railed against totalitarian regimes so as to gain access to new markets are on the verge of becoming totalitarian themselves—but perhaps not so ironic if these railings were merely rhetorical stances, the result of concerns with expediency rather than conviction.

The increased concentration within the international press is a symptom of Postmodernism, especially in the sense of commodification; in a Postmodern world, everything—even information—is commodified (Jameson, 1991). A Modernist no doubt greets such concentration with fear and trepidation, since it embodies the limitations of the system to be orderly and self-regulating in a way that promotes diverse opinions, democracy and a marketplace of ideas. Postmodernists are perhaps just as fearful about the concentration, but less surprised, given their expectancy of an inherent messiness to human affairs.

Other Concerns. Other concerns which are frequently cited as issues in domestic journalistic ethics are also important for international journalism, albeit in slightly different ways. Journalistic bias, of perpetual concern to American media observers, takes on a new dimension in the international media marketplace, where social orientations and linguistic coloration which might be perfectly obvious in one culture cannot be similarly decoded in another. Gatekeeping is another matter for consideration in journalistic ethics, but in the international context, gatekeepers may know little or nothing about the cultures to which their information is disseminated; this would be particularly true of media services like Sky News on satellite, which is available throughout Europe, but which exhibits distinctly British gatekeeping. Emotional appeals are no more acceptable in an international context, but they may be decoded in any number of unintended ways in different cultural contexts. Privacy, too, is an issue in international journalism, but one which extends to information gathering in general. These ethical considerations, then, all have both domestic and international aspects.

With the dawning of a new medium, the World Wide Web on the Internet, the ethical problems surrounding international journalistic practices will become even more salient: The Web allows users to visit web sites around the world in apparent privacy, but all the while transferring important information about themselves to the host site. As on-line casinos, banking and shopping become more popular, issues of privacy, appropriate appeals, and the opportunity for fraud, will be compounded. It has even been argued that in this technologically evolving new media environment, the concept of privacy is rapidly dying and should be abandoned (Brin quoted in Teitelbaum, 1995)—an almost unfathomable and unaddressable prospect for traditional ethics. Another issue concerns access: More people around the world are gaining access to more channels of information via broadcasting and satellite, but computer ownership and Internet access are confined to economic elites, particularly in the developing world.

International journalism, then, presents us with many ethical issues for consideration, although they are no more numerous and only slightly different than issues related to domestic journalism. Far more complex, from an ethical standpoint, than the issues raised when we deal with the international dissemination of information, are those connected with entertainment. Although this subject matter has been considered far less in the scholarly and popular literature than journalistic ethics, nothing may be of greater moral urgency than a consideration of the relationship between ethics and narrative.

Encountering Narrative

The tremendous volume of visual entertainment imports and exports, and the paucity of scholarly consideration of them, has tended to obscure the fact that the most significant transnational media ethical issues concern narrative rather than journalistic media. This relative neglect may have resulted because traditionally the effects of narrative are more subtle, or because policy makers are more interested in and involved with journalism than visual fictions. Another reason may be that the literature on the effects of transnational narrative upon indigenous cultures is so polarized and contentious: One camp, epitomized by Schiller (1989), asserts that imported media—particularly of the American variety—are destructive to indigenous economies and cultures; another camp, epitomized by Ang (1985), argues that readings of the media are so varied among different audiences that they have a negligible effect on local cultures. Either way, there can be no question that the international export of film and television fiction raises varied and pressing ethical questions that are of a different nature from those related to international journalism.

Certainly, the most significant of these ethical debates concerns cultural survival: Does the economic right of media-producing nations to create and export media products outweigh the right to survival of cultures threatened by media imports? Indigenous culture could, theoretically, be threatened in many ways. One of these factors is that their ability to produce and disseminate their own television programs or movies is threatened by cheaper and flashier imports, one of Schiller's (1989) concerns. The loss of indigenous values, beliefs, and narrative structures is another concern (see, for example, Kapoor & Kang, 1995 and Kang & Wu, 1995). It seems clear that the French government considered both of these concerns when it insisted on capping the volume of U.S. film and television imports to Europe during the General Agreement on Trades and Tariffs ("GATT") debates (Cohen, 1993).

What is not clear, however, is that the right-to-export versus the right-to-survival debate is framed properly. It proceeds from the presumption that cultures are transformed by the introduction of foreign media. At a superficial level this is almost certainly true—people might stay home to watch a program when before they did not—but whether it is true at a deeper structural level is questionable. The debate continues as to whether or not culture is transformed or reinforced by imported narrative media. Certainly Klapper's (1960) famous assertion that the media reinforce rather than transform should give the ethicist some pause, even when the artifact in question originates in a different culture.

Transparency. Elsewhere (Olson, forthcoming) I have argued that the international success of the American media is due to their ability to reinforce indigenous beliefs rather than their ability to introduce new ones, a textual device I call "transparency." It seems that the American cinema, in particular, is designed to function as though it is indigenous in whatever context. Of course, this is not the result of any deep concern for the cultures which import its products, but because this approach greatly increases its profit potential. Those films and television programs which successfully exploit transparency are likely to do well in the international media marketplace, in conjunction with other marketing and distribution factors.

The transparency factor makes clear that the nature of global media consumption underscores the limitations of the Modern notion of meanings intended, possessed, and controlled. What is called by Fiske (1987) and others "polysemy," by Raschke (1992) the "plurisignificative," and by Bloom (1975) "misprision" refers to the multiplicity of meanings that any text, but particularly iconic media, engenders. Any media text generates numerous readings ("meanings") within its own cultural context, and these multiple meanings explode exponentially in the international media marketplace. It is a rather complex question to ask what *Dallas* (CBS TV) means to Americans, but it is much more complex to ask what it means to Nigerians, Netherlanders, Nicaraguans, or New Zealanders. The diversity of meanings created by audiences in interaction with media texts has been extensively observed (see among many others: Shekwo, 1984; Ang, 1985; Fiske, 1987; Jenkins, 1992; Bacon-Smith, 1992; Liebes & Katz, 1993; Yoshimoto, 1994; Miller, 1995; Allen, 1995). In this chaos of simultaneous, manifold and mutually exclusive meanings, what place do Modernist ethical rules have? Any talk of "universals" becomes problematic, to say the least.

The question of whether ethical frames, or cultural orientations themselves, are exported along with the media product is still being debated. To the extent that there is a consensus, it seems to be gathering around the notion that while broad cultural biases can be readily identified (e.g., "family is important"), more particular messages are read in vastly different ways. Audience members from different cultures may interpret the same episode of *Dallas* (CBS TV) to say "capitalism is good," or "capitalism works most of the time," or "capitalism is evil" (see Liebes & Katz, 1993). This observation suggests that ethical frames can neither be exported within a media narrative nor can they be easily appropriated from it. Ethics are not like Greeks crouched within a media-Trojan Horse, waiting to jump out and overpower the moral values of viewers. This is not to say that audience values may not change. They may, but in ways that can neither be fully planned nor anticipated. Our tenuous consensus on media impact, then, is situated somewhere between the dichotomized extremes of Schiller (1989), for whom only the dominant, hegemonic meaning is significant, and Ang (1985) for whom only the indigenous, subaltern readings are significant.

In fact, cultures and texts must really be considered the same thing, rather than one being an artifact of the other. As Raschke (1992) has argued,

> texts are no longer bare runes to be puzzled over. They are at once an intricate braid of the latent and the manifest, of form and function, of intimation and opacity, of word and image, of grapheme and difference. Indeed, textuality and culture—regarded in the primitive sense of all that is somehow 'indicative'—now emerge as reciprocal constructs. (p. 101)

For the ethicist, media texts do not exist only as artifacts of the culture which produced them, but as an active and covalent aspect of every culture in which they are consumed on the terms of that culture. As Miller (1995) has indicated,

The Young and the Restless must be treated from a cultural standpoint as a Trinandian television program, in spite of the fact that it happens to have been produced in the United States. This means that in evaluating the exporting and importing of media narratives, at least two judgments are needed: one from the perspective of the exporter, the other from the perspective of the importer.

The concentration of power and control within the media is as big a concern in the realm of narrative as it is in the realm of journalism, although its study has not advanced as far in the former. With Disney merging with ABC Cap Cities and a planned merger between Turner and Time-Warner, not to mention numerous joint ventures (including a Microsoft/NBC partnership), decreasing numbers of entertainment media providers do present ethical problems in terms of diversity of voices and democratic participation. Still, it is apparent that at the present time, there are many more actors involved in international entertainment, with successful domestic and export industries thriving in India, Hong Kong, Australia, Brazil and elsewhere, whereas there are effectively only two players in international journalism: Turner and Murdoch.

The ethical responsibilities in the realm of international narrative production, distribution, and consumption are best parceled out by mode of agency. There are producers, distributors, regulators and audiences, each with their own ethical obligations. Each mode of agency can be analyzed from Modern and Postmodern perspectives.

Creators and Distributors. What are the ethical responsibilities of the creators and global distributors of narrative media programming? It is possible to identify several such areas of obligation, although the obligations themselves vary depending on the ethical standards used. Several notions from both Modernist and Postmodernist perspectives can be readily identified, including the Modern notions of quality, respect and the obligation to address genuine needs, and the Postmodern notion of semiotic openness or polysemy.

From a Modern perspective, one of the main challenges faced by a media producer is the responsibility for quality—what Johannesen (1990) would call "the best language"—although this concept is obviously hard to define. Quality is an important notion in discussing what is and is not ethical and appropriate, but even if it is agreed that audiences have a right of access to the highest quality media, how do we define that term? Masterman (1995) cautions that

> there can be no return to a narrow, exclusivist, class-based notion of quality . . . we will all have to work with a much more generous, pluralistic and inclusive notion of value. This probably means

ditching any transcendental notion of value, and recognizing the
transitive nature of value terms. (p. 8, italicized original)

Quality, then, exists only in context. It can only be defined from within, not
from without. Any ethical system of global media distribution must recognize
the grassroots, indigenous, participatory notions of quality.

Similar to the imperative for high quality, a Modern ethicist would argue
that media producers need to respect their audiences. This means, presumably,
not using emotional and inflammatory appeals, and addressing the audience in
a mature and responsible fashion. Given the wide ranging distribution that
many films and television programs receive, this turns out to be a difficult
directive: What might strike an audience from one culture as well-developed
and useful might strike an audience from another as childish and silly (see, for
example, Liebes & Katz, 1993). Similar to the admonition for respect, a
Modern ethicist would assert that ethical media production must address the
genuine needs that the intended audience has. It is difficult to conceive of most
Hollywood productions in these terms, but many national cinemas around the
world promote just such an approach. The Korean film *Our Twisted Hero*
(1992) which examines culturally appropriate uses of power, or the Mongolian
film *Heritage* (1993) which meditates on the virtues of traditional Mongolian
rural life, are two specific examples. Entertainment is, in these cases, merely a
secondary concern; they are intended to address some perceived social need of
the audience. The Hollywood product, on the other hand, has entertainment as
its primary objective almost all of the time, so unless one constructs an
argument that entertainment is an essential need of the audience, then from a
Modern perspective it is a morally inferior communication (Funiok, 1995, gets
out of this Modernist conundrum by arguing that entertainment is in fact a
legitimate audience need).

The Postmodern ethicist might see a single imperative for media
producers where the Modern one sees many. If numerous readings of media
narratives are possible, is polysemy a coincidental and unfortunate byproduct
(the Modern perspective) or the essential essence of communication (the
Postmodern perspective)? Measuring how well, in an ethical sense, a producer
of a media narrative has done would certainly depend on which of the
perspectives an evaluator or critic were to adopt. It seems that from a Modern
perspective, and particularly in circumstances related to national development,
the "best" media texts would be those which did the most effective job of
limiting alternative readings, in a sense forcing the dominant reading ("less is
more"). From a Postmodern perspective, the "best" media texts would be those
which enabled rather than restricted a multiplicity of readings, allowing

viewers to create any number of meanings out of the same text ("too much is never enough").

Take, for example, the Disney film *The Lion King* (1994). From a Modern perspective, the film's "meaning" can be measured in fairly simple political, economic, and ideological terms: it meant to promote Western notions of patriarchal family responsibilities while maximizing profit for Disney stockholders. Concluding that the film, therefore, lacks respect for the audience, is dishonest about its purpose, has no genuine concern for the needs of the audience and uses inappropriate techniques and appeals, the Modernist might conclude that *The Lion King* is an unethical utterance, at least in the global context. From a Postmodern perspective, on the other hand, the film's "meaning" might be seen as much more elusive and complex. While it certainly "means" profit to Disney, the particular images in the film might have vastly different significance for viewers from different cultures. The opening sequence of the film, for example, in which the baboon Rafiki spreads melon juice and dust over the baby lion Simba's head, can be read as any number of different initiation rituals, including a baptism, a bris and several traditional Native American and African shamanic practices. Which ritual is it? Which is the correct reading? To the Postmodernist, they all are, since meaning is created in the listener/reader. To the extent that this polysemy is deliberate on the part of the creators of *The Lion King*, their action in designing the film as they have can be deemed ethical from this Postmodern perspective, since it enabled rather than restricted interpretation, and to that extent is for-the-Other.

Indeed, from the Postmodern perspective, limiting or restricting readings is the unethical act. Bauman (1993) calls the attempt to limit cognitive and aesthetic space "proteophilia" (p. 168), a form of control which denies strangers their strangeness. The consumption of media is a ritual, and rituals create meaning rather than respond to it. Indeed, ritual takes a world which is "shifting, human, and untidy" and gives it "unity, mastery, and control" (Cupitt, 1992, p. 153). Postmodernism itself is rife with ambivalence and ambiguity, yet the well-designed Postmodern media product is capable of indigenous recoding throughout the world, becoming—like *The Lion King*—a sort of localized ritual, which then masks the very Postmodern chaos that allowed the film to come into being, with a veneer of order and familiarity.

The role of international media distributors is roughly analogous to the role of producers in Modern and Postmodern terms. The Modern ethicist will judge them well if in matching a product to a market they have made available films and television programs of the highest quality, at a fair price, respecting and addressing genuine programming needs of the intended audience(s). This could affect the way a distributor, for example, deals with a film like *The Last*

Temptation of Christ (1988), which might be considered disrespectful of audiences in Ireland or Poland, and consequently might not be distributed there. A Postmodern ethicist would most likely be unconcerned about distribution except from an economic and political perspective; he or she would doubt the ability of the distributor to ascertain what constitutes quality, respect or genuine needs in any intercultural situation.

Regulators. The role of the producers and distributors of media programming is where most discussions of media ethics begin and end, but they are not the only ones when considering ethical concerns. The ethical responsibilities of the leaders of a media importing country are similarly a contested site. For example, the French government has sought to limit American media exports to Europe through quotas attached to the General Agreement on Trades and Tariffs (GATT). How is this to be measured from an ethical perspective, particularly when one considers that limiting imports is usually unnecessary if there is no domestic demand? The limitations are needed precisely because demand is great, so the regulators in such an instance are actually limiting the choices available in the market, and in some cases they are prohibiting the first choice of many consumers. Such regulators are clearly operating out of a Modern conception of how the communication process works—the imported product, usually a Hollywood product, is thought to communicate something foreign and unsavory, and it is seen as capable of changing the indigenous culture in the direction of the culture whose product has been imported.

Audiences. A final agent in the production and consumption of global media narratives are the audiences, which have ethical responsibilities just as the producers and distributors of the media do. Indeed, they may be the only actors capable of determining the ethicality of the media (Thayer, 1980). Funiok (1995) has identified several principles which undergird any evaluation of the ethicality of audience behavior: Audience members must be aware of the significance of their viewing choices in a broad social context; they must be aware of the private/personal and public/social aspects of their choices; and their legitimate need for entertainment must be considered. These principles lead Funiok (1995) to a rather Modern construction of the audience's "co-responsibility" in ethical media use. For him, audiences have an ethical responsibility to be competent, self-controlled and self-educating in their own media use, and they have an ethical imperative to make sure children are similarly competent.

Funiok's (1995) assessment is a Modern one, then, given its emphasis on universal imperatives and rules. It may work *within* a cultural context, but is problematic *across* contexts. From a Postmodern perspective, these imperatives may be difficult—how competent can one be in viewing media imported from another cultural context? Is it possible to self-educate, or to educate children when the media represent alien cultures and contexts? Consider, for example, the disparity in VCR penetration in 1994 between the developed and developing world. In the United States, 82.9% of households own at least one VCR, compared to Mexico and the Philippines with penetration under 25% and India and the Czech Republic where it is closer to 10% ("Emerging-Market Indicators," 1995). Such data make media literacy programs seem a great imperative in the U.S., but not nearly as pressing in India or the Czech Republic where access to programming is much more limited.

The international production, distribution and consumption of film and television narrative, then, raises numerous ethical issues for the various actors in the process. The ethical obligations of any one of them are difficult to pinpoint, however, because different ethical frameworks indicate different judgments for the same behaviors. The focus of this chapter to this point has been on the ethicality of only one direction of the communication process, the direction from production to consumption. Communication always involves an element of mutuality, though, so there is another direction which needs to be considered as well. What response, what feedback is possible for the audience which has received international media programming?

Routes for the Subaltern

In the face of an overwhelming volume of imported media, what options do members of an indigenous culture have, and what ethical considerations resonate from them? The extreme responses—terrorism on the one hand and complete cultural submission on the other—seem outside the realm of what could be considered moral options. But what of the possibilities, the strategies, that lie in between?

Subalterneity is the state of being subordinate, and those in such a state have been called by Postcolonial theorists (Spivak, 1995; Bhabha, 1994) "the subaltern," a term which is both a noun and an adjective, and can refer to either a particular person or to a social group, just as the word "dispossessed" can. Derrida (1981) has sometimes used "*antre*" as its synonym. Spivak (1995) uses the term "subaltern" to refer to non-elite, dominated social classes in postcolonial India, a use broadened by Parry (1995) and Chakrabarty (1995) to refer to those in similar situations in other cultural contexts, or to a particular agent or actor, such as a certain peasant woman.

Subalterneity raises a third, non-dialectical alternative to Modernism and Postmodernism—the possibility of a Postcolonial ethics. In true Postcolonial fashion, the route may be neither/nor (see for example Bhabha, 1994). In any case, there are three primary routes available to a subordinate culture in reaction to dominant imported media with which it interacts: acquiescence, disinterest or resistance.

Acquiescence and disinterest. When the subaltern are willingly merged into the dominant culture, when it acquiesces and loses its identity and adopts the dominant culture, the process is called absorption (Schmookler, 1984). Presumably, the values and practices of the dominant culture will be affected and recreated by this absorption in proportion to the strength of the subaltern culture; that is to say, a trace of the subaltern will impact the dominant culture even though they have disappeared into it (Bhabha, 1994; Spivak, 1995). To the extent that American media exporters have inculcated communication patterns and other norms of the cultures to which their media are exported, this "trace" remains, detectable by the subaltern and maybe by the dominant culture as well. Subtle but recognizable references to folkways in Hollywood movies might act in this way. Is this ethical? A Modern perspective doesn't suggest a categorical problem here; the viewer is respected to the extent that the trace exists. Whether Hollywood films are created to use "the best possible language" is, of course, subject to debate.

Assimilation describes the situation in which the subaltern is swallowed up by the dominant culture against its will. Almost always the situation will be absorption rather than true assimilation because a trace of the subaltern culture will remain to help shape the dominant culture in some way. The assimilation of the subaltern assumes that the subordinate culture will surrender itself to the dominant one, losing all distinctiveness; in terms of the media, this would mean that all meanings become the dominant meanings. As Hall (1980) has shown, this virtually cannot occur: There will almost always be resistant readings and oppositional decoding. Trace elements prevent complete assimilation, however absorbed a culture may be. Transnational media will never have universal meanings. From a Modern or Postmodern ethical standpoint, assimilation is as undesirable as it is unlikely; how can one be "for the Other" when the Other has ceased to exist?

Occasionally, in a acquiescence scenario, the dominant culture gives a voice to the subaltern out of a sense (possibly misplaced) of superior moral responsibility, even pity. Such a situation can be described as pater/maternalism. Research on the relationship between Sweden and the Samifolken ("Lapps") regarding broadcasting power revealed a pater/maternalist pattern, one which, while ostensibly well-intentioned, effectively hobbled indigenous attempts at cultural and linguistic preservation (Olson, 1985). The Samifolken were smothered by "parental" love. The actions of the dominant culture would be judged to be positive by Modern ethical standards because of the belief that such actions are motivated by the genuine needs of the audience, but from a Postmodern perspective, the action actually makes the Other's situation more difficult.

If the subaltern culture's attempt to disconnect itself from the imported media, if it detaches from and ignores it, secession occurs, or what Schmookler (1984) has called "withdrawal." From a communication perspective, subcultures would ordinarily be the source of this withdrawal. Many such subcultures have been extensively studied by Cultural Studies scholars, including punk, gay and lesbian subcultures; because the media rarely, even never depict these cultures from their own point of view, because they tend to be seen as secessors from the dominant culture. A particularly poignant example is the gay/African-American/poor/drag/Manhattan subculture portrayed in the film *Paris is Burning* (1991). The process of "outing" is essentially a secessionist strategy; it is the name used by radical homosexuals for their practice of making public the names of homosexuals who might otherwise want to hide their identity (Gross, 1991). Such a practice raises innumerable ethical issues. Whatever the merits of its motive of making the world aware of the ubiquity and contributions of gays and lesbians are, outing respects neither the subject of the communication (who wants his or her sexuality to remain private) nor the receiver of the communication (who probably isn't interested in receiving this message). In short, the ethics of a secessionist strategy are highly contentious; in the case of outing, the Other has not been respected.

Another type of detachment is the creation of an alternative media reality. Hyperreality, a sort of self-enclosure described by Baudrillard (1985) and de Certeau (1984) and observed by Meyrowitz (1985), creates a more fatalistic situation as the subaltern culture creates for itself a pseudo-environment which is often called solipsism. From a purely cognitive perspective, solipsism is the purest variety of self-empowerment, since power is actually created, rather than shifted from one point to another. Such power is somewhat ephemeral, however, since solipsism remains a personal response to saturation by the media. One example are the Otaku, young Japanese men who live in a self-contained virtual reality which they created (Greenfeld, 1993). This computer subculture has essentially disassociated itself from any direct contact with actual human beings, all contact confined to the electronic media. This group and others like it have coopted the dominant media's hardware and software for their own self-enclosed, antisocial, reality-generating purposes, gaining power by imposing subjective meanings and structures over hegemonic meanings, erasing them in the process at the cognitive level. From a libertarian ethical perspective, it is difficult to find anything to debate here, since each participant is communicating with self and others in a consensual and generally respectful manner. From more communitarian approaches to ethics, however, some complications can be seen. Do geographic neighbors have the right to completely isolate themselves from the rest of their community, replacing it with connections to other geographies, some of them virtual? Is there a moral obligation to be merely aware of (let alone tolerant of or "for") the Other? These ethical questions will become more pressing as the electronic media increasingly enable non-contiguous, synthetic, even "pretend" communities. What will ethics be when community has no geographic location?

Resistance. If the subaltern culture should opt to strategically resist the dominant meanings in imported media, it has several options. Sholle (1988) has elaborated several strategies which the dominant media—in this case imported media—use to muffle or silence other voices, including sedimentation, reification, adaptation, mollification, and legitimation. These can be observed through textual analysis of media exports. What Sholle (1988) did not consider were the subaltern strategies and tactics which might be used in resisting dominant ones. The subaltern can resist dominant culture devices by using countervailing ones: eruption, deconstruction, mutation, intensification and illegitimation (Olson, 1994). Each of these can and has been used, and each raises ethical questions.

Stuart Hall is credited by Sholle with identifying sedimentation, the process by which only certain types of discourse are allowed to exist by the dominant culture, restricting the social options available to a few. Sedimentation is resisted by eruption (Olson, 1994), a subaltern strategy which expands discourse into new formats, forces unasked questions and puts the discourse onto new ground. In America and elsewhere, subaltern cultures have resisted dominant media messages by making use of new media (the World Wide Web and other internet possibilities, for example), public access television, or sabotage techniques. Because eruption increases the volume and variety of discourse forms and topics, it must be considered fundamentally ethical, although particular uses may lack respect "for otherness."

Sholle (1988) attributes reification, the process through which the existing social order is made to seem not manufactured but natural, to

Horkheimer and Jameson. In reification, the media are used by the dominant culture to present images and ideas of what is, rather than what could be. The reinforcement aspect of the media was clearly established by Klapper (1960), so it is easy to see the potential power of reification. Yet such images in the media can and are resisted and denaturalized. The subaltern cultures do this with deconstruction, a process of textual analysis which reveals how images are produced within linguistic, conventional, and ideological codes. Efforts at media literacy are efforts in this direction, by creating a space in which audiences may contextualize and dissect what they see. This requires a fairly high level of literacy, however—a level at which the relationship between signs and meanings is understood semiotically. Since deconstruction means education, and since it creates rather than restricts meanings, it can be considered ethical from both a Modern and Postmodern perspective.

Adaptation has occurred when media images have been slowly manipulated by the dominant culture so as to engineer conformity. This can be done in a number of ways, but most predominantly when the Other is portrayed as threatening to the dominant culture. American television sit-comedy uses this technique quite commonly; the strange or foreign is portrayed as something in need of containment (e.g., Latka on *Taxi* [NBC TV]). The strategy of mutation can be used by the subordinate culture, however, as a way of counteracting adaptation; mutation is an attack on predominant sentimentalization and convention through stereotype-bashing and nonlinear representations of time designed to disorient the viewer. Such disorienting widens the cognitive possibilities of the audience through art (Fleming & Wilson, 1987) or "trash" (Weldon, 1983; Vale & Juno, 1987). Because it broadens the range of discourse, mutation must be considered fundamentally ethical from a Modernist perspective.

Subaltern attempts to set traps for and play tricks on the media subvert the dominant media environment and are often a kind of mutation, but often go by other names. "Culture jamming" is the phrase used by Dery (1993) to describe a variety of monkey-wrenching techniques which each raises its own ethical considerations. Pirate radio—clandestine commercial or political radio stations which operate without the permission of the state to which they broadcast—are more clearly a kind of intellectual sabotage. Depending on the intention of the pirate broadcasters, these stations are either a pesky nuisance (Radio Caroline commercial broadcasts of rock and roll music to England in the 1960s) or revolution itself (Basque separatist radio in the 1980s). The ethics of pirate radio are best judged by the nature of the message, not the medium; depending on what is being advocated, the breaking of national broadcasting laws may be reprehensible or fully justified, the latter particularly when it gives voice to some suppressed perspective, culture, language or opinion. Broadcasting laws generally serve the interests of the ruling elite, who may themselves be fundamentally unethical.

There are other sabotage possibilities as well. "Poaching," coopting existing media messages for alternative and contradictory purposes (Jenkins, 1992; de Certeau, 1984), is one example. Frequently cited in this regard is the way *Star Trek* fans have "poached" (i.e., stolen from the king/queen's land) copyrighted characters and concepts for home-made books and magazines (Bacon-Smith, 1992). Media hoaxes, as practiced by Alan Abel and Joey Skaggs (Juno & Vale, 1987) use the media's own laziness and sensationalism to trick them into reporting false and absurd stories, such as houses of prostitution for dogs. Another type of sabotage is "billboard banditry," which involves defacing and manipulating billboards into new messages which contradict the original one; one particularly prolific such "artist" is Mark Pauline (Juno & Vale, 1987). All of these pranks are an irritation to the dominant political and commercial structure, but since they actually expand and elaborate the number of messages communicated in the culture, they are, in general, fundamentally ethical. Since they occasionally involve the destruction or manipulation of private property, they should be questioned more in the realm of law than of ethics. The extent to which these are used internationally is unclear, but the Berlin Wall, for one, was adorned with many mutational sentiments.

Sholle (1988) credits Benjamin and Ellul with observing the strategy of mollification, the process through which participants in a culture are made to feel more like observers and audiences than agents and actors. Discussions of how the media "desensitize" viewers to any number of social ills are too common to cite. It is possible for the subaltern culture to use the process of intensification, however, to act as antidote to mollification. Intensification would be any process which compels viewers to adopt active agency. Propagating images which make the viewer feel empowered, angry, capable and active would be one approach. For example, gory videos and postcards have been sent to random recipients separately by animal rights activists and anti-abortion activists, encouraging intensification. The ethics of such a strategy are worthy of considerable debate—from both a Modern and Postmodern perspective this technique has some dubious aspects. Can the practice be said to be "for" the Other when it doesn't address any or their perceived legitimate needs? On the other hand, actions such as these have little hope of mobilizing public action without intensification.

The process of legitimation, often described by Frankfurt School theorists, occurs when certain genres of discourse and certain types of messages are rendered "official" by the dominant culture. These may take a number of forms depending on the level of control over and involvement in the media that the government may have, so it can range from the direct and authoritarian to the indirect and subtle. Illegitimation is the logical approach of those seeking to counteract legitimation, and it is best accomplished through public demonstrations that legitimacy is conferred, not inherent. This is not easy to do, especially in those instances when alternative access to the media is unavailable. Recognizing that illegitimation acts essentially to dramatize the complexities of communication, and by providing alternative voices, it is not inherently unethical.

Whether they acquiesce to, ignore or resist imported media, indigenous cultures or subcultures must confront basic moral questions. Given the diversity of cultures which would find themselves in the position of confronting imported media, the question of whether Modern or Postmodern approaches are relevant and applicable to them is important. On the other hand, can there be no generalizations about what constitutes ethical behavior in the international media? Are right and wrong particular to every culture, or are there commonalities? In spite of all indications to the contrary, it may be possible to construct a rule deontology for global media production, distribution, and consumption.

The Road to Rule Deontology

Modernist communication deontology is easy enough to construct, provides clear rules for behavior, and neatly informs the agent whether he or she has lived up to his or her ethical responsibilities. It is easy to see how these rules could be applied to global media—easy and probably wrong. Because it proceeds from the presumption that an utterance has inherent meaning, a meaning created in deliberate fashion by the utterer, and that the ethical obligations of the sender and receiver have to do with ferreting out this intended and inherent meaning, Modernist ethics builds it foundation on a naive, simplistic and outmoded model of the communication process. Modernism's inherent dualism between mind and world creates problems which disconnect ethics from real human experience (Cronen, 1991). Whatever meaning is implied, inference is ultimately more important. This is nowhere more true than in the universe of global media, a universe in which the American soap opera *The Young and the Restless* (CBS TV) became the most popular program in Trinidad, where it has a cultural significance never imagined, let alone intended by its creators, a significance which has everything to do with indigenous and traditional Trinidadian cultural norms

(Miller, 1995). In such a universe, is it possible to measure ethics by intended meaning? Modernist deontology, then, doesn't really fit the global media scenario; this seems to leave Postmodern deontology, or no deontology at all, as the only alternatives.

But is a Postmodern deontology possible? If premodern morality was a set of disconnected admonitions, and Modernist ethics was a code of interrelated, rational rules, is any Postmodern deontology possible? Rules seem to require transcendent meaning. Both premodern morality and Modern ethics were predicated on some form of transcendent meaning (Makau, 1991, for example, uses fidelity and veracity as transcendent values), but Postmodern theorists have generally been quick to deny the possibility of transcendence. Some Postmodernists, such as Joanna Hodge (1992), have begun to reconsider this denial, however:

> My suspicion is that an ethics for a postmodern community will have
> to retain some of the characteristics of a morality of transcendental
> subjectivity and transcendent value, alongside the incompatible
> emphases on location more characteristic of the postmodern. The
> task for . . . a postmodern ethics is then to explain how such a
> conjunction of incompatible elements can be thought about at all. (p.
> 135)

It is not the purpose of my chapter to resolve this contradiction, but only to indicate that it may be possible in the future to reconcile the purely subjective and local/indigenous cultural aspects of Postmodernism with some meanings which are shared between subjective beings and different cultures. Whether this intersubjective reality can be labeled transcendent or not is less important to a discussion of contemporary ethics than is the deontology which any shared meaning enables.

Bauman (1993) worries that the Postmodern era may also mean a post-ethical era, what he calls "a social life absolved from moral worries" (p. 3), and the "ethics" displayed by international media companies such as Microsoft do give any ethicist pause. Microsoft's philosophy seems to be that if something isn't expressly illegal, it must de facto be ethical (Gleick, 1995). Further, Bauman (1993) argues that rules may be contradictory to ethics, since rules tell us when we have done enough, when we have met our duty, whereas for him the truly ethical stance is analogous to Oscar Schindler's: No matter what good I may have done, I could have done more. "The moral self is always haunted by the suspicion that it is not moral enough" (Bauman, 1993, p. 80).

Unlike the Modernist approach, Postmodern deontology is not about measuring intended meanings. Being-for-the-other isn't a meaning in a message, it is a purpose behind the message-making. Postmodern ethics are well suited to the global media marketplace, not only because the media themselves create and sustain Postmodernism, but because in the global media, meanings are neither possessed nor controlled. There is a problem, however, in measuring ethical compliance to the one Postmodern rule: Compliance is personal and subjective, not social and objective. Who can measure what is in people's hearts?

So Bauman (1993) does, perhaps unwittingly, illuminate a trail for Postmodern deontology, but it is a journey each of us takes alone. Encouragingly, he concludes that the Postmodern moment may present a ripe opportunity for infusing ethics into all aspects of everyday life, rather than the segregation of the ethical from the everyday that Modernist ethics tended to produce. This everyday ethics can proceed because each person is capable of moral choice, and the intersubjectivity of moral choices adds up to a code: "personal morality . . . makes ethical negotiation and consensus possible" (Bauman, 1993, p. 34). Perhaps in the intersubjective realm, Postmodern deontology gains a prescriptive status beyond the mere subjective, but something still short of a rule—a common but unsaid and unsayable "understanding" which grows out of discursive community (Antczak, 1991). This Berry (1992) has called "a new capacity for ethical action . . . love, compassion, altruism, or care" (p. 5) and Wyschogrod (1990) has called "radical saintly generosity" (p. xxiv).

What might be elements of this personal Postmodern morality? Bauman (1993) identifies self-limitation, moral responsibility for one's own ignorance, the ability to see the long-range effects of technological behavior, and the conscious embracing of uncertainty (pp. 220-222). Krippendorff (1989) has looked for personal Postmodern moral elements, too, and identifies a new "ethics of constructing communication" which repudiates the Modern perspective. For Krippendorff (1989), ethical communication recognizes that one constructs one's own reality, encourages one to invent alternative constructions and to see one's own role in them, grants others the right to their own constructions, and increases the number of choices possible (pp. 76-93). These are, essentially, a detailed elaboration of being-for-the-Other.

In the final analysis, the ethics of Modernity are constructed on a belief that there is no Other, that the Other is either fundamentally like me or is irrelevant. Postmodern ethics, on the other hand, are constructed on the belief that there is only an Other, that we are all Others, and that the most fundamental measure of ethicality is the extent to which we are for that Other. Bauman (1993) indicates a possible ethical path in Postmodern times: "I am for the Other whether the Other is for me or not; his [or her] being for me is, so to speak, his [or her] problem, and whether or how he [or she] handles that problem does not in the least affect my being-for-Him [or Her]" (p. 50).

In the end, must an ethical sojouner make a choice between one path or the other, between the Modern and the Postmodern? It is possible that the road may not be forked; it may not come to a choice between these two, because they may be engaged in a dialectical struggle. Such a struggle need not be of the Hegelian variety. Bhabha (in Mitchell, 1995) has indicated that seeing synthesis as the only outcome of a dialectic is a failure to recognize richer possibilities: that of "interstitial articulations" that "come between" the opposition because "there may be a way of thinking generality not in that binary and mimetic way" (p. 110). As a result of the tension between thesis and antithesis, more than just synthesis is possible:

> Something opens up as an effect of this dialectic, something that will not be contained within it, that cannot be returned to the two oppositional principles. And once it opens up, we're in a different space, we're making different presumptions and mobilizing emergent, unanticipated forms of historical agency. (Bhabha quoted in Mitchell, p. 114)

In other words, the Modernism/Postmodernism schism may produce neither a fork in the road, nor a single widened highway, but a new and hitherto unconsidered direction: a new dimension in which to travel, a tesseract, a new ethics.

If a new dimension is opening up, traveling in it will be disconcerting to say the least, but we may take some comfort in the knowledge that the elements of premodernism inherent in Postmodernism (Lyotard, 1984; Raschke, 1992) will help to orient us. Is it possible that a new route might, as Berry (1992) predicts, bridge the Judaic/Hellenic passages, and possibly even the Eastern/Western ones? Because many of the signposts will have traces of something familiar, there may be a way through this daunting and unanticipated landscape after all. It seems the deontological foundation of this new ethics is at heart a recapitulation of one of the central tenets of the Tanakh (Leviticus 19:18) and the Bible (Luke 6:31): "Do unto others . . ." The nature of the encounter is transformed. The pilgrim may make progress after all.

REFERENCES

Allen, R. (1995). Introduction. In R. Allen (Ed.), *To be continued . . . Soap operas around the world* (pp. 1-26). New York, NY: Routledge.
Ang, I. (1985). *Watching Dallas*. London, England: Methuen.

Antczak, F. (1991). Discursive community and the problem of perspective in ethical communication. In K. Greenberg (Ed.), *Conversations on communication ethics* (pp. 75-85). Norwood, NJ: Ablex.

Auletta, K. (1995). Annals of communication: The pirate. *The New Yorker, LXXI* (36), 80-93.

Bacon-Smith, C. (1992). *Enterprising women: Television fandom and the creation of popular myth.* Philadelphia, PA: University of Pennsylvania Press.

Baudrillard, J. (1985). *Simulations.* New York, NY: Semiotext(e).

Baudrillard, J. (1993). *The transparency of evil.* J. Benedict (Trans.). New York, NY: Verso.

Bauman, Z. (1993). *Postmodern ethics.* Oxford, England: Blackwell.

Berry, P. (1992). Introduction. In P. Berry & A. Wernick (Eds.), *Shadow of spirit: Postmodernism and religion* (pp. 3-8). New York, NY: Routledge.

Bhabha, H. (1994). *The location of culture.* New York, NY: Routledge.

Bloom, H. (1975). *A map of misreading.* New York, NY: Oxford University Press.

Chakrabarty, D. (1995). Postcoloniality and the artifice of history. In B. Ashcroft, G. Griffiths, & H. Tiffin (Eds.), *The postcolonial studies reader* (pp. 383-388). New York, NY: Routledge.

Cohen, R. (1993, December 8). U.S.-French cultural trade rift now snags a world agreement: Paris talks of film onslaught from Hollywood. *The New York Times*: pp. A1, D2.

Cronen, V. (1991). Coordinated management of meaning theory and postenlightenment ethics. In K. Greenberg (Ed.), *Conversations on communication ethics* (pp. 21-53). Norwood, NJ: Ablex.

Cupitt, D. (1992). Unsystematic ethics and politics. In P. Berry & A. Wernick (Eds.), *Shadow of spirit: Postmodernism and religion* (pp. 149-155). New York, NY: Routledge.

de Certeau, M. (1984). *The practice of everyday life.* Berkeley, CA: University of California Press.

Derrida, J. (1974). *Of grammatology.* G. Spivak (Trans.). Baltimore, MD: Johns Hopkins University Press.

Derrida, J. (1981). *Dissemination.* B. Johnson (Trans.). Chicago, IL: University of Chicago Press.

Dery, M. (1993). Culture jamming, hacking, slashing, and sniping in the empire of signs. *Open pamphlet, 25* (July), 1-16.

During, S. (1987). Postmodernism or postcolonialism today. *Textual Practice, 1* (1), 32-47.

During, S. (1993). The culture industry: Enlightenment as mass deception: Editor's introduction. In S. During (Ed.), *The cultural studies reader* (pp. 29-30). New York, NY: Routledge.

"Emerging-market indicators." (1995, December 2). *The Economist*, p. 108.

Fiske, J. (1987). *Television culture.* New York, NY: Routledge.

Fleming, J., & Wilson, P. (1987). *Semiotext(e) U.S.A.* New York, NY: Columbia University Press.

Funiok, R. (1995). Basic questions concerning audience ethics. *Media Development, XLII* (4), 37-40.

Gleick, J. (1995, November 5). Making Microsoft safe for capitalism. *The New York Times Magazine*, pp. 50-57, 64.

Grant, M. (1992). Gibraltar killings: British media ethics. *Journal of Mass Media Ethics, 7* (1), 31-40.

Greenfeld, K. (1993). The incredibly strange mutant creatures who rule the universe of alienated Japanese zombie computer nerds. *Wired, 1* (1), 66-69.

Gross, L. (1991). The contested closet: The ethics and politics of outing. *Critical Studies in Mass Communication, 8* (3), 352-388.

Grossberg, L. (1992). *We gotta get out of this place: Popular conservatism and postmodern culture.* New York, NY: Routledge.

Hall, S. (1980). Encoding/decoding. In S. Hall, D. Hobson, A. Lowe, & P. Willis (Eds.), *Culture, media, language* (pp. 40-52). London, England: Hutchinson.

Hodge, J. (1992). Genealogy for a postmodern ethics: Reflections on Hegel and Heidegger. In P. Berry & A. Wernick (Eds.), *Shadow of spirit: Postmodernism and religion* (pp. 135-148). New York, NY: Routledge.

Hutcheon, L. (1987). Beginning to theorize postmodernism. *Textual Practice, 1* (1), 10-31.

Jameson, F. (1991). *Postmodernism or, the cultural logic of late capitalism.* Durham, NC: Duke University Press.

Jenkins, D. (1992). *Textual poachers: Television fan and participatory culture.* New York, NY: Routledge.

Johannesen, R. (1990). *Ethics in human communication.* 3rd edition. Prospect Heights, IL: Waveland Press.

Juno, A., & Vale, V. (1987). Pranks. *Re/search, 11*, pp. 36-50, 103-109.

Kang, J., & Wu, Y. (1995). Culture diffusion: The role of U.S. television programs in Taiwan. Unpublished conference paper. International Communication Association National Conference, Albuquerque, NM, USA, May.

Kapoor, S., & Kang, J. (1995). Use of American media and adoption of Western cultural values in India. Unpublished conference paper. International Communication Association National Conference, Albuquerque, NM, USA, May.

Klapper, J. (1960). *The effects of mass communication.* Glencoe, IL: Free Press.

Krippendorff, K. (1989). On the ethics of constructing communication. In B. Dervin, L. Grossberg, B. O'Keefe, & E. Wartella (Eds.), *Rethinking communication: Paradigm issues* (pp. 66-96). Newbury Park, NJ: Sage Publications.

Liebes, T., & Katz, E. (1993). *The export of meaning: Cross-cultural readings of Dallas.* Cambridge, MA: Polity Press.

Lyotard, J. (1984). *The postmodern condition: A report on knowledge.* G. Bennington & B. Massumi (Trans.). Minneapolis, MN: University of Minnesota.

Makau, J. (1991). The principles of fidelity and veracity: Guidelines for ethical communication. In K. Greenberg (Ed.), *Conversations on communication ethics* (pp. 111-120). Norwood, NJ: Ablex.

Masterman, L. (1995). Media education worldwide: Objectives, values and superhighways. *Media Development, XLII* (2), 6-9.

Meyrowitz, J. (1985). *No sense of place: The impact of electronic media on social behavior.* New York, NY: Oxford University Press.

Miller, D. (1995). The consumption of soap opera: *The Young and the Restless* and mass consumption in Trinidad. In R. Allen (Ed.), *To be continued . . . Soap operas around the world* (pp. 213-232). New York, NY: Routledge.

Mitchell, W. (1995). Translator translated: W.J.T. Mitchell talks with Homi Bhabha. *Artforum, 23* (7), 80-83, 110, 114, 118-119.

Olson, S. (1985). Devolution and indigenous mass media: The role of media in Inupiat and Sami nation-state building. Doctoral dissertation. Evanston, IL: Northwestern University.

Olson, S. (1994). Strategies and tactics of communication empowerment: Toward a descriptive tautology. In A. Malkiewicz, J. Parrish-Sprowl, & J. Waskiewicz (Eds.), *Komunikacja spoleczna w procesach transformacyjnych [Social communication in the transformation process]* (pp. 31-38). Wroclaw, Poland: Osrodek Badan Prognostycznych Sp.z. o. o.

Olson, S. (forthcoming). The global audience for American media exports: A reception approach. *Polish-American Journal of Social Communication, 1* (1).

Parry, B. (1995). Problems in current theories of colonial discourse. In B. Ashcroft, G. Griffiths, & H. Tiffin (Eds.), *The postcolonial studies reader* (pp. 36-44). New York, NY: Routledge.

Raschke, C. (1992). Fire and roses: or the problem of postmodern religious thinking. In P. Berry & A. Wernick (Eds.), *Shadow of spirit: Postmodernism and religion* (pp. 93-108). New York, NY: Routledge.

Said, E. (1993). *Culture and imperialism.* New York, NY: Knopf.

Schiller, H. (1989). *Culture, Inc.: The corporate takeover of public expression.* New York, NY: Oxford University Press.

Schmookler, A. (1984). *The parable of the tribes: The problem of power in social evolution.* Boston, MA: Houghton Mifflin.

Shekwo, J. (1984). Understanding Gbagyi folktales: Premises for targeting salient electronic mass media programs. Unpublished doctoral dissertation, Northwestern University, Evanston, IL.

Sholle, D. (1988). Critical studies: From the theory of ideology to power/knowledge. *Critical Studies in Mass Communication, 5*, 16-41.

Spivak, G. (1995). Can the subaltern speak? In B. Ashcroft, G. Griffiths, & H. Tiffin (Eds.), *The postcolonial studies reader* (pp. 24-28). New York, NY: Routledge.

Stavrianos, L. (1976). *The promise of the coming dark age.* San Francisco, CA: W.H. Freeman and Company.

Taylor, M. (1992). Reframing postmodernisms. In P. Berry & A. Wernick (Eds.), *Shadow of spirit: Postmodernism and religion* (pp. 11-29). New York, NY: Routledge.

Teitelbaum, S. (1995). Privacy is history—get over it. *Wired, 4* (2), 124-125.

Thayer, L. (1980). Ethics, morality, and the media: Note on American culture. In L. Thayer (Ed.), *Ethics, morality, and the media: Reflections on American culture* (pp. 3-42). New York, NY: Hastings House.

Vale, V., & Juno, A. (1987). Incredibly strange films. *Re/search, 1* (10), pp. 4-6.

Weldon, M. (1983). *The psychotronic guide to film.* New York, NY: Ballantine Books.

Wyschogrod, E. (1990). *Saints and postmodernism.* Chicago, IL: University of Chicago Press.

Yoshimoto, M. (1994). Images of empire: Tokyo Disneyland and Japanese cultural imperialism. In E. Smoodin (Ed.), *Disney discourse: Producing the magic kingdom* (pp. 181-199). New York, NY: Routledge.

A Developing-Region-Based Model of Proto-Norms for International and Intercultural Communication

Cornelius B. Pratt and Folu Ogundimu
Michigan State University

The purposes of this chapter are threefold. First, it examines the philosophical foundations of proto-norms, that is, fundamental moral norms that undergird the ethics of the mass media in developing nations. Second, it argues that classical moral theories, as global universals, are relevant to the continuing search for improved news coverage and analyses in international communications. Third, it proposes a preliminary model for ethical communications about developing nations in the international mass media and for cross-cultural communications within such nations.

These purposes are underscored by two realities. First, in the eyes of the world, developing nations, particularly those of South America and Africa, have earned the notoriety of being economically and politically troubled, wasting countries. Second, ethics-driven cross-cultural communications within a state are critical to diffusing ethnic problems, particularly at national levels.

As presented by the international news media, the problems of developing countries revolve around four overarching issues: political instability, economic decay and corruption, human-rights abuses, and inter-ethnic group violence. Whether the countries deserve this image is a different matter, considering that those pathologies have complex origins, causes, and consequences. The inadequate reporting of the Third World by the international media led to demands for a new information and communication order during the 1970s. For the Third World in general the main complaint was that coverage by the international media lacks context and failes to provide a more balanced and representative picture in at least three important ways.

First, the media's fixation with crisis and the exotic—-coups, wars, natural disasters, hunger, wildlife, corruption, economic failures—-ignores the accomplishments of the modern state and undermines efforts to build nations from fundamentally flawed colonial heritages and global economic systems.

Second, media coverage of the countries' political and economic failures has, for the most part, excluded the consequences of international geopolitical and economic discontinuities in which a number of developing countries were caught, both as willing pawns and as proxies of colonial and Superpower interests during the Cold-War era. Consequently, many developing nations found themselves saddled with corrupt, authoritarian, and decadent regimes and with culturally disparate groups. Moreover, critics complain that international communications fail to note the inequities in the international division of labor and economy. This division ensures that, with only a handful of exceptions, the countries have remained at the periphery of global economic transformations. Their status as the world's poorest countries is confirmed by World Bank indicators, and, as in the colonial era, the developing countries, particularly those of Africa and South America, remain primary exporters of commodities and importers of finished products.

Third, attempts to revitalize the countries' economies and to reverse decades-old misfortunes primarily represent failures to transplant Western institutions and ideas to the Third World without taking into account the region's unique cultures, traditions, and circumstances. In Africa, for example, the record of failed development projects during the U.N. Development Decade of the 1960s and 1970s and current difficulties with implementing structural adjustment and reconstruction programs during the 1980s and 1990s are symptomatic of these failures (Adebayo, 1993; Chenery, Ahluwalia, Bell, Duloy, & Jolly, 1981; Economic Commission, 1989).

Of course, dissatisfaction with imbalances in the global flows of information and the quality of information about different parts of the world predate the new information order debate of the 1970s. U.S. complaints about European monopoly of international telegraph news and the consequent distortion of U.S. image in the international media were common in the late 1800s and early 1900s (Altschull, 1995; Merrill, 1995). But the debates of the 1970s culminated more than 30 years of renewed concern by scholars, jurists, statesmen, and international advocacy groups that the world was being shortchanged by the lack of a representative picture in the reporting of global issues. For developing countries, the issue was cast in terms of victimization from "cultural colonialism" (MacBride & Roach, 1993). The United Nations asked its agency, UNESCO, to look into the matter (Altschull, 1995; Gerbner, Mowlana, & Nordenstreng, 1993; MacBride Commission, 1980; Merrill, 1995). The resulting study and report by the MacBride Commission led to calls for a New World Information and Communication Order (NWICO), perhaps one of the most controversial and ideologically divisive issues in international communications during the last 30 years.

Arguably, concerns generated in the 1980s by NWICO heightened global sensitivity to the nature of reports about the developing regions. Within the decade, NWICO was proclaimed dead for practical purposes (McPhail, 1989). As the 1990s began, there was evidence that the pattern of limited coverage of Africa, for example, continued (Hultman, 1992). Even though international media staffers had been cognizant of the limitations of reporting developing countries, no model, let alone an ethics-based type, had been formulated to help them adopt communication decisions that were at once responsive to ethical and societal issues so immanent in the NWICO debates and formulations.

This chapter is divided into four parts. The first outlines issues in international and intercultural communications. The second presents the universals in classical theories of ethics, whose relevance to the developing countries is discussed. The third analyzes three coexisting elements of the cultural foundations of African moral philosophy. Similar elements guide intercultural communications in developing countries. And the fourth proposes a model for communicating ethically about the developing world in the international mass media and cross-culturally within developing nations.

Issues In International And Intercultural Communications

A major issue in the use of the mass media and national development is the social impact of communication technologies. Since the 1970s, communication technologies have been an integral part of that development. So effective were such technologies in influencing the knowledge and attitudes of rural residents in, say, India, that a number of developing countries adapted experiences from India's Satellite Instructional Television Experiment (SITE) to their development programs. SITE was credited with improving primary school education; providing teacher training; distributing information on agricultural practices, health, hygiene, and nutrition; and contributing to family planning and national integration (Agrawal, 1984).

The impact of such technologies have rubbed off on improvements in international communications about the developing region. However, even though improvements in the speed of delivery and in the diversity of news sources can be attributed to the increasing use of communication technologies, it remains to be seen if such improvements would, in the long run, improve the quality of reporting about the region. Technological improvements have been encouraged for two reasons: (a) they diversify the range of news sources and program formats, and (b) they are coopted into national development programs to provide much-needed community or national development.

However, society's dependence on communication technologies has been criticized by contemporary philosophers such as Ellul (1964, 1989) and Hastedt (1994). Ellul (1964, 1989), for example, argues that humanity's dependence on technology has created a technicist society, in which there is a modern world-weariness; an ever-increasing escalation of power, which always brings about a questioning, declining and an abandoning of values; and an ethics of non-power and superficial freedom, which generates tension and conflicts.

Hastedt (1994), noting that technology is a whole way of life that requires ethical reflection, concludes that, until we develop better ways to use technologies in accordance with ethical principles, we will continue to live in a state of mental immaturity.

Postman (1992), a social critic, views technology as a friend whose gifts are not without a heavy cost. He uses "Technopoly" to describe a state of culture that deifies technology by which culture seeks and takes its authorization and orders from technology and finds its satisfaction in technology. On the rise of "Technopoly" in the United States, Postman (1992) wrote that "nothing is so much worth preserving that it should stand in the way of technological innovation" (pp. 53-54). Yet, "Technopoly" reduces the meaning of history, religion and human life to machinery and technique and submits all forms of cultural life to technology, thereby depriving societies of their past, their culture, their Old World sources of belief, and their psychic tranquility and social purpose.

Increases in the use of technologies such as mainframe and personal computers as communications media in the Third World are not without difficulties. In that region, technologies could produce new forms of dependency and exacerbate inequities in the distribution of goods and services (Mukasa, 1992). Berman (1992) notes that their use "is likely to reinforce existing distributions of power and wealth, create reified images of society based upon quantitative data of dubious value and accuracy, and accentuate the authoritarian relationship between the state and an increasingly marginalized populace" (p. 227).

Whereas the preceding paragraphs highlight the dangers of information technologies, particularly in industrialized societies, technology-induced problems, as a sequela of those immanent in technology-rich nations, have emerged vis-à-vis developed nations' reporting about developing countries.

For major example, international media coverage of the Third World has suffered from the twin problems of scarcity and decontextualization. What was true at the time of the NWICO debate remains true today. Merrill (1995) pointed to Giffard's (1982) finding that U.S. wire services typically covered developing countries as being more prone to internal conflicts and crisis, and more likely to be associated with disaster relief and with military and economic aid. Similarly, Lent (1977) reported the crisis orientation of news about the Third World. And Golding and Elliott (1974) observed that much of the coverage was about repetitive crises or military conflicts. Larson (1983) found in an extensive analysis of U.S. network news coverage from 1972 to 1981 that, whereas 41 percent of stories mentioned some foreign country (international stories), the Third World was grossly underreported compared to the industrialized countries. And what coverage there was of the Third World (27 percent) tended to be crisis-oriented.

But Weaver and Wilhoit (1984), in their extensive study of news in Western agencies, concluded that although their data did not support Third-World claims of neglect in the foreign coverage of two U.S. regional wire services, the findings were supportive of the conflict and crisis-orientation of coverage (Weaver and Wilhoit, 1984). Media scholars provide several reasons for such coverage. "What is 'known' about Africa," writes Fair (1993), "is created, filtered, and reproduced through dominant (ideological) conceptions of 'we' and 'they,' 'Self' and 'Other'" (p. 18). Another is the inadequate infrastructure and telecommunication facilities in many developing countries, the reluctance of potential news sources to collaborate with non-local journalists, and the latter's adherence to news values that are occasionally different from those of the reported communities. Ultimately, the distorted images of the Third World add to the global inequities in the distribution of benefits. Altschull (1995) argues that

> attempts by the advancing (developing) countries to correct the global imbalance both in economic power and in control over information are two parts of the same struggle; they are inseparable. Believing that information is power, many Third World nations view the news agencies as enormously significant in adding to the power imbalance in both economics and information. (p. 306)

In the intercultural milieu, conflicts, disagreements, and violence characterize countries such as Burundi, India, Lebanon, Liberia, Rwanda and Sri Lanka. Since independence from Belgiumin the 1960s, The Tutsi-dominated governments of Burundi and Rwanda have, for example, been generally unable to contain deadly ethnic-inspired conflictsbetween the Hutu and the Tutsi. In the face of international scrutiny, the governments of these two contries have usually refused to accept culpability for the ehnic-inspired atrocities.

In Lebanon, 17 years of civil war has turned a country that was once the "Switzerland of the Middle East" into one whose economy has been marred with ethnic-based violence. Similarly, Liberia's seven-year civil war, a result of ethnic rivalries, has plunged a country once regarded as the model of political stability in Africa into anarchy.

In Sri Lanka, a 12-year-old conflict between the government and Tamil militants, who initially advocated the interests of the minority Tamil population, has pitted the latter against the majority Sinhalese. Similarly, caste, religious and political conflicts are rife in India. Peace talks have focused on cross-cultural communications aimed at fostering understanding and acceptance and emphasizing cultural commonalities through negotiation and dialogue. Ethics issues, namely, symmetry and openness in the communications process, have slowed the resolution of cultural conflicts that have political implications.

Ethical Universals And Theoretical Considerations

The ethical precepts adopted in this chapter are based on the notion that there are universal moral rules and principles. Such a notion has little intellectual support among scholars who pride themselves "in championing diversity and pluralism, trotting out ethnographies . . . to show that different cultures have different moralities and that to argue otherwise foists one's intentions on others in an act of moral or ideological imperialism" (Christians, Ferré, & Fackler, 1993, p. 58). Christians, Ferré and Fackler's (1993) response to that argument is that "[t]here are moral universals, but only a handful of them. Plenty of room remains for tolerance, respect, and even admiration of cultural differences" (p. 59).

Arguably, classical moral thought has its roots in Western societies. Nonetheless, it is undergirded by universals: the search for truth, fairness, justice, free expression, and the public interest; and the emphasis on nonmalficence, that is, the responsibility to avoid harm. Therefore, these universals are as inherently relevant to Western philosophy as they are to non-Western moral thought (Cooper, 1989); they are, in essence, cross-cultural proto-norms.

The following five classical moral theories, as universals, have potential relevance to the ethics of the mass media in the Third World:

1. Kant's categorical imperative, which tests the morality of action through three criteria: universalizability, reversibility, and dignity (Velasquez, 1992). Universalizability means that "I ought never to act except in such a way that I can also will that my maxim should become a universal law" (Kant, 1964, p. 70). Reversibility means that a person's reason for acting must be those that the person would be willing to have all others use, even as a basis of how others treat her or him. Dignity means that a rational person should be treated with respect, that is, as an end.

2. Rawls's (1971) veil of ignorance which states that justice emerges in the absence of social differentiations; therefore, each person has equality of liberty, opportunity, and access to positions and offices.

3. Aristotle's (in McKeon, 1947) virtue-based ethics in which moral virute is amean between two vices, that which depends on excess and that which depends on defect.

4. Mill's (1951) "Greatest Happiness Principle," which holds that "actions are right in proportion as they tend to promote happiness, wrong as they tend to promote the reverse of happiness" (p. 8).

5. Judeo-Christian ethics of love, which holds that the basic ethical imperative, to love, is the wellspring of all other eithical imperatives (Frankena, 1973).

Each falls into one of two broad categories: deontology or teleology. Deontology, of which Kant's categorical imperative is the best-known example, is a duty-based, nonconsequentialist theory of ethics. It asserts that certain human actions are inherently right or wrong. Rawls's (1971) veil of ignorance, a nonconsequentialist theory of justice, governs the assignment of rights and duties and regulates the distribution of social and economic advantages. People, he argues, "have an equal right to the most extensive basic liberty compatible with a similar liberty for others" (Rawls, 1971, p. 60). Rawls (1971) suggests that, to accomplish equal justice in society, everyone be placed in a hypothetical "original position" behind a "veil of ignorance," which requires that, in evaluating situations, people step from their everyday, status-based traditional roles into an egalitarian position behind a veil. The goal is to develop a conception of justice or of the good from a disinterested, "equal" perspective.

Both these Kantian and Rawlsian theories seem inappropriate for Africa's modern mass media, for four reasons. The first is the susceptibility of the

African mass media practitioner to groupthink, that is, "a mode of thinking that people engage in when they are deeply involved in a cohesive in-group, when the members' striving for unanimity override their motivation to realistically appraise alternative courses of action" (Janis, 1982, p. 9). Breed (1960) refers to this process as newsroom socialization. Understandably, the effects of such a phenomenon are not unique to Africa; what is unique is the extent to which they define the ethics of African communications. Obeng-Quaidoo (1985) describes "groupthink" as the non-individuality of the African. But both these perspectives "socialization and non-individuality," are best interpreted in a relative rather than in an absolute sense, for two reasons.

The first is that even though Africans are bound by social control and strong ties of kinship, they nevertheless exert their autonomy. Among Ghana's Tallensi, who are primarily farmers, lineages, not individuals, own the land and land rights are distributed according to male seniority in a lineage. Nonetheless, the Tallensi exercise some degree of autonomy, which is limited by the complex nature of their social relationships. Conflicts may occur between people with a common lineage.

Among the communalistic Batswana of Botswana, a strong sense of autonomy and individual industriousness exists even within the context of strong social ties with others (Alverson, 1978). Roe (1988) reports that Batswana values of individualism and communalism may appear conflicting at one level; however, at another level, both encourage the same Batswana responses toward their environment.

The second reason is that, even among peoples of the industrialized countries, the pursuit of self-realization and individual pleasures is not devoid of an ethics of communal responsibility (Berger, 1989). In fact, Fromm (1969) questions Western views about individualism and asserts that they are an illusion because they foster the loss of the self and increase the propensity to conform to the expectations of others by, for example, disregarding an individual's spontaneous feelings and wishes and eliminating spontaneity in the acquisition of information.

In sum, the hostile, unpredictable environment within which African journalists editorialize makes them susceptible more to groupthink than in, say, Western societies, where the media have higher levels of freedom and independence from governmental interventions.

The second reason for the incompatibility of deontology with African communications is rooted in the African value system, which emphasizes "wholesome human relations," an "altruistic moral philosophy," "community fellow-feeling," and a "live-and-let-live philosophy" (Sofola, 1973).

Third, because a number of African cultures have a preference for first-person, self-denying plurals "we," "ours," and "us" ethics tends to be group-centered rather than individual-centered.

Finally, culturally, communications in developing countries demonstrate non-situationism in that they adhere to absolute truths. This ontological ethic has been undermined by the media-government interface. A similar conclusion has been drawn by Moemeka and Kasoma (1994): "The bulk of the African journalists, in their individual capacities, would apply the categorical imperative, but in their practice of the profession in the media organizations do not" (p. 42). The adversarial environment in which Africa's modern media function is based on anything but non-absolute truths, as indicated in the results of a study of Nigerian journalists (Pratt, 1990). African communicators who adhere to non-situation ethics will, at an instant, be out of favor with both their clans and local government élites. The assassination of Nigeria's Dele Giwa in October 1986 and of Angola's Ricardo de Mello in January 1995, and the threats to outspoken Burundians—Rwandans and Liberians, all suggest that demonstrating ethical principles that disregard the consequences of one's actions can be a risky proposition for communicators developing countries.

Utilitarian ethics, a consequential theory of teleological ethics, assesses the greatest good through cost-benefit analyses. Businesses generally adopt the utilitarian ideology (Scollon & Scollon, 1995). One variant of that theory is Aristotle's theory of the golden mean, a virtue-based ethics, which strikes a moral balance between two extremes, one indicating excess, the other deficiency. The mean, in this context, is not a statistical mean but a willingness on the part of the decision maker to exercise moderation or temperance a virtue. Such a mean relates to the individual's particular situation, her or his status, strengths and weaknesses (Christians, Rotzoll, & Fackler, 1991).

Contemporary philosopher MacIntyre (1984) defines virtue as "an acquired human quality the possession and exercise of which tends to enable us achieve those goods which are internal to practices and the lack of which effectively prevents us from achieving any such goods" (p. 191). The two characteristics of virtue are that it is acquired and that it advances certain internal goods such as serving the public interest, telling the whole story, and reporting the news with fairness. Other professional virtues, according to May (1984), include perseverance, integrity, courage, candor, fidelity, prudence, public-spiritedness, justice and humility.

Donaldson and Dunfee's (1994) communitarian-based social contracts theory posits that there are hypernorms, that is, global norms that apply to *all* people and that macrocontractors use as fundamental principles in evaluating lower-level moral norms. At the community level, microsocial contracts endorse cultural specifics insofar as they do not violate universal rules, that is, the macrosocial contracts.

The Foundations of Africa's Moral Thought

The model proposed in the last part of this chapter is based on the notion that international communications about developing countries will be continually constrained by a disregard for the underlying moral principles of national thought. Writing about the importance of understanding the principles that undergird communications in Nigeria, Okigbo (1989) makes an observation that is applicable to the rest of the world: "Making sense of . . . communication necessitates proper understanding of the underlying principles that guide the conduct of communication professionals" (p. 136).

Admittedly, the definition of African philosophy, as are those of a number of anthropological and ethnographic concepts, is fraught with disagreement. One such disagreement is that to think about an African philosophy is to play unwittingly into the hands of colonialists who would be tempted into defining African values with respect to European values (Hountondji, 1983, 1991). Another disagreement is that because myths and folklore are antithetical to Western concept of philosophy, it is improper to incorporate them into a discussion of philosophy. Hountondji (1991) writes that when the word "philosophy" is applied to Africa, " . . . it is supposed to designate no longer the specific discipline it evokes in its Western context but merely a collective worldview, an implicit, spontaneous, perhaps even unconscious system of beliefs to which all Africans are supposed to adhere" (p. 117).

Yet another disagreement is that, to the extent that African myths are not written but are passed from generation to generation, they cannot stand the test of scientific and objective scrutiny. While it is true that cultural differences occur among various cultures, it is also true that *all* cultures have universals, albeit interpreted differently. One such universal is our existence in a metaphysical or an ontological world, which defines our moral (and societal) values. In industrialized societies, for example, the universal of metaphysics is based on a static conception of being; in the African philosophical thought, however, being is dynamic and it is not separated from forces such as divine, celestial, human or even mineral forces (Adegbola, 1969; Onyewuenyi, 1991).

Philosophy is related to culture. In general, philosophy may be defined as the worldview of an established order among various phenomena that are based on a culture. It is a culture's perception of life; and because no culture has a monopoly over *the* order and *the* last word, one can write about European, Asian, Indian, American or African philosophy (Onyewuenyi, 1991).

However, because of the interrelationships among nations, groups or societies, the philosophy of a people is a consequence of multiple influences, sometimes of multiple worldviews.

Therefore, Africa's moral philosophy is a coalescence of at least three factors: (a) indigenous religions, that is, ontological morality; (b) universal religions and Western political influences; and (c) post-colonial political and social influences. Across these factors, however, is the pre-eminence of religions in whatever activities, intellectual, physical, or spiritual, Africans engage. Mbiti (1990) emphasizes this point: "Religion in Africa has produced its own society with a distinctly religious set of morals, ethics, culture, governments, traditions, social relationships and ways of looking at the world" (p. 266). The underlying significance of religion to the worldview of the African encourages Mbiti (1990) to describe Africans' approach to understanding their universe as ethnophilosophy.

1. *Indigenous religions as the bases of ontological morality.* Indigenous religions, Christianity, and Islam coexist in Africa to produce a sense of spirituality that satisfies the moral needs of Africans. To the African, ethical conduct is the essence of religious spirituality. Inarguably, in spite of the challenges of Christianity and Islam, African traditional spirituality and moral values are very much alive. The immanent and intrinsic character of the ethics of Africans suggest their ontological value. Within the rubric of indigenous influences are cultural and indigenous religious foundations of ethics. Culture iterates an African's loyalty to her or his cultural heritage; indigenous religions focus on myths and taboos, which provide the African with ontological sanctions for moral consciousness.

To the African, God is pre-eminent, all-powerful, ever-present, immanent, omniscient, and omnipotent. The African worships God through songs, plays, proverbs, sacrifices, offerings, and prayers. The African believes that intermediaries, e.g., priests, oracles, elders, the living-dead, spirits, and divinities, should approach God in behalf of the people. Success in making and maintaining spiritual contacts with these intermediaries is contingent on an understanding of African ontology: the belief in a hierarchy of forces which interact with one another and in forces such as God, spirits, and ancestors. One might argue that such beliefs impose a number of do's and don'ts, that is, sanctions, on the day-to-day life of the African. But judging by the debate in the philosophy of the social sciences, religious scholars and sociologists are uncertain about whether a radical distinction is to be made between African thought and the positivist tradition of the West. As Buchowski (1995) writes in his critique of Horton's (1993) work:

[T]here is not a real difference between personalized concepts of African systems and depersonalized concepts of Western science. Spirits and atoms have equally imperceptible status and explanatory function. Cognitive function is fulfilled in the West by science and in Africa by religion. . . . The concept of a supreme being is surely an assertion that beneath the diversity and apparent haphazardness of the world of appearance, there is an ultimate unity and an ultimate consistency. This is why we should speak about continuity and analogy rather than contrast and inversion of intellectual life in all types of human societies. (p. 387)

Hence, we argue that the syncretism between traditional religions and Christianity or Islam in Africa is central to African moral thought. The influence of African ontology on the ethics is noted by Adegbola (1969), who avers that the ethical sense of the African is related to the African people's idea of what being is: the metaphysically or ontologically good is the ethically good.

The African places a lot of weight on fostering communal relationships and in building ontological relationships, not just with the living, but with the living-dead. (The living-dead is one who is physically dead, but still lives on the minds of his or her descendants or ethnic group.) The African is part of the whole. Social Darwinism and rugged individualism, both economic and social hallmarks of most Western societies, are usually not revered. Anyanwu (1984) observes that the African exists at three levels: as an individual, as a member of a group, and as a member of a community. But most cultures in Africa fuse all three levels in the belief that all are perpetually interacting with one another.

African normative ethics, therefore, has a communal tone, by which "I" becomes "We" as the individual is synthesized with the whole community (Anyanwu, 1984), and "for me" becomes "for us." It is this community that imposes sanctions on morality, expressed as reward or punishment (Parrinder, 1969). Such sanctions are the bases of the ethics of the traditional mass media.

2. Universal religions and political influences. Universal religions in Africa are Christianity and Islam. At about the first century, Christianity had a marked influence in Egypt, where Alexandria was home to theologians whose writings influenced the beginnings of Christianity in Africa. Parrinder (1969) argues that this early and continuous presence of Christianity in Egypt and Ethiopia makes it a traditional African religion.

Christian missionary influences in Africa date to the 15th century. During that period, missionaries sought the help of their home governments to maintain political stability in the colonies. Such stability was necessary for the simultaneous exploitation of the territories as well as for evangelism.

The unwritten nature of African mythologies and myths spawned the earlier notion that African philosophy was nonexistent (e.g., Ruch & Anyanwu, 1984). As the natives of the new colonial territories imbibed the culture and philosophy of the colonizing power, they soon recognized the contradictions between the moral certitude of Western religious philosophy and church-sanctioned acquiescence to the colonizer's expropriation of native resources. This recognition had two major consequences. First, it fuelled the rise of religious syncretism, with Africans drawing substantially from their own indigenous cultures in attempts to customize the newly adopted evangelizing religions of Islam and Christianity. Second, it consecrated nationalism as a moral and religiously-sanctioned crusade for independence, and consequently allowed the syncretic religious movements to play a vital role in liberating the African state from colonial rule. These two developments would have major significance for the continuing role of religion and the newly-emergent African in the post-colonial state.

Regarding religious syncretism, one might conclude that one reason for the quick and widespread adoption of syncretic behavior was the African perception of racial discrimination among the leadership of the colonial Christian churches. For one thing, to the African, a missionary and a colonist were of the same breed. For another, some of the preaching of missionaries were inconsistent with their actions, which indicated a reluctance to share church leadership with colonial indigenes. As Haynes (1995) notes, the simple fact is that the senior Christian leaders in sub-Saharan Africa were overwhelmingly European. Consequently, they supported colonial rule not only because they shared racial bonds, but, more important, because they were members of the colonial socioeconomic élite with a stake in the continuation of the status quo. "Thus there were class, racial and institutional bonds which bound senior Christian figures to the colonial regimes" (Haynes, 1995, p. 90). Moreover, unlike the Europeans who were uncomfortable with Africa's traditional (animist) religious practices, the emerging African religious élite found ways to incorporate tradition with Christianity. For example, Ipenburg (1992) shows that among the Lubwa Christians of Zambia, the Lumpa Church of Alice Lenshina had an effective pastoral response to the problem of the belief in, and practice of, witchcraft. This was in contrast to the rival Catholic White Fathers missionary. Gifford (1995) concludes that "the missionaries' preoccupation with the personification of evil, evil spirits had a very minor role in Bemba traditional religion, may even have increased belief in witchcraft" (p. 518). In time, the Catholic Church would adopt some of the methods of the indigenous churches. In the case of Bembaland, Gifford (1995) says the Catholic Church "adopted large gatherings like processions, developed local music, and effected a move from a Latin to a Bemba church culture" (p. 519).

Regarding the role of religion in consecrating African nationalism, one might cite several examples from different parts of the sub-continent to support this claim. The more recent experience of Mozambique is perhaps illustrative of this relationship. Rossouw and Macamo (1993) note that during the colonial era, the Portuguese government treated the Roman Catholic Church as the official Church of Mozambique:

> The image of the Catholic Church was further strengthened in the minds of the Frelimo supporters when the Catholic Church turned down a request by Frelimo to minister to them in their bush camps during their guerrilla warfare against the colonialist regime. This resulted in severe antagonism against the Catholic Church, especially on the part of the Frelimo leadership (p. 538).

As with Christianity, Islam was similarly transformed and adapted to African realities on the sub-continent. Thus, one finds that Islam in sub-Saharan Africa is, in fact, a multifaceted term that covers a number of Muslim interpretations of the faith (Haynes, 1995). These interpretations correspond to extant social, cultural and historical divisions (Haynes, 1995). Hence we argue that the recognition by Africans that the orthodox religions were bereft of the African ethos and the need for a religion that was relevant to the African culture and was sensitive to the African sense of spirituality led to uniquely African interpretations of Christian and Islamic orthodoxies. In other words, the African was unwilling to have traditional ethos play second fiddle to an alien religion. It is the vehemence with which Africans held on to traditional beliefs that underlies the continuing popularity of the African moral thought. Mazrui (1977) observes that because Christianity has become an Afro-Western religion and Islam an Afro-Asian religion by the second-half of the 20th century, Africa has become a kind of religious melting pot. "Christian, Islamic and indigenous beliefs and values have sometimes competed and sometimes merged with each other to create a new African synthesis" (Mazrui, 1977, pp. 90-91). An outcome of that synthesis is African morality.

Before the 19th-century scramble, Africa had attracted white settlers. When the Dutch arrived in South Africa in the 17th century, there were Bushmen, who may have preceded the Dutch by some 3,000 years.

The British had widespread influence in West and East Africa; the French in West and Central Africa; the Dutch in southern Africa; the Germans in Cameroon, then-Tanganyika, and South West Africa (Namibia); the Belgians in Congo and Ruanda-Urundi (which, after 1962, became the separate countries of Rwanda and Burundi); the French and the British in much of west and sub-equatorial Africa; Germans in the then-South West Aftrica and the then-Tanganyika; the freed black slaves from southern United States of America in Liberia; the Portuguese in Angola, Cape Verde, Guinea-Bissau, Mozambique, and in São Tomé and Príncipe; and the Italians in Somalia and Eritrea. Two countries, Ethiopia and Liberia, did not have duly constituted foreign governmental influences.

The European scramble for Africa and the economic-centered activities of European businesses left Africa primarily as a source for raw material rather than as a region of immense development potential. Therefore, the economic and political structures that were established made possible the fulfillment of economic benefits to the West and the subjugation of the continent to the control of the West, a subjugation that made the former phenomenon even more attainable. The modeling of African political administrations after those in the colonists' home countries was done for political and economic expediency: it was economically feasible to use a structure with which the colonists were familiar; it was politically expedient because it exemplified the expansionist interests of the colonial powers. The hallmarks of a foreign political system, as a signal of dominance and occupation on a foreign soil, was a message to another competing power not to meddle in the affairs of a colony. Long before the arrival of colonial bureaucracies in Africa, the continent relied on a political administration that was based on social systems of kinship or lineage. Indigenous, pre-colonial African governments had institutional structures, which, even though complex and efficient, were far from bureaucratic. In fact, it was the complexity of the lineage arrangements that helped Africans resist European expansion in Africa. A "contract" between Europeans and African chiefs did not necessarily translate into a unanimous agreement among all subjects; subjects could announce their loyalty to a competing lineage and continue the resistance to a foreign power.

In most African cultures, however, hierarchy was the overriding concept; day-to-day duties were conducted by chiefs and their councils of elders who revered kingship and its trappings, and abhorred blatant opposition to lineage authority. This translated into traditional systems and domestically constituted authorities that created wide public acceptance of local governments, which functioned efficiently, in the absence of any massive bureaucracy. Taboos (for example, that something undesirable will happen to a violator of a taboo) and myths (for example, that the all-seeing God is omnipresent, omiscient) provide built-in systems of checks and balances that ensure that a society operates largely in the public interest. The myths that underlie taboos engendered perceptions of the possibilities of evil consequences; such possibilities act as moral sanctions. Even a ruler was not above the sanctions of his subjects. Regicide, the killing of a king who was autocratic or stepped out of line, was prevalent in African kingdoms such as that of the Margi in Nigeria until the early part of this century.

When the colonists arrived in Africa, some were impressed; others were surprised by the kinship structures already in place. For example, Lord Frederick Lugard introduced into Nigeria indirect rule, by which the traditional emirs of northern Nigeria and the "obas" (or kings) of Western Nigeria formed the bases for British rule in parts of Nigeria and in other British African colonies. Attempts to apply the system to the Igbos of southeastern Nigeria in 1928 were unsuccessful. The appointment of "warrant" chiefs as liaisons between the British and the people led to suspicion and hostility that culminated in several local riots, such as the Aba women's riots of 1929, during which the "warrant" chiefs were attacked, native courts were destroyed, and many women were killed.

Among stateless societies such as those of the Igbo of Nigeria, the Kru of Liberia, and the Konkomba of Togo, respect for others is based on kinship rather than on kingship. Yet, societal matters are handled even handedly, with elders expressing free-speech rights by voicing opinions prior to reaching a consensus. Even though such people are largely individualistic, governance is still democratic in the African scheme of things. In sum, one might say despite the introduction of colonial rule and the subjugation of the sub-continent, the pattern of colonial administration throughout the sub-continent was extremely variegated, ranging from the system of direct and indirect rule in much of the British-held territories, to the direct assimilationist policies pursued by the French, to the highly centralized and proprietary rule of the Belgians and the Portuguese in central and southern Africa. All of the contradictions of the colonial state and the introduction of repressive controls and regulations to check dissent and control communications, would later be manifested in the post-colonial African state.

3. *The media and post-colonial influences.* To the extent that freedom of religious worship was tolerated by the state, religion-both Islam and Christianity—was often ambivalent toward both state repression and exploitation (Haynes, 1995). Africa's indigenous mass media, the printed press in particular, were often bastions of nationalist and anti-colonial criticism. Collectively, the press pointed out the contradictions between colonial regime policies and the native condition. True, Africa's mass media, as social institutions, are a consequence of both endogenous and exogenous factors. Even though cultural contacts with colonial powers had been present during the three centuries preceding 20th-century occupation, it was not until the first decade of the 1900s that any major forms of pre-independence mass media were established. Of course, missionary activities were largely responsible for this development. Africa's first regularly published, local-language newspaper, *Iwe-Irohin Yoruba*, was published in 1859 by the Reverend Henry Townsend of the Church Missionary Society in Nigeria. The society also published *Leisure Hours* (1917). Similar church-affiliated publications were *African Church Gleamer* (1917), *African Hope* (1919), *Nigerian Methodist* (1925), *African Christian* (1931) and the *Catholic Life* (1936). These publications not only helped create a local cadre of enlightened newspaper journalists, but also exposed them to the tenets of Christian morality.

In Ghana, the colonial government made the first attempt at establishing a newspaper in the colony, where, on April 2, 1822, Sir Charles MacCarthy (1822-1824), first Crown Governor of Gold Coast Settlements, published the *Royal Gold Coast Gazette*. Hachten (1971) notes the importance of the colonial influence on the founding of Africa's mass communications:

Mass communications . . . are not indigenous to Africa. A crucial element in the development of mass communication in Africa, both past and present, is the nature and extent of European influences. Differences in colonial experiences help explain differences in media systems. (p. xv)

Similarly, Golding and Elliot (1974), in describing the effects of the international media culture on the media of the developing nations, state that such culture "contains models and standards for the 'good' or 'successful' story or programme, based on examples from British and American media" (p. 236).

Some of the continent's colonial papers were owned and published by Africans. The general editorial policy of the African-owned colonial media was based on the reasoning that, in the absence of democratically elected governments, such media regarded themselves as institutions for critical discourse of public policy. This tradition evolved into what was regarded by the colonial administrations as adversarial and even subversive communications, which eventually shaped the ethics of media in post-colonial Africa.

Omu (1968) notes four reasons for the adversarial ethic of Africa's early mass media in British colonies. First, Africans did not constitute an alternative government in the British democratic tradition. Second, public attention was almost exclusively directed toward political issues. Third, Africans attached some prestige to severe criticisms of colonial government. Regardless of the form of government established by the colonial powers in their overseas territories, the latter's economies were geared toward the interests of those foreign powers. In time, the colonial élites began questioning the wisdom of that form of exploitation, resulting in nationalist movements. Media criticism of colonial regimes boosted media operations and their political influence. Despite several restrictive statutes designed to limit anti-colonial advocacy, colonial African media were nevertheless enmeshed in politics and policy debates, a pattern that remained largely unchanged in the post-colonial state despite restrictive laws, continued harassment, and harsh sanctions by post-colonial African governments (Agbese, 1990; Elias, 1969; Faringer, 1991; Ogbondah, 1994; Ogundimu, 1990). Whether the active role being played by the post-colonial African media in public discourses has been significantly hampered or curtailed when compared to their role in the colonial era is debatable, considering the media's current role in public-policy issues in many African states. This role seems fulfilled despite state-engineered sanctions and terrorism against members of the press, and despite sizable government ownership and controls instituted over wide areas of mass media production and distribution.

Three Proto-Norms

First, a caveat. We acknowledge the diversity of cultures, political systems and religions; that, for example, the peoples of the Arabic North have religious inclinations and media patterns and challenges that are different from those of countries that are to the south of the Sahara. For one thing, Islamic influences are more pervasive in the north than in equatorial and sub-equatorial Africa. For another, there has been more political stability in the north; the instability in the south makes the challenges for social and economic development even more daunting. Even so, our analyses make no strong attempts to distinguish between media patterns in the North and those south of the Sahara.

Our discussion focuses on three forms of proto-norms that underlie media ethics in Africa. The first form of proto-norms is related to the traditional media; the second to the modern print and government-run broadcast media; and the third to the increasing number of private broadcasting stations that are an emerging reality in Africa.

1. *Proto-norms of the traditional mass media.* Doob (1961) identifies the communication value of rumors, folk tales, folk drama, dance, music and songs in Africa. Ugboajah's (1972, 1979, 1985a, 1985b) research developed and advocated the concept of "oramedia" or folk media. He also argues that such media, for example, the "gongman" or puppetry, should be used in Africa's national development because they are forceful, effective, and credible and motivate multi-ethnic societies. Wilson (1987) similarly argues that traditional news agents are the only credible sources of information for rural residents because such agents signify Africans' resistance to Western media's efforts to cannibalize them. Commenting on the importance of traditional media systems, Oduko (1987) bemoans the local limits of their range, whereas Orewere (1991) and Yankah (1992) note that they will continue to play major roles in transmitting knowledge and information about development issues. More recently, Riley (1993) outlined the essential features of traditional media and suggested methods for incorporating them into community and social development and health education.

Undoubtedly, these still-largely pristine media attract a high degree of response from audiences because, as prime disseminators of culture, their messages have symbolic meanings that are understood by all (Ugboajah, 1985b). But the ethics of the use of these media are governed by those reflected in the social-ethical order by which the absence of subjectivism is accompanied by the use of deontological sanctions of myths and taboos.

For example, the belief among the Ashantis that God is everywhere, means that, regardless of the communication one engages in, one is under the unfailing supervision of the metaphysical powers of God. This is the essence of the Ashanti, and perhaps most African ontological morality in Africa.

Obeng-Quaidoo (1988) attributes the success of one such project to its sensitivity to traditional ethos. In the Wonsuom rural newspaper and radio broadcast project in the Swedru district of Ghana, Wonsuom clubs were used as public education and information channels. Club members used proverbs, performed concerts, and sang folk songs with developmental themes (Obeng-Quaidoo, 1988). The success of the education project resulted in part from the ethics of the purposive communication strategies employed by project planners. The strategies, demonstrably utilitarian, were based on the application of indigenous resources to development challenges.

2. *Proto-norms of the print and broadcast media.* Perhaps the more disturbing proto-norm that affects print and government-run broadcasting stations is that on the relations between the government and the modern mass media. It is a proto-norm of unpredictability. African journalists have been harassed, arrested, tortured, and killed for blind-siding governments with their interpretive reports on various laws, policies and actions. Sometimes, the dispute was over the amount of leeway journalists should exercise in analyzing government actions.

In pre-Mandela South Africa, conditions under which most black journalists worked were so unpredictable that the journalists' professional independence was blunted. Because black journalists, in the minds of the English and the Afrikaner "became identified with agitation, not only for racial equality, but also for the communist cause" (Phelan, 1987, p. 69), they were forced to work in racially mixed groups which then began editing their own publications. This media development resulted in the demise of the independent black press in South Africa. Such development is compromised by the government's overreaction to the seeming challenges to the apartheid regime's stronghold on the country.

3. *Proto-norms of the private radio and television stations.* Comparatively, these stations are a novelty in Africa. Their numbers, while increasing, are still very much a rarity on the continent. Private television stations are much fewer than private radio stations. Because of the inherent dissemination speed of these electronic media, the license-granting government agencies have, at best, given the station operators a short leash. Conditions for the granting and revoking of licenses are harsh in some of the countries. This calls into question the extent to which these stations are indeed "private."

In May 1970, Radio Syd of The Gambia became the first private-enterprise radio station to go on the air in Africa. Mali, Nigeria, Uganda, and Zambia, to name of few, have granted licenses to private organizations or groups to operate radio and television stations and many of the stations were already on the air as at the time of writing. Ghana was in the process of awarding some 40 private broadcasting licenses. Whereas this development may augur well for the future of private-enterprise broadcasting, it remains to be seen to what extent some of the restrictive regulatory provisions made in respect of the licenses may affect the independent operation of private-enterprise broadcasting. For example, in the case of Nigeria, Article 9 of Nigeria's National Broadcasting Commission (1992) Decree 1992, states that the Commission must be satisfied that an applicant for a private license

> can give an undertaking that the licensed station shall be used to promote national interest, unity and cohesion and that it shall not be used to offend the religious sensibilities or promote ethnicity, sectionalism, hatred and disaffection among the peoples of Nigeria (p. A319).

If the letter of the provision of the regulatory decree were enforced, it could significantly constrain the operation of independent commercial broadcasting in Nigeria, perhaps to the same extent as the operation of the state-owned Nigerian broadcasting system is constrained. The significance of government interference and implications for control of the press in sub-Saharan is illustrated by the case of the Nigerian *Newswatch* magazine. *Newswatch* is regarded as Africa's pre-eminent and most widely-read news publication. Its weekly paid circulation is 150,000. It is circulated in Africa, in Europe, and in North America. Agbese (1989) notes that it "changed the form of print journalism in Nigeria [and] introduced bold, investigative formats to news reporting in Nigeria" (p. 331). Consequently the Nigerian government had reason to clamp down on the magazine.

In light of the aforementioned incompatibilities, what, then, is the ethical preference of Third-World mass media staffers? Cast against the background of the coalescence of indigenous and universal religious influences, it stands to reason that utilitarian ethics seem emphasized by the media. This ethical orientation is preferred to others for two reasons. First, it emphasizes the welfare of the group, not just that of the élite. Research on the ethics of the Nigerian daily press found that utilitarian ethics was the preferred ethical approach used in editorial analyses about development issues, and was perceived by the journalists as the preferred methods for resolving such issues (Pratt, 1990; Pratt & McLaughlin, 1990). Second, its tenet is consistent with Mbiti's (1975) observation that African religious practices expect community members to contribute to community welfare.

All three reasons underscore the Third-World orientation for the group rather than for the self; however, such penchant is more strongly apparent in the use of traditional mass media than in that of the modern, urban-based media, which are more likely than the traditional media to challenge established social and political practices.

A Proposed Ethics Model

U.S. journalists are reluctant to make ethical decisions based on a systematic application of moral philosophy (Singletary, Caudill, Caudill, & White, 1990). In the latter study, for example, respondents agreed on four out of 77 Q-statements, suggesting that there is no uniform code of ethics in journalism, that not all journalists subscribe to any of such codes, and that journalists' ethical standards and professional practices are debatable.

Therefore, Childers (1988), Bovee (1991) and Swain (1994) have developed models to help journalists make consistent and ethically defensible decisions. But no such model exists for reporting international news. Because our intent was to propose an ethical standard that could aid international media coverage of the Third World, we suggest that such a model better serve journalists' attempts to rehabilitate the region's image in the international media. Such a rehabilitation will improve the region's image by presenting its administrative and development issues within appropriate contexts, thus lessening criticisms now being levelled against Western reporting regarding its negative, crisis-oriented bias.

What could be the key elements of such an ethics model for presenting news stories and analyses about the Third World in the international news media? We propose a preliminary model that builds on the following propositional inventory.

Proposition 1: *To improve the strategic importance of international communications about and of intercultural communications within developing nations, communication professionals should understand that, regardless of their communications interest, certain apparent ethical universals are apparent in developing countries. Even so, the interpretation of these universals should be based on the culture or society of the communicators' foci.*

This proposition is based on the universality of certain proto-norms, that is, fundamental moral rules and moral principles, as stated in the second part of this chapter. It recognizes the influence of classical moral thought and the applicability of moral universals such as the search for truth, fairness, justice and the public interest. This is our domino proposition.

Proposition 2: *To improve the strategic importance of international communications about and of intercultural communications within developing nations, communication professionals should understand that, even though the African, for example, exists at three levels (as an individual, as a member of a group, and as a member of a community [Anyanwu, 1984]), the concept of singularity assumes the African individual simultaneously fuses all three roles.*

This implies that international and intercultural communicators be cognizant of and sensitive to dealing with a Third-World source as both a multiple entity and as a representative of the self and of the community. Hence we argue that in the case of the African in particular, communications about a specific individual is seen as a commentary on an entire society. An insult to one individual, is an insult to a nation. Praise and credit for one individual are regarded as praise and credit in a collective sense, that is, for an entire society. The strong, sometimes fanatical, kinship that is demonstrated among, say, the Hutu extremists (Burundi) and the Tamils (Sri Lanka) create for them a uniform, unidimensional worldview. This is our singularity proposition.

Proposition 3: *To improve the strategic importance of international communications about and of intercultural communications within developing nations, communication professionals should regard contemporary moral thought as a synthesis of, say, Western, Afro-Asiatic and indigenous thought.*

The consequence of this syncretism is the expectation of a push and pull in the daily polity of the Third-World nation. This is a highly complex, multipolar, and variegated pattern of responses by the Third-World government to situations and events that might strike the Western reporter as the region's demonstration of illogical thought, inconsistencies, and spatial rationality in the allocation of resources as well as the stability of its systems. This is our syncretic proposition.

Proposition 4: *To improve the strategic importance of international communications about and of intercultural communications within developing nations, communication professionals need to demonstrably appreciate the unique role of the social, cultural, and political institutions in the developing environment, especially as many of the nations struggle to survive in extremely fragile political, social, and economic circumstances.*

In the absence of such demonstrated appreciation, governments in developing countries would necessarily regard as hostile adverse criticisms and coverage on the part of domestic and international media and the pronouncements of interest groups regarding governments' failings. Such negative reaction does not, of course, imply that the media, domestic or international, and interest groups, should be intimidated or cowed into silence on the failings of Third-World administrations. However, it does mean that such institutions or groups should seek to balance both negative and positive communications about the Third World. This is our balanced ethos criterion and proposition.

Three elements comprise the basic model: media and interest-group ethical values, principles and roles; ethical decision-making process; and public pronouncements. A major characteristic of the model is that it provides the international media staffer and the domestic interest groups with opportunities to "weave in and out," meaning that communication professionals can observe or assess how Third-World societies arrive at their criteria for making information public, and how best to present communications content. The communicator is encouraged to listen and to observe more, making a message a product of multiple worldviews.

Media and interest-group ethical values define the good and the bad; principles define the right and the wrong; and roles define how communications function in specific circumstances and situations. While ethical values and principles are largely universal (for example, tell the truth or serve the public interest), roles tend to be unique to a society's development stage and its political and social realities. Hence, while the media in a number of developing countries tend to be co-opted into government public-information programs, those in the developed West tend to play more of an adversarial role than their Third-World counterparts.

The second element in the basic model, ethical decision-making, encourages communication professionals to synthesize the universal elements of moral theories, of societal values, and of the ethical decision-making processes used in the developing region.

A feedback loop provides an opportunity for monitoring the sensitivity of the product to professional and moral values that preceded and subsequently shaped actual communications.

In visual terms then, the top one-half of the model (international communications) is separated by broken lines from its bottom one-half (developing nation). This suggests the globalization of the entire communications environment in which events and occurrences in one region are truly a sequela of an interface on a global scale.

In its extended form, the model posits that societal, organizational, and personal factors influence values of both international and intercultural communication. For the African, for example, the cultural value of the "I" becomes the "We," as the individual is synthesized with the whole community (Anyanwu, 1984), and the "for me" becomes the "for us." Thus, an individual-focused event is in reality a community event that involves more than just the obvious subject of the event.

Organizational factors in the form of ethics codes and personal factors in the form of the intensity of one's religious or spiritual beliefs influence the workplace formulation of and reverence for media values. Thus these factors are windows for events and occurrences and media treatment of them.

According to Lambeth (1992), right and wrong are defined by the principles of truth-telling; by humaneness, that is, preventing harm wherever appropriate; by justice; by freedom; and by the stewardship of free expression. At various levels, all five principles are apparent in Third-World communications; however, to engage in ethically sensitive communications, the principles of the development role and of community orientation of communications need be integrated into the list.

Thus, international communication staffers need to determine how developmentally supportive of society's interests is, say, a report. Does it prevent direct harm to the government? Does it render some assistance to governments' development programs?

Because every communications program is an opportunity for stock-taking, international and cross-cultural communications are yet further opportunities for summative evaluation: How reflective of our social and professional values and principles is a particular communication?

CONCLUSION

This chapter outlines international communication issues that are still apparent in the international news media even though NWICO debates focused attention on them beginning in the late 1970s. It outlines ethnic conflicts as presenting challenges for the ethics of intercultural communications. It argues that the absence of an ethics model for covering international news has resulted in the extant nature of problems associated with reporting the Third World. It suggests a society- and a values-based model for that type of coverage. It illustrates, with examples from sub-Saharan Africa, the philosophical foundations of the ethics of the traditional and modern mass media in the Third World. Those foundations comprise three elements: indigenous religions as ontological morality, universal religions and Western political influences, and post-colonial political and social influences. It argues that indigenous religious influences are significantly more apparent among the traditional media than among the urban-based mass media.

Drawing on situations in Africa, it also presents three proto-norms of mass media ethics. The first proto-norm relates to the traditional mass media; the second to the modern print and government-run broadcast media; the third, still largely unfolding, relates to the increasing number of private broadcasting stations. It notes that previous research reported that government restrictions tend to influence media ethics in ways that are not sensitive to media-ownership patterns (Pratt & McLaughlin, 1990). Such a finding has major implications for assessing the call for private print and broadcast stations, whose ethics may not be significantly different from those of government-run media.

This chapter also brings to the fore the impact of the political environment in shaping the ethics of communications in developing countries. Whereas indigenous religious influences are more pronounced on traditional media, which are commonly used in rural communities, the urban mass media are subject to ethical influences that emanate from earlier indigenous influences but are at once political, social and technological. Third World and other international journalists occasionally work under politically sensitive circumstances that are a threat to their professional values.

Regarding distribution of and access to communication content, the available technologies are so unevenly distributed that information gathering oftentimes focuses on sources with access to communication technologies. This limited access brings into question the extent to which utilitarian interests are being addressed. This chapter has spelled out the limitations of deontology as an ethical principle of the mass media in developing countries. It argues for utilitarian ethics, which seeks the greatest good for the largest number of Third-World citizens. But the international reporter, even if she or he had weighed the utilitarian benefits and disadvantages of a report, may not be able to estimate accurately all the consequences of the report on society. However, the extent to which utilitarian ethics, as a development-related ethical approach, can be balanced with the evolving constraints that are the hallmarks of the mass media is largely contingent on the evolving relations between the government and the media.

It is against this backdrop that this chapter proposes a preliminary model that could enhance the ethical sensitivities of international communicators whose reports, inadequate at best, provide, for most audiences, their only accounts of developing nations. The model is premised on societal influences on the occurrences and interpretation of events, influences that tend to be overlooked in international communications. On the one hand, it is the recognition, or perhaps the demonstrated appreciation, of societal values, and, on the other, of their influences on ethical considerations that need to be the focal point of any attempts toward improving the international coverage of the region.

It is suggested that future research test and refine the model and extend it to other forms of international and intercultural communications. The continuing restructuring of mass-media operations, their continuing efforts at redefining communications content and the evolving changes in the marketplace all place demands on both the domestic and international media staffer. Those demands occasionally manifest themselves as shortcuts toward ethical conduct. Thus, future research could also test the influences on such organizational and market constraints on ethical reporting of Africa in the international media.

REFERENCES

Adebayo, O. (1993). *The politics of structural adjustment in Nigeria*. Portsmouth, NH: Heinemann.
Adegbola, E. A. A. (1969). The theological basis of ethics. In K. A. Dickson & P. Ellingworth (Eds.), *Biblical revelation and African beliefs* (pp. 116-136). London: Lutterworth Press.
Agbese, P. O. (1990). The military and the privatization of repression in Nigeria. *Conflict, 10*, 239-266.

Agbese, P. O. (1989). State, media and the imperatives of repression: An analysis of the ban on *Newswatch. International Third World Studies Journal and Review, 1*, 325-334.

Agrawal, B. C. (1984). Satellite Instructional Television: SITE in India. In G. Gerbner & M. Siefert (Eds.), *World communications: A handbook* (pp. 354-359). New York: Longman.

Altschull, H. J. (1995). *Agents of power.* New York: Longman.

Alverson, H. (1978). *Mind in the heart of darkness: Value and self-identity among the Tswana of Southern Africa.* New Haven, CT: Yale University Press.

Anyanwu, K. C. (1984). African political doctrine. In E. A. Ruch & K. C. Anyanwu (Eds.), *African philosophy: An introduction to the main philosophical trends in contemporary Africa* (pp. 369-384). Rome: Catholic Book Agency.

Berger, P. (1989). *Bill Moyers: A world of ideas.* New York: Doubleday.

Berman, B. J. (1992). The state, computers, and African development: The information non-revolution. In S. G. Lewis & J. Samoff (Eds.), *Microcomputers in African development: Critical Perspectives* (pp. 213-229). Boulder, CO: Westview.

Bovee, W. G. (1991). The end can justify the means, but rarely. *Journal of Mass Media Ethics, 6,* 135-145.

Breed, W. (1960). Social control in the newsroom. In W. Schramm (Ed.), *Mass communication* (2nd ed., pp. 178-194). Urbana, IL: University of Illinois Press.

Buchowski, M. (1995). Back to cognitive foundationalism? *Philosophy of the Social Sciences, 25,* 384-395.

Chenery, H., Ahluwalia, M., Bell, C. L. G., Duloy, J., & Jolly, R. (1981). *Redistribution with growth.* Oxford: Oxford University Press.

Christians, C. G., Ferré, J. P., & Fackler, P. M. (1993). *Good news: Social ethics and the press.* New York: Oxford University Press.

Christians, C. G., Rotzoll, K. B., & Fackler, M. (1991). *Media ethics: Cases and moral reasoning* (3rd ed.). New York: Longman.

Childers, D. (1988). Media practices in AIDS coverage and a model for ethical reporting on AIDS victims. *Journal of Mass Media Ethics, 3,* 60-65.

Cooper, T. W. (1989). Global universals: In search of common ground. In T. W. Cooper (Ed.), *Communication ethics and global change* (pp. 20-39). White Plains, NY: Longman.

Donaldson, T., & Dunfee, T. W. (1994). Toward a unified conception of business ethics: Integrative social contracts theory. *The Academy of Management Review, 19,* 252-284.

Doob, L. W. (1961). *Communication in Africa: A search for boundaries.* New Haven, CT: Yale University Press.

Economic Commission for Africa. (1989). *Africa's alternative framework to structural adjustment programs for socio-economic recovery and transformation (AAF-SAP).* Addis Ababa: Author.

Elias, T. O. (1969). *Nigerian press law.* Lagos, Nigeria: Evans.

Ellul, J. (1964). *The Technological Society.* New York: Alfred A. Knopf.

Ellul, J. (1989). The search for ethics in a technicist society. In F. Ferré (Ed.), *Research in philosophy & technology: Ethics and technology* (pp. 23-36). Greenwich, CT: JAI Press.

Fair, J. E. (1993). War, famine, and poverty: Race in the construction of Africa's media image. *Journal of Communication Inquiry, 17,* 5-22.

Faringer, G. (1991). *Press freedom in Africa.* New York: Praeger.

Frankena, W. K. (1973) *Ethics.* (2nd ed.). Englewood Cliffs, NJ: Prentice-Hall.

Fromm, E. (1969). *Escape from freedom.* New York: Avon.

Gerbner, G., Mowlana, H., & Nordenstreng, K. (Eds.). (1993). *The global media debate.* Norwood, NJ: Ablex.

Gifford, C. A. (1982, August). Coverage of developed and developing nations in American wire services to Asia. Paper presented at the annual convention of the Association for Education in Journalism and Mass Communication, Athens, Ohio.

Gifford, P. (1995). Bemba Christians. *The Journal of African History, 36,* 518-520.

Golding, P., & Elliot, P. (1974). Mass communication and social change: The imagery of development and development of imagery. In E. de Kadt and G. Williams (Eds.), *Sociology and development* (pp. 229-254). London: Tavistock.

Hachten, W. A. (1971). *Muffled drums: The news media in Africa*. Ames, Iowa: Iowa State University Press.

Hastedt, H. (1994). Enlightenment and technology: Outline for a general ethics of technology. In G. Allan & F. Ferré (Eds.), *Research in philosophy & technology: Technology and everyday life* (pp. 205-217). Greenwich, CT: JAI Press.

Haynes, J. (1995). Popular religion and politics in sub-Saharan Africa. *Third World Quarterly, 16*, 89-107.

Horton, R. (1993). *Patterns of thought in Africa and the West: Essays on magic, religion and science*. Cambridge: Cambridge University Press.

Hountondji, P. (1983). *African philosophy: Myth and reality*. Bloomington, IN: Indiana University Press.

Hountondji, P. J. (1991). African philosophy: Myth and reality. In T. Serequeberhan (Ed.), *African philosophy: The essential readings* (pp. 111-131). New York: Paragon.

Hultman, T. (1992). Dateline Africa: Journalists assess Africa coverage. In B. G. Hawk (Ed.), *Africa's media image* (pp. 223-236). New York: Praeger.

Ipenburg, A. T. (1992). *'All good men': The development of Lubwa mission, Chnisali, Zambia 1905-1967*. Frankfurt, Germany: Peter Lang.

Janis, I. L. (1982). *Groupthink*. Boston, MA: Houghton Mifflin.

Kant, I. (1964). *Groundwork of the metaphysic of morals*. (H.J. Paton, Trans.). New York: Harper Torchbooks. (Original work published 1948).

Lambeth, E. B. (1992). *Committed journalism* (2nd ed.), Bloomington, IN: Indiana University Press.

Larson, J. (1983). *Television's window on the world*. Norwood, NJ: Ablex.

Lent, J. (1977). Foreign news in American media. *Journal of Communication, 27*, 46-51.

MacBride Commission. (1980). *Many voices, one world: Toward a new more just and more efficient World Information and Communication Order*. London: Kagan Press.

MacBride, S., & Roach, C. (1993). The New International Information Order. In G. Gerbner, H. Mowlana, & K. Nordenstreng (Eds.), *The global media debate: Its rise, fall, and renewal* (pp. 3-11). Norwood, NJ: Ablex.

MacIntyre, A. (1984). *After virtue: A study in moral theory* (2nd ed.). Notre Dame, IN: University of Notre Dame Press.

May, W. F. (1984). The virtues in a professional setting. *Soundings, 67*, 245-266.

Mazrui, A. A. (1977). *Africa's international relations: The diplomacy of dependency and change*. Boulder, CO: Westview.

Mbiti, J. S. (1975). *Introduction to African religions*. New York: Praeger.

Mbiti, J. S. (1990). *African religions & philosophy*. Oxford: Heinemann.

McKeon, R. (1947). *Introduction to Aristotle*. New York: Modern Library.

McPhail, T. L. (1989). Inquiry in international communication. In M. K. Asante & W. B. Gudykunst (Eds.), *Handbook of international and intercultural communication* (pp. 47-66). Newbury Park, CA: Sage.

Merrill, J. C. (1995). *Global journalism: Survey of international communicatio*. White Plains, NY: Longman.

Mill, J.S. (1951). *Utiliatarianism, liberty and representative government*. New York: E.P. Dutton. (Original works published 1859, 1861).

Moemeka, A. A., & Kasoma, F. P. (1994). Journalism ethics in Africa: An aversion to deontology? In F. P. Kasoma (Ed.), *Journalism ethics in Africa* (pp. 38-50). Nairobi, Kenya: African Council for Communication Education.

Mukasa, S. G. (1992). Towards pan-African cooperation in satellite communication: An analysis of the RASCOM project. *Africa Media Review, 6*, 13-30.

National Broadcasting Commission. (1992). Decree No. 38, National Broadcasting Commission Decree 1992 (Extraordinary Federal Republic of Nigeria Official Gazette, No. 33, Vol. 79). Lagos, Nigeria: The Federal Government Press.

Obeng-Quaidoo, I. (1985). Culture and communication research methodologies in Africa: A proposal for change. *Gazette, 36,* 109-120.

Obeng-Quaidoo, I. (1988). Assessment of the experience in the production of messages and programmes for rural communication systems: The case of the Wonsuom project of Ghana. *Gazette, 42,* 53-67.

Oduko, S. (1987). From indigenous communication to modern television: A reflection of political development in Nigeria. *Africa Media Review, 1,* 1-10.

Ogbondah, C. W. (1994). *Military regimes and the press in Nigeria, 1966-1993.* Lanham, MD: University Press of America.

Ogundimu, F. (1990). They don't teach survival skills: Journalism education in Africa. *Gannett Center Journal,* Fall, 81-91.

Okigbo, C. (1989). Communication ethics and social change: A Nigerian perspective. In T. W. Cooper (Ed.), *Communication ethics and global change* (pp. 124-136). White Plains, NY: Longman.

Omu, F. I. A. (1968). The dilemma of press freedom in colonial Africa: The West African example. *Journal of African History, 9,* 279-298.

Onyewuenyi, I. (1991). Is there an African philosophy? In T. Serequeberhan (Ed.) *African philosophy: The essential readings* (pp. 29-46). New York: Paragon.

Orewere, B. (1991). Possible implications of modern mass media for traditional communication in a Nigerian rural setting. *Africa Media Review, 5,* 53-65.

Parrinder, G. (1969). *Africa's three religions.* London: Sheldon.

Phelan, J. M. (1987). *Apartheid media: Disinformation and dissent in South Africa.* Westport, CT: Lawrence Hill & Company.

Postman, N. (1992). *Technopoly: The surrender of culture to technology.* New York: Alfred A. Knopf.

Pratt, C. B. (1990). Ethics in newspaper editorials: Perceptions of Sub-Sahara African journalists. *Gazette, 46,* 17-40.

Pratt, C. B., & McLaughlin, G. W. (1990). Ethical dimensions of Nigerian journalists and their newspapers. *Journal of Mass Media Ethics, 5,* 30-44.

Rawls, J. (1971). *A theory of justice.* Cambridge, MA: Harvard University Press.

Riley, M. (1993). Indigenous resources in a Ghanaian town: Potential for health education. *The Howard Journal of Communications, 4,* 249-264.

Roe, E. M. (1988). A puzzle solved: Individualism versus community in Africa? The case of Botswana. *The Journal of Modern African Studies, 26,* 347-350.

Rossouw, G. J., & Macamo, E. (1993). Church-state relationship in Mozambique. *Journal of Church and State, 35,* 537-546.

Ruch, E. A., & Anyanwu, K. C. (1984). *African philosophy: An introduction to the main philosophical trends in contemporary Africa.* Rome: Catholic Book Agency.

Scollon, R., & Scollon, S. W. (1995). *Intercultural communication: A discourse approach.* Cambridge, MA: Blackwell.

Singletary, M. W., Caudill, S., Caudill, E., & White, A. (1990). Motives for ethical decision-making. *Journalism Quarterly, 67,* 964-972.

Sofola, J. A. (1973). *African culture and the African personality.* Ibadan, Nigeria: Heinemann.

Swain, K. A. (1994, August). *Beyond the Potter Box: An ethical decision-making model for media managers.* Paper presented to the Qualitative Studies Division, annual convention of the Association for Education in Journalism and Mass Communication, Atlanta, GA.

Ugboajah, F. O. (1972). Traditional-urban media model: Stocktaking for African development. *Gazette, 18,* 75-95.

Ugboajah, F. O. (1979). Developing indigenous communication in Nigeria. *Journal of Communication, 29,* 40-45.

Ugboajah, F. O. (1985a). Inspirational cultural symbols in nation-building: Introduction to part II. In F. O. Ugboajah (Ed.), *Mass communication, culture and society in West Africa* (pp. 87-94). New York: Hans Zell.

Ugboajah, F. O. (1985b). "Oramedia" in Africa. In F. O. Ugboajah (Ed.), *Mass communication, culture and society in West Africa* (pp. 165-176). New York: Hans Zell.

Velasquez, M.G. (1992). *Business Ethics: Concepts and cases.* (3rd ed.). Englewood Cliffs, NJ: Prentice-Hall.

Weaver, D. H., & Wilhoit, G. C. (1984). Foreign news in the Western agencies. In R. L. Stevenson & D. L. Shaw (Eds.), *Foreign news and the New World Information Order* (pp. 153-185). Ames, IA: Iowa State University Press.

Wilson, D. (1987). Traditional systems of communication in modern African development: An analytical viewpoint. *Africa Media Review, 1*, 87-104.

Yankah, K. (1992). Traditional lore in population communication: The case of the Akan in Ghana. *Africa Media Review, 6*, 15-24.

6

Toward a Dialogic Ethic in the Context of International Business Organization

Stanley Deetz, Deborah Cohen, and Paige P. Edley
Rutgers University

No one familiar with the international business situation today needs to be told that contemporary issues of ethics and responsibility are complex and critical. They include important issues such as human rights, environmental protection, equal opportunity and pay for women and various disadvantaged minorities, stakeholder rights, and fair competition. These broad issues become instantiated in activities such as using prisoners as workers, moving operations to environmentally less restrictive communities, offering and taking bribes and payoffs, creating environmentally unsound or wasteful products, growing income disparity, malingering harassment, advocating consumerism and closing of economically viable plants in takeover and merger games. Transportation and information technological developments and the concurrent growth of internationalization of business create a complex, high speed business environment that is not very conducive to value debate and the type of value-based decision making that benefits the wider community (see Deetz, 1995 a, b; King & Cushman, 1994). Furthermore, the massive growth and consolidation of commercial corporate ownership and sponsorship of mass media can restrict and distort such debates.

Much of the problem in discussing ethics today rests in the continued reliance on conceptions and practices of ethics and responsibility which provide little guidance during a period involving fundamental social changes and the centering of much of life in an economic context. These conceptions and practices of ethics include both those based on traditional beliefs and values and those based on rational discussion and instrumental reasoning. The former assumed relatively stable and homogeneous communities and the latter assumed relatively predictable relations between actions and consequences as well as equal opportunities to engage in such discussions. Neither of these conditions hold true today in large areas of human endeavor. Textbook discussions, as well as those in trade magazines like *Business Ethics,* make use of narrow and under-theorized conceptions of ethics. Sages and passions often substitute for careful analysis, providing everyday common sense for specific problems without a deeper exploration of embedded values or larger social contexts. In this chapter, we will side-step some of the more technical definitional issues that make up the profession of ethics today to get deeper into the inter-related concerns of values, morality, social responsibility and the negotiation of value-based lives. In the new international business situation, we find ourselves in a profoundly different moral and ethical situation which entails new responsibilities, one which call for a new discussion of central issues.

Unfortunately, the conceptual legacy of organizational ethics, which situates the site of ethics in the individual agent's conscious/conscience and which is backed by legal statutes and social practices, makes starting a new and more productive consideration of organizational ethics difficult. Discussing organizational ethics is challenging because of its politically and socially charged nature; what is "right" often represents the interests of those who are politically powerful. In a national and international corporate environment how can the interests of those who are less powerful, "less advantaged," or marginalized (for example, minorities, the elderly, women, and children to name a few) become represented? How do we address concerns regarding organizations' responsibilities (e.g., environmental preservation, the use of international natural resources, exploitation of labor forces, health care, and child care, again to name only a few) in an international organizational context when these are peripheral concerns for such organizations? While these questions seem extremely difficult to answer and while the hope for achieving a shared ethic in an international and multicultural climate is hardly assured, we believe that a meaningful ethical discussion is possible and necessary.

This chapter enters that discussion with rather modest goals. Initially, we will explore our current situation, briefly noting the problems this situation poses for our standard western, and now often international orientation to ethical discussions. Of principal interest to us is the enlightenment legacy with its emphasis on the separation of the private and public and the resulting positioning of ethical responsibility in the individual. With this positioning, traditional community-based ethics no longer directed the entire system but were relegated to the home and local communities. As a result, the business corporation was conceptualized as independent from the realm of private values. Business activities were seen as rational and the individual and values became subservient to organizational goals. The "manager" emerged as a personally moral but corporately amoral operator. These concepts constituted the foundation for the difficulties found in developing a meaningful ethic for an international free-market system. Next, we will look at various contemporary attempts to provide an adequate discourse on ethics. In doing so we demonstrate the difficulties we face when addressing particular problems in international business today. We will examine and critique concepts such as social responsibility, silencing the marginalized and multicultural voices, privatized values, such as emotivism, and the potential for a universal value and ethical system within each theoretical territory, as well as within both a multicultural organizational context and an international business environment. Finally, we will explore a dialogic or communicative basis for ethical discussions emerging out of feminist and postmodern social philosophies. Looking to the dialogic or communicative site of ethics offers important possibilities for our contemporary condition. Dialogic conceptions focus on the relational and discursive origin of ethics rather than communal, individual or rational ones. We feel that such a position overcomes the theoretical problems inherent in both traditional and enlightenment ethical conceptions, as well as a subtle but limiting patriarchy embedded within these positions. Enriching our ethical discussion can lead to more creative, responsive and responsible international business choices.

Rather than focusing on the individual as the site of ethics, we will suggest that the commercial business context is perhaps a more significant, productive and meaningful site for ethical discussion. In most modern societies corporations make crucial decisions for the public regarding the use of resources, development of technologies and products, and working relations among people. Increasingly social/political decision making in family, community and state processes is replaced by economic decision making organized in corporate practices (Deetz, 1992). The interlacing of commercial corporations and commercial mass media completes the loop of influence (see Deetz, Fisher & Power, 1995). Corporate practices and propaganda have significant effects on social conceptions, values and personal self-definitions. Every contemporary political philosophy or investigation of ethical decision making must consider the logic of the market economy and the internal decision processes in corporations. Perhaps it should come as little surprise that in this situation value, moral, ethical and aesthetic considerations should be taking on additional significance. Organizations must be evaluated by criteria richer than profitability.

We believe that Gergen (1992) is right; organizational research and theory need to be evaluated as much by a question of "how shall we live?" as by verisimilitude and methodological rigor. At the minimum, a general theory of ethical communication in organizations should (1) provide a unified way of understanding the complex processes of organizational life, (2) direct the evaluation of existing organizational forms and activities, and (3) provide guidance for the education of members and the redesign of organizational structures and practices. Before getting into these larger issues of business ethics in an international context, it is instructive to see the crises of ethics in contemporary society at the individual level.

The Crisis of Contemporary Individual-Focused Ethics

In western societies common sense provides us with three ways of accomplishing individual ethical behavior. The first rests on the inculcation of community values and reasoning processes in each new generation. The second rests on utilitarian criteria requiring the assessment of the consequences of action, and the third rests on the development of systems of regulation. In looking at these three approaches, it is clear why common sense fails us so completely in the discussion of ethics and why a fresh analysis is necessary.

The Community Stance. In traditional society, the community developed basic values and expectations and these were maintained through active socialization. Ethical behavior was a developmental issue and the responsibility for maintenance was shared by community members. In opposition to the secular society, certainly the more conservative elements of contemporary society place considerable faith in the recovery of such communities. Even if recovery were possible, many have questioned the ethical quality of traditional communities. For example, owing to the vast oppression of women throughout the world, male domination is not only accepted in many cultures but protected through generations of exclusion, institutional domination, and physical violence toward women (including rape, murder, and maiming of women and young girls). Even acknowledging the ethnocentrism of human rights claims, clearly most human rights "violations" occur in "strong" traditional communities. In effect, industrial and postindustrial societies owe much of their continued "glass ceilings" and various relatively subtle forms of "human rights" violations in sexual, class, ethic, racial, religious, physical, and age discriminations to their cultural traditions. Male domination is a characteristic of most traditional communities and most community ethics have a decisive patriarchal character.

However, even if strong traditional communities could provide positive ethical conceptions and action, such systems require three conditions which are rarely present today: agreement, surveillance and social consequences. Especially in closed traditional communities, agreement was easy to reach. The community's way of seeing, thinking, valuing and acting had little competition, and the community's particular mode of being could easily be treated as that which was dictated by nature. The growth of science and global contact undermines such a naive faith. If the community's way of being is understood as a set of historical choices and alternative communities are readily available to members, much of the spontaneous voluntary compliance disappears. As the arbitrary and discriminatory nature of many community standards becomes clear, legitimacy is often lost and embarrassing questions are asked regarding who benefits from these standards. Such issues are most clearly developed in feminist writings.

But, it is not only agreement that is strained. Surveillance of member conduct is difficult in complex institutional settings, especially in businesses which often maintain a proprietary cloak over member behaviors. Further, as will be shown, the private/public split which has developed in the western world, limited the domain in which community standards were considered relevant. Even if surveillance were possible, the social consequences associated with such behaviors are weak, for the large complex communities of today grant much anonymity. Even if one were held accountable to a relevant community, the possibilities of moving unscathed, or even as a hero into a new community, are great. This can be observed over and over again in the actions of savings and loan officials, actors in the Watergate scandal, insider traders and others. Professional codes appear fairly weak as members slide from one profession to another in instances where community standards have been violated.

Just as importantly, in an international context it is unclear as to whose community standards are relevant. Neither ethnocentrism nor the cosmopolitan advice "when in Rome do as the Romans do" offer much help. As we will show, the hope for grounding any community's standard in universal conditions is not great and to impose any standards without such a grounding means building on shaky ground. While those working from a "human rights" stance have often been successful in reduction of practices that most of us consider repugnant, the concept of human rights is itself a kind of community standard. Such conceptions often are based on western ideals and they rarely have taken on western corporate-interests' violations of democracy or mental and physical health. In fact, the economic sanctions which are central to human rights advocates' clout, would rarely be effective against corporate business organizations. Ethnocentrism, even in the name of human rights, favors dominant groups in dominant societies. The relativism of the cosmopolitan offers little more. Problems of violence and environmental damage stretch across communities. Unfortunately, in the world of commerce, communities granting greater member protection are penalized as jobs and resources flow to areas encouraging more individual opportunism. Corporate leaders today have little sense of allegiance to people or communities; international business based on using the least ethical standards is common.

The Utilitarian Stance. Given the various problems of community standards, many have given up altogether on value-based decision making. Rational choice-making may overcome traditional prejudices and the decline of strong communities. Clearly, in the modern period community standards have been augmented by a second common-sense faith that, even in the absence of surveillance and social enforcement, good behavior pays off in the long run. Unfortunately, in the international business world of today, there is no long run (see King & Cushman, 1994). In the open system of modern commerce, time is irreversible and irrelevant. Systems rapidly transform and no one is around to realize the long term consequences. Not only is the notion of time different from our classical and common-sense models, but highly complex systems have highly complex action chains. Hence, the consequences of particular choices are virtually impossible to determine. Informed, politically correct shoppers, for example, struggle over the use of paper or plastic bags only to be confronted with so many contingencies and unpredictable co-determinative elements that no preferrable choice seems possible. Anyone who has been involved in social actions knows the rude awakenings that come with following through on any action program.

Furthermore, in the corporate context the increased importance of images and symbolic events make rational assessment nearly impossible. Jackell (1988) perhaps summarized this idea best in his description of moral decision making in corporations:

> What, however, if men and women in the corporation no longer see success as necessarily connected to hard work? What becomes of the social morality of the corporation-the everyday rule-in-use that people play by-when there is thought to be no fixed or, one might say, objective standard of excellence to explain how and why

winners are separated from also-rans, how and why some people succeed and others fail? What rules do people fashion to interact with one another when they feel that, instead of ability, talent, and dedicated service to an organization, politics, adroit talk, luck, connections, and self-promotion are the real sorters of people into sheep and goats (p. 3).

Not only are individuals in the corporate context in a difficult place regarding the possibility of rational choices, but we will show the same dilemmas exist for corporate officials when acting on behalf of the corporation.

The difficulties with utilitarianism are deeper than the assessment of the connection between choices and consequences. Rational choice making still relies on the acceptance of underlying, if not hidden and unexplored, values. These values are subject to the same group/ethnocentric qualities as community standards. The focus on the success of attainment, rather than on the quality of that which is to be obtained, has become a common source of distortion in individual choice making. The values supported are rarely explored and often benefit the dominant group. As will be explored later in this chapter, when such a conception is expanded from the individual to the system, market choices are treated as if they were able to represent rationally the values of various relevant communities, money-substitutes for substantive accomplishment as a measure of good. The idea that market choices accomplish representation and that money measures it is a very naive one. Thus, markets are value-laden rather than neutral representation processes, but the values are rarely explored (see Schmookler, 1992). As a result, market-place decisions provide us with some of the thinnest and most ethnocentric ethical systems available (Deetz, 1995 a, b).

The Regulation Stance. A third common-sense position suggests that, if community standards and voluntary compliance are weak and if utilitarian assessments do not lead to desired outcomes, law and regulatory policy can fill the gap. The hope that ethical and responsible decision making can be accomplished by value codification in governmental and other public regulation however is also dim. Regulation becomes a pricey way, at best, to accomplish ethical and responsible behaviors. Most often the attempt is not only expensive but it also fails. As detailed elsewhere, governments usually lack the resources, micro-knowledge, capacity or legitimacy to provide proactive value-based regulation (see Deetz, 1995 a, b). Most often they provide crude guidance at best, and are left to clean up the mess left behind by the socially irresponsible actions of others. Furthermore, the entanglement of dominant groups (especially commercial ones) with regulatory agencies leaves little hope that policies and enforcement will match the values more widely shared in a society (see Laumann & Knoke, 1987). To reinforce this point, as anyone who has dealt with a building department knows, codification and regulation lead to red tape and generic solutions which defy good common sense in their particular applications. Each of these difficulties undermine any liberal hope of government successfully guiding moral behavior.

The Context of Forming an Ethic Appropriate for International Business

The real problem today, however, lies not so much in the difficulties related to guiding individual behavior, but in providing an ethic for corporate behavior. When the individual is the focus, most attention is given to issues of compliance, while the value of the policy or procedure to which compliance is directed receives little or no attention. Additionally, the largest issues of responsibility and value relate to systemic problems and collective actions. Clearly this is also the case in international business. There are unethical employees and they do harm (judged by any number of standards and measures), but their compliance to laws and corporate policies will not solve many of today's difficult problems. Corporate goals and activities are themselves the issue. The difficulty lies in creating an adequate public rather than simply a private ethic (see Deetz, 1985). Today, many lament the weak morality of commercial corporations. Thus, an adequate discussion of ethics must focus on both the individual and corporate levels. But the discussion of corporate responsibilities has been severely hampered by dominant social conceptions which make such a discussion difficult. Central to these conceptions has been the growth of enlightenment rationalization and the accompanying "managerialism." While rationalization was meant to help overcome the difficulties of individuals acting on the basis of community value-standards, the consequence has been a strange value-laden rationality in its own right.

The Enlightenment and Progressive Rationalization. MacIntyre (1984) provides probably the best known discussion of progressive rationalization and managerialism in regard to ethics. But while his work has been much discussed, he is a rather late entry in a long list of writers attending to the disenchantments and progressive rationalizations of modern society. Heidegger (1961) and Weber (1958) certainly stand out as earlier, key figures in our contemporary understanding of this process, though Habermas' (1984, 1987) conception of the domination by "technical reasoning" and Lyotard's (1984) demonstration of the rise of "performativity" serve as the most challenging recent expressions. All these scholars share with MacIntyre a historical interpretation that goes something like this:

Decision making in traditional societies was dominated by authority and strongly held beliefs and values. The emergence of modern societies, described as enlightenment societies, enacted a system where a particular form of scientific knowledge replaced authority as a basis for understanding. New "procedural values" like "due process," "democracy," "progress" and "increased consumption" replaced "end-state values" which defined, in advance, the good life, proper behavior or what was good to consume. The residue of traditional values (as well as emotions, pleasures, the feminine and body processes) were privatized and assigned to the individual and home. This was the birth of what has been called "emotivism." They were outside the public quest for truth and rational decision-making but an important supplement to them. With this came liberalism—a new tolerance for the culturally different, as long as the difference stayed private-and the capacity to interact globally within new integrative and presumed value-neutral metasystems such as science and market economy. Value conflicts and debates gave way to calculations in presumed value-free representational codes. This left two presumed-to-be independent realms, a rational public one and a traditional private one. Appropriate experts and institutions arose to care for each realm with safeguards created to protect each from the other.

With this conception, business ethics were most often either privatized or instrumentalized. In the privatized conception, organizations and society counted on individuals to behave ethically by following selected supportive principles from the home community. This included honesty in work processes as well as in dealing with various publics, following professional codes and corporate policies, commitment to social services and philanthropic giving and attempting to be socially and environmentally responsible to the extent that it did not infringe on business interests.

Basically, the individual was assumed, or even commanded, to pursue self-interests within certain social limits, in other words, to be appropriately opportunistic. The fundamental command was to do "good business" rather than to do "good," but one should still obey the rules. Business leaders especially were expected to be "good," even God-fearing, people. With their power came a basic responsibility to be social stewards. How that was to be accomplished was left to their private determination. Even with their private conception, ethics were also instrumentalized. Doing good could also be seen as good business. This is most clearly seen in various forms of social and environmental marketing. Here ethics are reclaimed as a part of organizational decision making but subservient to its instrumental consequences. The difficulties of both positions will be discussed later.

Clearly, the privatization of values and rationalization of the public are interdependent on a macro as well as the micro level. Weber (1958) showed this most clearly in the confluence of capitalism with Protestantism. His point was reinforced by Habermas' dual demonstration of the dependence of the system world (and its technical instrumentalism) on the life world for legitimation and the way life-world processes constrained the run-away technical control potential in the system world (Habermas, 1975, 1987). Recently, the power of life-world institutions (such as family and community) and of private voluntary constraints have weakened, thus potentially creating disorder, motivation and legitimation problems (Habermas, 1975). Technical systems have responded to the increasing dislocation and social disintegration both through further system development and an attempt to colonize the life-world to elicit support (Deetz, 1992). Much of this has taken place through active value and cultural management programs in business (see Alvesson, 1987; Deetz, in press).

The Rise of Managerialism and the Eclipse of Ethics. Modern organization processes and management are both constituted by and have an impact on this historical situation. The combination of instrumental logic with the support of science and technological development lead to an unbalanced position with both nature and other people becoming transformed into merely means for corporate system perpetuation and profitability. Managerialism, as a term, draws attention to the way upper managers both confuse or unify their identity and the company identity, and reduce all corporate rationality to instrumental rationality.

Many studies of organizations have documented the development of a technocratic consciousness (e.g., see Fischer, 1990; Alvesson, 1987). Such studies indicate a narrowing of conceptions of rationality, a tightening of control systems, and a loss of social responsibility. Other studies have indicated that with the growth of multinationals a kind of manager has developed who is "more distant, more economically driven . . . more coldly rational in their decisions, having shed the old affiliations with people and place" (Reich, 1991, p. 77). Yet, the apparent loss of ethics arises more from the type of values pursued rather than the absence of values. The proclaimed presence of a new super-rationality often hides the value-laden and personally interested rationalities that invade managers' decisions. Yet, implicit questions remain: economically rational for whom and in regard to what? It is not just the coldness and distance that is an issue. It is their rationality! Managers have been both excused from moral scrutiny based on their perceived neutrality or at least economic rationality, and they have carefully used their attachment to science to support this image. Clearly, managers are not value neutral or simply economically rational, they make decisions in conditions of uncertainty and rely greatly on decision-making routines.

Contemporary organizations have developed a discourse where particular values are already integrated into work processes and decisions, but they remain invisible. Even the presence of "diversity training" can be better seen as a way to reduce "irrationality" arising from traditional communities, rather than a genuine attempt to consider alternative value systems for corporate life. The presumption of value neutrality is important for instrumental control since separating the values for explicit consideration disrupts the control systems which are internal to organizations and from which managers benefit in particular ways. As control systems are challenged-challenged far more by the growth of speed, complexity and broken means-ends chains, than by critics-"performativity" alone, rather than values, provides public legitimacy for managers. The moral problem is not just one of managers treating people as means rather than ends, but also one of reducing concern with competing values. Once such a logic is in place, all people-managers, workers, the public-appear willing to treat themselves as means (rather than ends) to an increased consumption potential. As Jackell (1988) showed in his study of corporate ethics, it was not the lack of values (or there would not have been any moral *dilemma*) which was the central problem, but rather the idea that one had to work in systems where subordination to expedience was the limit of thinkable agency. Burawoy (1985), Knights and Willmott (1989; Willmott, 1994) and others (Deetz, 1995a; in press) have developed this point at length elsewhere.

The market narrative completes this instrumental logic. The success of managers is measured by success in the marketplace. The public believes that market economy, rather than values or political action, keeps managers (who they accept as self-interested) in line with the public's own interests. Clearly, management groups use this public way of structuring the issue in order to deflect attention from their own moral failings and to increase internal corporate control. Thus, management's ability to articulate interests and choices in the economic code (rather than efficiency or satisfying public interests) has led to public support. As long as the system continues to pay off through its self-promoted good of increased consumption, management is tolerated.

Corporation and Moral Responsibility. If the system rewards the promotion of increased consumption, why should we look to commercial corporations as the site of the moral discussions? The answer rests in the role such organizations have inherited in society, rather than in the moral or ethical character of the manager. Presuming a purely economic realm, placing the questions of morality and good in the domain of the state, religion or private person, obscures this role. In addition, the conception of organizations as mere tools for the production of goods and services also obscures the organization's role. Value questions rest at the heart of the contemporary business enterprise.

First, as shown, neither managers nor the market economy are economically rational (see Gorz, 1987; Schmookler, 1992). Dominant groups gain considerably from treating their conceptions and practices as neutral and/or universal. Concepts of efficiency, effectiveness and performativity have been treated as if they were goods or ends in themselves without recognizing that their quality is grounded in the ends they serve and ultimately in relation to some conception of social good (Carter & Jackson, 1987). The question is, effective and efficient toward what? Additionally, whose and what interests should count for how much in formulating goals (Cameron & Whetten, 1983)?

Second, while perhaps instituted for economic reasons, organizational colonization of the private realm and influence on the state have considerable social effects. Modern corporations have developed processes, some intentional and others not, for colonizing the life world through political action and various forms of cultural management and often soliciting employee's self-colonization on their behalf (see Deetz, 1992; in press). The problem is not just the instrumental reasoning of managers but their size and clout with no competing institutions to moderate or counter-balance their effects. Corporate economic effects are felt in worker's lives, child rearing practices, income distribution and general economic cycles. Such public decisions need public discussion because the home and community are dependent on corporate money, corporate goods and corporate stability. This often reduces the meaning of life to the accumulation of goods, the only apparent certain thing in an uncertain world.

Finally, commercial organizations in most western societies have been given many of the legal rights and legal standing of persons. Yet, the rights of a person and citizen clearly carry some responsibilities. Corporations could become positive social institutions providing a forum for the articulation and resolution of important social conflicts regarding the use of natural resources, the production of desirable goods and services, the development of personal qualities and the future direction of society. By focusing primarily on narrow economic outcomes (usually profitability), the broader social and economic effects of our way of making business decisions have been missed.

Where to Begin the Discussion of Ethics?

Even if we can agree on the nature of the moral malaise, the way management currently works in modern societies, and the appropriateness of taking on moral decision making in the corporate site, the nature of the moral discussion appears open to much dispute. Several responses to these new conditions are possible. Five have emerged: *the cynical, the new traditionalist, the modern/rationalist, the communitarian, and the dialogic.*

The *cynical* response is the opportunistic use of new freedoms without commitment, guilt, or responsibility. The loose situation of fluid images and virtual facts leaves personal gains as the most certain and calculable of ends. The *new traditionalist* response decries the decline and holds out the hope, the last hope, for a return to authority and traditional values. The *modern* response follows the managerial discourse. More science, more technology, more control over the "irrational" forces can solve the problems. The *new universalists* response demonstrates fear of the uncertainty in our situation and the cynical response and hopes to recover some foundation without falling to the excesses of either the traditional or modern response. The *dialogic* response acknowledges at the outset the impossibility of a substantive foundational/universal ethic. Rather, we as a world community have to make it up as we go. But in order to do that, we must have the kind of negotiative discussions that provide for the inclusion of the full variety of human life. Value debate needs to be enabled through a recovery of those things feared–the body, the emotions, the feminine and pleasure, all suppressed by traditional and modern rationality. We have paid enough attention to the cynic and new traditionalists, but both the modern/rational response and communitarian deserve some commentary before we look to the dialogic alternative.

The Modern/Rationalist Response. Rational decision making models, which emphasize individualistic approaches to ethical decision making, suggest that it is the "economic man" (Bullis, 1993) who makes "rational" decisions. Rational decisions are seen as those which maximize economic gains and minimize economic losses in organizations. In this perspective, the behavior of the individual is "atomistic" and "egotistical"-individuals in organizations engage in interaction for the sole purpose of advancing their own goals and interests, as well as those of the organization (Mangham, 1995). Yet, it is important to point out that these organizational goals and interests are in large part thought to be shaped by the "invisible hand" of the market-place in which these organizations function. Therefore, efficiency, the ultimate goal guiding the decisions made by the rational actor, is in part shaped by the outside forces of the market-place.

This model asserts that through a reliance on the authority of objective, scientific knowledge or statistical information, which serves to characterize the state of the market-place in quantifiable terms, an orgaanization's decision makers can harness, or begin to understand and to predict the fluctuations of the market-place. With the use of this "objective information" about the market-place, "rational actors" are believed to be in a position to make informed and logical organizational decisions that are thought to be value-free or value-neutral. By virtue of their scientific basis, these decisions supposedly require no ethical scrutiny.

Based on such a position Rawls (1971) developed his theory of justice, and Martin (1994) his own position related to the study of organizations. While such a position has merit and deserves considerable discussion, we will only briefly consider it here. We agree with Habermas (1990) in dismissing the logic of the "fictitious original position" where a rational agent "situated behind a veil of ignorance" is best suited to ethical decision making (Rawls, 1971, p. 136). It seems untenable that such a person could remain unaware of the position he or she might occupy in the future social order, and remain equally unaware of the impact or benefit value-related decisions will have on his or her own situation. Such an "ignorance," which on one hand bypasses the problem of creating a theory of justice which is self-benefiting, is problematic for at least two other reasons.

First, such an "ignorance" is an idealistic fiction for it is impossible to ensure the impartiality of any moral judge. How could it be that one would be entirely removed from the values and beliefs in which individuals are so embedded? Secondly, such a theoretical position is monologic; Rawls is suggesting that we rely on the judgments of a few moral experts rather than on community participation. It is in light of the first problem, that is, the impossibility of removing any individual from the values and beliefs in which he or she is embedded, that the reliance on a few moral experts becomes increasingly problematic, because these individuals are always in some way morally and ethically situated. By limiting the ethical decisions to a few experts their positions will always remain privileged.

Rational actor models, in general, face a similar problem. There are limitations inherent in a model which privileges that which is objective and scientifically quantifiable. Scientific method is critically important to management, but as Buchholz (1991) suggests, "it is not sufficient to provide an ethical or moral philosophy for management. Such a philosophy cannot be built solely on the notion of economizing"(p. 21). Rational actor models value organizational rationality and economy, and in doing so unrealistically privatize or marginalize factors such as emotions, pleasures and body processes, which in many human circumstances might profoundly influence the decisions we make. In rational actor models these factors are placed within the individual, outside the public quest for truth and rational decision making, and they are, therefore, not considered to be influential in organizational decision making processes.

The keystone in beginning to understand the implications of "rationally" motivated decisions lies in a recognition that emphasizing the efficiency, performativity and effectiveness of organizational decisions is only one particular way of seeing this decision-making process, and, therefore, making decisions from this perspective is clearly a choice. Additionally, it is a choice which serves to represent the interests of the organization. Other stakeholders such as employees, non-working community members and children, to name just a few, as well as the community at large, will undoubtedly be affected by the decisions made by the organization. Thus, we would suggest that the concerns and interests of these stakeholders must be accounted for when organizations make their decisions. Yet, the primary concern of such stakeholders is quite often not the economic efficiency of the organization alone. Rather, these stakeholders have different interests, beliefs, feelings, and approaches for addressing organizational issues which directly impact the community. It is these ideas, beliefs, and interests which remain unrepresented in rational actor models.

Thus, what are purported to be value-free and neutral decisions by virtue of being objective, scientifically-based and economically rational, are clearly value-laden for at least three reasons: First, rational actor models assume that the scientific, quantitative information used in the decision-making process is objective and value-free. All research, including scientific, quantitative research, is conducted from a particular perspective or way of seeing the world and, therefore, represents the interests and values of a certain limited number of powerful stakeholders while ignoring the interests of other less powerful stakeholders.

Second, questions arise in regard to an individual's ability to make decisions that are disconnected from any sense of personal belief of what is right or wrong. Rather than being a question of the reliance on value-laden research when making decisions, this is more directly a question which concerns the environment in which organizational decision makers have to act. That is, research has indicated that ethical or value-laden decisions are often split-second choices for which managers rely on "instinct" rather than rationale. Such decisions are made in a context of ambiguity, and difficulty is experienced in any attempt to directly apply scientific information and an organization's predetermined policies and beliefs to solving problems (Conrad, 1993). This suggests that under such circumstances reason and rationale unavoidably, and often unknowingly, combine with individual, personal ethical beliefs in the decision making process. In such cases, these decisions do not serve to represent the community's or the organization's interests but rather the interests and personal moral and ethical beliefs of the individual decision maker. Again, one cannot claim that decisions made under such circumstance are value-free.

Third, these organizational decisions impact the whole community. Yet, as we have previously mentioned, the information that decision makers rely on is steeped in personal and organizational values, ethics and beliefs in regard to what is good and right. On this basis, one can suggest that such decisions are unquestionably made from a singular perspective, one which only represents the interests of the organization and its leaders. On the other hand, we need to recognize that within any society people are engaged in many discourses, forms of reasoning and ways of seeing what is socially good and right that compete for a position of centrality as ethical and moral standards, and which help to shape our decision-making process.

Rational actor models of organizational decision making, however, only privilege the lens of the technical and scientific. In so doing, other non-organizational interests and ways of seeing and understanding what is ethically, morally and socially good are marginalized. This becomes increasingly problematic when we consider that these decisions impact all members of the community. This being the case, we would suggest that non-organizational voices, that is all community members external to business organizations, have the right to participate in moral conversations and decision-making processes in order to have their interests represented in decisions which will invariably have an impact on their lives. Rational actor models do not facilitate such participation.

An example may help to clarify this issue. When large manufacturers decide to move a plant to another country, they do so, in the economic interest of the organization. That is, the manufacturer will be more efficient and have a greater margin of profit (for those in control of the organization) if the manufacturing plant is relocated, because taxes, wages and other costs are reduced. Yet, the impact this move will have on communities is great effecting both the community from which the plant is moving, as well as the community in which the plant is relocating. Moving the plant means that many of the community members employed by this manufacturer will be left unemployed.

On a large scale, such a massive wave of unemployment is not only devastating to the individuals that have been fired (and their families), but such a relocation also has a potential negative effect on the entire community, both socially and economically. In addition, relocating a plant will unavoidably have a significant impact on the new community in which this plant will operate. The social structure and culture of the community will be altered. In addition, in some parts of the world where poverty is a severe problem, the potential exists for both the exploitation of the work force and contamination of the environment.

Such social, economic, environmental, and emotional effects on communities are generally not considered by the organization. An interest in what is good for the community is outside of the purview of the rational actor, and economically motivated organizational decision maker. While rational and economically efficient decisions may make sense from within the discursive community of the "rational" organization—and in fact from this limited perspective decision makers may not see the potential for other viable options because concepts like emotions and the social impact of decisions are not easily or objectively quantifiable—such decisions will impact the life of the community. By failing to consider both the social and emotional repercussions of such decisions, rational actor models fail to be socially responsible when making decisions, they silence the voices of community members, and privatize the emotional nature of moral values and ethics. Thus, not only do these decisions tend to be socially irresponsible, in that they do not consider the social ramifications of such decisions, but also because they are determined from the perspective of the organization only; these decisions privilege a particular discourse and a particular way of seeing and acting. The privileging of this organizational discourse, therefore, serves to devalue or to privatize critical emotional aspects of these decisions, and to silence and to marginalize a large segment of the community who will be affected greatly by such decisions.

Without such a critique, economically rational decisions initially seem justified and unproblematic. Yet, we need to recognize that organizations do not exist in a social vacuum. Decisions regarding issues such as health care, child care, and the environment, are just a few which serve to exemplify the impact organizational decisions can have on the larger society. If we excuse managers and organizations from moral scrutiny by suggesting that decisions made within the organization are value-free, we passively adopt organizational ethical perspectives which shape our moral and ethical social life. In so doing we ignore the moral and ethical beliefs of various other social groups or stakeholders within society that are not positioned as key organizational decision makers.

The New Universalist Response. For centuries the appeal of a universal ethics has been great. Generally three tacks were taken to found such an ethics-a universal religion, a human essence, and cultural universals. Owing to the rather obvious ethnocentrism of a privileged or universal religion, most scholars have pursued the two latter directions. Grounding ethics in an essence sought an understanding of distinctly human qualities and argued that these served as categorical or inalienable rights. Kant's (1959) categorical imperative-that every person should be treated as an end and never as a means-represented the most discussed and advanced position. Much of today's human rights discussion today maintains a similar reasoning process. As already argued, such principles have aided the development of civil liberties and granted protection to oppressed people but rarely have been applied to international corporations. One can hardly imagine a strategic management program or personnel department where people are treated as anything but means. The search for cultural universals has fared little better. Universals to guard against claims of ethnocentrism, and to apply to commercial organizations have been difficult to find (Waltzer, 1987).

More recently a "new foundationalist" literature has arisen focusing more on human tasks and bodily experiences (see Johnson, 1987). Again MacIntyre and his followers (see Mangham, 1995) have been most explicit in the applications to business enterprises. MacIntyre, in opposition to the individualistic, rational models of organizational ethics, suggests that one of the legacies of individualistic, enlightenment models is decreased emphasis on community as an essential part of life. In this way the "new foundational" literature has a clear communitarian quality. He hopes to recover some shared foundation in which individuals are grounded in a connected community of shared traditions (MacIntyre, 1984). He suggests that it is within this connected community (local, national and international) that organizational goals, as well as ethical and moral decisions can be made by organizations and communities that will represent the values of the collectivity rather than merely the values and ethical concerns of the "powerful" individuals. Integrated and complete people grounded in connectedness and tradition are able to engage in a discussion aimed at a more rational social order.

Frederick (1986) followed a similar analysis in considering business responsibility in his corporate social rectitude (CSR3) model. He suggested that moral and ethical questions arise during periods of particular social stress. The most significant stresses occur when "the norms or standards defining and controlling human consciousness, human community, and human continuity are affected" (1986, p. 127).

Frederick's (1986) strategy for dealing with the decisions that must be made (either by actions or inaction) in these contexts is to pursue core values and normative principles that are deeply embedded in general culture or humankind itself. The strategy seems to work in the right direction, but there are a number of difficulties with pursuing substantive values of this sort. Many of the moral platforms he discusses are distinctly western and perhaps male in character, and philosophers for generations have had difficulties in suggesting universal ones (see Mangham, 1995). Further, the problem remains of applying them to specific contexts where the same value is open to alternative interpretations, and where different core values suggest different actions. Further still, the core values are often treated as if they were immune to the processes of everyday life, where the dominant speakers and messages of the time might have considerable influence on the nature of these values and their interpretation. And finally, rarely do these conceptions entail an adequate theory of power. Even if analysis could display the presence of core values, what force of compliance do they carry? Might not powerful groups do what they wish if the core values were not in their interest? As suggested, Kant's (1959) categorical imperative is well argued and widely accepted, yet much of organizational life and entire corporate human resource departments work in direct opposition to it. This model provides no easy way to determine whether the promotion of corporate values through mass media, for example, is good or bad, or if such discussions are considered problematic, how media and available discussion forums might be reformed.

Generally these new foundational and communitarian approaches demonstrate neither the ability to overcome the social/cultural/historical determinants of the configuration of modernity that set the malaise in play nor the discursive monopoly of corporations in modern society. The awareness of this, we believe, accounts for the pessimistic character of much of this work. Even if we were to agree that the contemporary problem in organizations and society at large that is that of a kind of "homeless" manager who has no community ties, who operates with an opportunistic self-interest, who uses the lack of a clear social identity and firm knowledge to build an imaginary world for personal advantage, the communitarian approach lacks a meaningful response.

Toward the Dialogic Alternative

MacIntyre's and Frederick's basic logic can be followed in another direction, however. The normative core pursued may not be *substantive, internalized values* held by a society, but rather *moral discursive procedures* already practiced in the community. This concept is more fully developed in works of critical theorists such as Habermas (especially, 1979, 1984) and Apel (1979). Moral procedural guidance for decision making is found in the immanent conditions of communicative action. Rather than ethics being biologically or psychologically grounded in the person or sociologically grounded in the tradition or community, ethics can be grounded in the communicative micropractices of everyday life. Since such a position requires a number of conceptual moves in the theory of communication and is easily misunderstood, we will provide some detail here.

Essentially we wish to ground business ethics in communication ethics. To do so we will begin with a brief review of the account of communication given in German hermeneutic and critical theory. We will then argue that despite the productivity of this approach as a point of departure, the work remains overly rational, idealistic, and ethnocentric. We will then turn to correctives offered by writers on feminist ethics. Using these reframed models we will combine them with a reformed stakeholder model of commercial organization to show how it could work in practice.

The Critique of Strategic Communication. Gadamer (1975) and Habermas (1984, 1987) have shown how strategic use of communication depends on a more basic communicative attempt to reach mutual understanding. While their conceptions differ regarding the nature of the process, they both emphasize the continual social formation of consensus in interaction beyond the intentions and opinions of the participants. Mutual understanding focuses attention on reaching openly formed agreement regarding the subject matter under discussion, rather than on the agreement of the perspective of the participants (see Deetz, 1990a). Habermas (1984) presented his position as follows:

> Processes of reaching understanding aim at an agreement that meets the conditions of rationally motivated assent [*Zustimmung*] to the content of an utterance. A communicatively achieved agreement has a rational basis; it cannot be imposed by either party, whether instrumentally through intervention in the situation directly or strategically. . . . This is not a question of the predicates an observer uses when describing processes of reaching understanding, but of the pretheoretical knowledge of competent speakers, who can themselves distinguish situations in which they are causally exerting an influence *upon* others from those where they are coming to an understanding *with* them. . . . [T]he use of language with an

orientation to reaching understanding is the *original mode* of language use, upon which indirect understanding, giving something to understand or letting something be understood, and the instrumental use of language in general, are parasitic (pp. 286-288).

An analysis of the attempt to reach mutual understanding includes a socially based description of morally guided dispute resolution and a description of communicative difficulties, (i.e., communicative processes which preclude mutual understanding). From a participation perspective, based in the pursuit of mutual understanding, communication difficulties arise from communication practices which preclude value debate and conflict, which substitute images and imaginary relations for self presentation and truth claims, which arbitrarily limit access to communication channels and forums, and which then lead to decisions based on arbitrary authority relations. Let us start by developing a conception of participation as a normative standard against which all communicational practices can be judged and consider objections to the primacy of this standard.

The support for participation as a normative ground is based on the presumption or anticipation of some ideal communication situation by each real communication community. It is internal to everyday communication (even though implicit and only partly realized) rather than external to it. The anticipation of the ideal community has been demonstrated in two ways. First, Gadamer (1975) in developing an ontology of understanding demonstrated the social character of the formation of experience which precedes each and every expression of it-the hermeneutic situation. Second, Habermas (1979, 1984) and Apel (1979) have shown that the illocutionary structure in discourse demonstrates the types of claims presumed as possible in a society and, thus, anticipates the forms of support and dispute in contested claims. In both cases the "hermeneutic" and "ideal speech" situation are counterfactual-that is, rarely fully realized-but each is a necessary anticipation even when violated.

Conversation and Mutual Understanding. Gadamer (1975) offers much to the development of the concept of participative meaning and interaction as productive in his ontological analysis of understanding. The full significance of his position requires a careful development of a hermeneutic description of language (see also Deetz, 1990). Central to his theory of language and implicit normative ideal is his description of the "genuine conversation." The genuine conversation is hermeneutically shown to be a special interaction among two persons and the subject matter before them. While most communication studies turn to consider what each person has to say about the subject matter, Gadamer focuses on what the subject matter "says" to each. In other words, the imaginary self and world produced in discourse is challenged by the excess of that which the discourse is about over the description of it. The communication question concerns how interaction is to proceed so that this excess is "remembered" or can make its claim.

In Gadamer's analysis the significance of conversation rests more in what it demands of us than in our capacity to say what we think. Conversation with a genuine other-someone culturally and experientially different-demands from us thoughts, feelings, the formation of concepts and evaluative criteria which do not precede its presence; it questions the adequacy of what we think and say. If a person wishes to bring an experience of the world to another, it is not his or her own feelings and concepts which are at issue. For these feelings and concepts are inevitably less than the possibilities in the world being experienced. The point of interaction is to help each person remove limitations to their own seeing so that the world may draw more thoroughly on them. Ideally other participants will help reveal aspects of the world which enrich one's own experience. The conversation has the character of progressively opening up the question of prejudicial certainty and the impelled imaginary self-directed experience. Such a discussion disrupts the totalizing character of experiences.

This productive, rather than reproductive, conception of communication shows the fundamental process by which mutual understanding arises in regard to the subject matter rather than in the sharing of opinions. Gadamer (1975) argued that the ideal is not "self expression and the successful assertion of one's point of view, but a transformation into communion, in which we do not remain what we were" (p. 341). While the dialectic of the genuine conversation requires a certain commonality of prior understanding, it works more to create and recreate a common language and experience as the tensions of difference question the adequacy of current understandings. More than sharing one's experience or point of view, it is the "art of seeing things in the unity of an aspect, i.e., it is the art of the formation of concepts as the working out of common meaning" (Gadamer, 1975, p. 331). It is not the insides of the other or the self that is to be understood for either would be covering up the objective demand of the subject matter with one's subjective reaction.

In this brief description it becomes clearer why a "successful" presentation of one's own meaning can limit rather than aid productive communication. To the extent that the object or other is silenced by the success, the capacity to engage in the reclaiming of difference and conceptual expansion to reach a more open consensus on the subject matter is limited. The "otherness" of the other and of the subject matter before us shows the one-sidedness and suppressed conflict in current perceptions, and forces a surrender of them to the development of consensual thought as a new momentary resting place. The fundamental indeterminacy of the subject matter itself feeds the progressive differentiation and development of experience, but must be conversationally recovered against self-directed perception. Levinas (1969) presented the understanding poetically: "The presence of the Other is equivalent to calling into question my joyous possession of the world" (p. 75). This loss and growth are critical to human social conduct. The culturally different is thus essential for productive communication rather than a problem for communication to overcome.

As an ontology of understanding, Gadamer is claiming the genuine conversation as the fundamental way all understanding happens. All reproductions rest on this fundamental production. Conversation is the ongoing process of creating mutual understanding through the open formation of experience. The communicative act should be responsive to the subject matter of the conversation and at the same time help establish the conditions for future unrestrained formation of experience. Such normatively based interaction is not willed or chosen by the individual; nor does it conform to some predefined or routine social practice. Rather, in its natural state the will is produced out of the demand of the subject matter in interaction.

Even if we wholeheartedly endorse Gadamer's description of the social development of human understanding, and even if we raise his characterization of genuine conversation to a normative ideal for all communicative interaction, we come up short of an adequate view of communication. While it is possible to participate in genuine conversations, such opportunities are relatively rare because of the limitations daily life imposes both on ourselves and others. Rarely is an experience so powerful that the disciplines, routines of life and ordinary ways of seeing are spontaneously overcome. And where are the experiences to come from which escape routinization and normalcy? There are real power relationships, manifested as institutional arrangements and structures of permissible discourse that preclude otherness and block conversation. Our shared history carries unexamined beliefs and attitudes which maintain preference for the expression of certain views of reality and of certain social groups. Under such conditions, genuine conversation cannot take place because there is no "other;" there is no means or forum for "otherness" to be expressed. We gain much from Gadamer's analysis of how new understanding is possible and how we can become open to the claims of the subject matter, but how do we construct situations where this is more likely? While Gadamer recovers dialectics and understanding from modern epistemological domination, he has no politics. Such a politics requires a more complete analysis of actual communication processes.

Discourse and Dispute Resolution. In what has been described as a hermeneutics of suspicion, Habermas took head on the issues Gadamer left aside. Since systems of domination usually preclude the genuine conversation, what is the nature of interaction where a new consensus does not emerge out of the interaction? What is the nature of the interaction by which competing claims can be resolved? In regard to the subject at hand, how can one distinguish consensus reached knowingly from that which is reached unknowingly or produced by authority or relations of power? Because of the capacity of Habermas's position to consider normative issues in the context of power and asymmetry, much like those in business organizations, his work has been used a great deal in organizational analysis (for review see Deetz, 1992; Alvesson & Deetz, 1996).

Basically, Habermas argued that every speech act can function in communication by virtue of common presumptions made by speaker and listener. Even when these presumptions are not fulfilled in an actual situation, they serve as a base of appeal as failed conversation turns to argumentation regarding the disputed validity claims. The basic presumptions and validity claims arise out of four shared domains of reality: the external world, human relations, the individual's internal world, and language. The claims raised in each are respectively: truth, correctness, sincerity, and intelligibility. Thus, we can claim that each competent, communicative act represents facts, establishes legitimate social relations, discloses the speaker's point of view, and is understandable. Any claim that cannot be brought to open dispute serves as the basis for systematically distorted communication. The ideal speech situation must be recovered to avoid or overcome such distortions. It should be clear that this conception applies not only to the everyday and ordinary acts of communication but also models the ideal processes by which collective decisions can be made. They can be used in this sense as a guide to defining institutions and practices which advance participation and democracy. Participation modeled in this way is central to our moral responsibility to decide what our society will be and what kind of people we will become. Such principles should be central to corporate design and human interaction within them (see Knights & Willmott, 1985). Four basic guiding conditions are necessary for free and open participation in the resolution of claims.

First, the attempt to reach understanding presupposes a symmetrical distribution of the chances to choose and to apply speech acts. This would specify the minimal conditions of skills and opportunities for expression including access to meaningful forums and channels of communication. When we extend these to a consideration of communication technologies, the initial focus needs to be on equal access, distribution of training opportunities, and development of technologies which can be used to express a full variety of human experiences. Such a principle argues against privileged expression forms and routines and rules which advantage certain experiences, identities, and expressions.

Second, the understanding and representation of the external world needs to be freed from privileged preconceptions in the social development of "truth." Ideally, participants have the opportunity to express interpretations and explanations with conflicts which are resolved in reciprocal claims and counter-claims without privileging particular epistemologies or forms of data. The freedom from preconception implies an examination of ideologies that would privilege one form of discourse, disqualify certain possible participants, and universalize any particular sectional interest. Communication technologies need to be examined with regard to how they function ideologically to privilege certain perceptions and forms of data and to obscure historical processes.

Third, participants need to have the opportunity to establish legitimate social relations and norms for conduct and interaction. The rights and responsibilities of people are not given in advance by nature nor by a privileged, universal value structure, but are negotiated through interaction. The reification of organizational structures and their maintenance without possible dispute and the presence of managerial prerogatives are examples of potential immorality in corporate discourse. Acceptance of views because of an individual's privilege or authority or because of the nature of the medium represents a possible illegitimate relation. Authority itself is legitimate only if redeemable by appeal to an open interactional formation of relations freed from the appeal to other authorities. Values and norms legitimately exist in society by the achievement of rational consensus. This consensus is subject to appeals and warrants supporting the assumed social relations. To the extent that particular technologies embody values, hide authority relations, or reify social relations, they participate in domination.

Finally, interactants need to be able to express their own authentic interests, needs, and feelings. This would require freedom from various coercive and hegemonic processes by which the individual is unable to form experience openly, to develop and to sustain competing identities, or to form expressions presenting them. Certain communication technology and structure can produce particular imagistic relations and establish a type of distance that denies the formation of "otherness" and the interrogation of self. In this sense they function immorally. The examination of technology in its structuring of the interior would be important to understanding its effect on the accomplishment of such an ideal.

The more serious violations of these principles are the invisible constraints to richer understanding. Here strategy and manipulation are disguised and control is exercised through manipulations of the natural, neutral and self-evident. In a general way, these can be described as "discursive closure" and "systematically distorted communication." Both concepts become central when we turn to look at the processes of domination in modern corporations and consider alternative communicative practices.

Following Apel (1979), a twofold foundation for ethical communication principles can thus be advanced:

> First, in all actions and omissions, it should be a matter of ensuring the *survival* of the human species *qua real* communication community. Second, it should be a matter of realizing the *ideal* communication community in the real one. The first goal is the necessary condition for the second; and the second goal provides the first with meaning. . . . [T]he task of realizing the ideal communication community [aims at] the elimination of all socially determined asymmetries of interpersonal dialogue (pp. 282-283).

The key issues for us here rest in the relation of the real and ideal communication community, and the nature of socially determined asymmetries. The significance of the ideal communication community rests in pre-acceptance by each interactant when engaging in communication. The argument here is not simply that we should believe in and try to create the ideal. Rather each and every interaction assumes the ideal as a background for each communicative act performed. Even the most strategic act of self-interested expression takes place in a language community where presumptions of reciprocity and symmetry exist.

The preferred hope is for more open participation and the evolution of more representative and responsive institutions. This is a change from seeing the individual as more or less effective to seeing the interaction as more or less productive-that is, the interaction is productive in the service of further understanding and agreement on the subject matter being determined by the nature of the subject matter itself (Deetz, 1990). The change is from seeing what the individual's point of view is and how it is presented, to determining whether the interaction includes all relevant positions and interests. Interaction cannot be effective in terms of social efficacy without representing the various interests, whether intentionally represented by the participants or not (Habermas, 1979).

The most frequent objection to Habermas is that he has overemphasized reason, particularly self-reflection and "mental" activities, and has only a negative view of power which hampers both the conception of social change and seeing the possible positivity of power. What Habermas does well is to give an arguable standard for normative guidance to communication as a critique of domination, even if his position is distinctly Western and intellectual. While both Habermas and Gadamer have been criticized as focusing too much on consensus at the expense of conflict and dissensus, the participatory issues do not depend on this nor the simple critique of false consensus. Lyotard (1984) has perhaps been the most suspicious of the consensus orientation found in Habermas. Essentially he argued that the language of consent is outmoded and incapable of doing justice to the full variety of experience and expression. However, he struggled to find his own moral ground for guidance. Implicit in Lyotard's as well as Gadamer's and Habermas' analyses is the recovery of conflict as an essential precursor to a new consensus and the perpetual critique of each new consensus as interaction continues. As shown in the feminist reformation, Habermas' description can be transformed from a faith in rational consensus to partial guidance on how conflicting knowledge claims, including those of the body itself, can be expressed to recover conflict from closure.

Following Apel (1979) and Habermas (1979), "ethics is really a form of socially produced practical knowledge, and discussion of ethics is as necessary and potentially as productive as discussion of any other knowledge claim" (Deetz, 1985, p. 254). If privatization and "emotivism" could be overcome, values and ethics could reenter the public discussion arena. Critical theorists have been useful partly because their analysis of the rise of instrumental reasoning was complete and persuasive, but perhaps more importantly, because they identified the key problem as the nature of the discussion itself rather than the participants. Universalist and communitarians like MacIntyre hold a grossly untheorized conception of discussion and dialogue. Thus, talk is treated as surprisingly unproblematic.

But the problem with the communitarian position is not only the weak dialogue mechanisms but the consensual goals they shared with the critical theorists. The solution to homelessness, insecurity, and self-interest may not rest in claiming the possibility for more rational foundations and social consensus. It may well rest in the acceptance of the loss of community and foundations and in being forced to use the freedom to seek more satisfying ways of living together (see Giddens, 1991). We do not need more integrative narratives. We need better discussions. Security may come more from finding ways to make decisions together than in recovery of a unified/solid identity. Opportunism may be constrained by better negotiations rather than by community principles. Lyotard (1984) and others may well be right. The faith in consensus (both the need for and possibility of), even in the procedurally guided sense of Habermas, perpetuates the problems it hopes to eradicate. The feminists have simply been much better in understanding both the interconnectedness of people and the situated nature of power and discourse. The avoidance of universalizing substantive or procedural claims and yet advancing a communication based ethics overcomes many of the weaknesses identified.

Feminist Dialogic Ethics

Jaggar (1989) defined feminist ethics as "a commitment to rethinking ethics with a view to correcting male bias" (p. 91; cited in Hekman, 1995, p. 62). Many feminists debate over whether or not ethics is a feminist issue at all since it has traditionally been theorized from a masculine, universalist, disembodied subject perspective. Frye (1991) argued that if ethics is defined as "getting it right" in moral theory, then feminists do not need ethics at all (cited in Hekman, 1995, p. 63). In addition, Walker (1989) vehemently states that feminists should define ethics as "connected human beings searching for shareable interpretations of responsibility" (p. 20; cited in Hekman, 1995, p. 63).

Gilligan's (1982) and Noddings' (1984) views of women's ethics of caring, have been attacked for essentializing women's morality development and, on the other hand, praised for celebrating a feminine form of ethics. Yet, Gilligan's *In a Different Voice* has inspired debate that still rages on in feminist texts. The multiple feminist camps each posit their own views of feminist ethics-some being more practical than others. Daly's (1990) radical feminist "metaethics" perspective links the global domination of women with the domination and exploitation of the earth in her take on ecofeminism. In her *Gyn/Ecology*, Daly (1990) describes the silencing of women throughout the world with detailed accounts of the violence against women throughout history and into the present (African genital mutilation, Indian dowry murders and suttee, Chinese footbinding, sixteenth and seventeenth century witch hunts, murder of female infants in Asia, rape, murder, etc.). However, her separatist solution of lesbian colonies to escape the domination of the patriarchy offers no escape for heterosexual women. Yet, her position informs and influences feminist resistance to patriarchal discourse. Other developments within feminist theorizing constitute ethics/morality as a relational phenomenon (Hekman, 1995), a voluntary communitarian prospect (Friedman, 1989a, b; cited in

Hekman, 1995), and as a respect and responsibility-oriented process of intersubjectivity between self and other (Benhabib, 1992).

The Relational Self. According to Hekman (1995), Gilligan's latter works take on a "coherentist, Kuhnian interpretation" (p. 31). Hekman states that a change in moral beliefs is a change in world view and is thus a paradigmatic change, and posits that Gilligan has revolutionized moral development theory with her concept of the relational self. Gilligan's research findings that women make moral decisions by discussing the moral dilemma with friends and family is an epistemology that replaces Kohlberg's "disembodied" self with a relational self. Gilligan hears "moral voices speaking from the lives of connected, situated selves, not the single truth of disembodied moral principles" (Hekman, 1995, p. 30).

Similarly McNay (1992) argues that ethics cannot be grounded in "a categorical imperative or in a respect for an abstract moral law" because feminist ethics is grounded in a "responsiveness to others and a respect for the particular [concrete] which leads to moral concerns connected to providing care, preventing harm and maintaining relationships" (p. 92). Many feminists base their notion of feminist ethics on Chodorow's (1978) theory of mothering, in which a relational self emerges in the early years through a child's interaction with a primary parent, usually the mother. This relational self is a key part of feminist discourse because of the connectedness and intersubjectivity within human interaction. Benhabib's view of the "situated self" is especially useful in working toward dialogic ethics in international business.

Habermas's Discourse and Benhabib's Situated Self. Habermas' ideal speech community assumes that all participants are considered to be equal. However, as illustrated by Benhabib (1992), Habermas' theory of communicative ethics breaks down with the reality of gendered and racial inequities. Habermas' ideal speech community and intersubjective communication can be developed in ways that foster the dialogic process in such contexts. Benhabib (1992) takes the domination and oppression of women and people of color into consideration when she posits a feminist, updated version of Habermas' ideal speech community. Habermas' theory is supposedly gender-neutral, but it assumes a political equality for everyone. That is simply not the case. Women, children and minorities (whether ethnic, gay, or lesbian others) are not treated with equal status in society, nor do they receive equal pay for equal work. And examples of discrimination, among both internal and external organizational communities, abound.

Benhabib (1992) criticizes Habermas in her discussion of the exclusion of women and their point of view as not only a "political omission and a moral blind spot but [it] constitutes an epistemological deficit as well" (p. 13). She sets out to improve upon Habermas' theory in a way that "both accommodate[s] feminist criticisms and also help[s] feminists in our own thinking about alternative public spheres" (pp. 13-14). Thus, Benhabib (1992) opens up the negotiative dialogue to the marginalized voices of others.

In the shadow of corporate exploitation and commercialization of women as objects across the globe, Benhabib (1992) extends the dialogue on this problem. In her discussion of the standpoint of the generalized other and of the concrete other in her critical approach to Habermas' universalism, Benhabib (1992) locates the ethical self on a continuum between rationality and communitarianism. She takes the situated critical approach to ethics, which is similar ideologically to Feminist Standpoint Epistemology (see Harding, 1991; Hartsock, 1983; Wood, 1992).

According to Benhabib (1990), the communicative ethicist asks not what the individual as a rational moral agent intends, but rather asks "what principles of action can we all recognize or agree to as being valid if we engage in practical discourse or a mutual search for justification" (p. 336). It is this practical discourse or mutual search for justification that lends itself to developing dialogic ethics. Benhabib (1990) states that with this reformulation universalizability can be defined as "an intersubjective procedure of argumentation, geared to attain communicative agreement" (p. 336). By reformulating Habermas' theory of discourse ethics, Benhabib turns universalizability from a "test of *noncontradiction*" into "a test of *communicative agreement*" (p. 336). Thus, she posits:

> We do not search for what would be nonself-contradictory but rather for what would be mutually acceptable for all. Furthermore, there is also a shift from the model of the goal-oriented or strategic action of a single agent intending a specific outcome to the model of *communicative action* which is speech and action to be shared with others (Benhabib, 1990, pp. 336-337).

In *Situating the Self*, Benhabib (1992) breaks down her concept of discourse ethics into simplistic terms: "we engage in communication, theoretical no less than everyday communication, to gain some basis of mutual understanding and reasoning" (1992, p. 216). She expresses an ideal of persons interacting with one another "through reciprocal recognition of subjectivities as a particular standpoint of moral autonomy" (Young, 1990; p. 308). Young (1990) suggests that Benhabib's standpoint of the generalized other "abstracts from the difference, desires and feeling among persons, to regard all as sharing a common set of formal rights and duties" (p. 309).

Benhabib's concept of the standpoint of the concrete other focuses on a person's "concrete individuality" (in Young, 1990, p. 309). Benhabib states:

> In assuming this standpoint, we abstract from what continues our commonality and seek to understand the other as he/she understands himself/herself. We seek to comprehend the needs of the other, their motivations, what they search for and what they desire. Our relation to the other is governed by the norm of *complementary reciprocity:* each is entitled to expect and assume from the other forms of behavior through which the other feels recognized and confirmed as a concrete, individual being with specific needs, talents and capacities. Our differences in this case complement rather than exclude one another (Benhabib, 1982; cited in Young, 1990, p. 309).

Thus, Benhabib's standpoint of the concrete other expresses community as the mutual understanding of each other that individuals achieve during interaction. Whereas the standpoint of the concrete other stresses individuality and one's relationship with the other "is governed by the norms of *equity* and *complementary reciprocity,*" the generalized other is "governed by the norms of *formal equality* and *reciprocity*" (Benhabib, 1992; p. 159). The standpoint of the generalized other is a universal commitment that every human being is worthy of universal moral respect. Although Benhabib (1992) states that the concepts of the generalized other and the concrete other are viewed as incompatible, as dichotomies, in contemporary moral theory, she sees the two as being spaced on a continuum within which the self is situated. And it is through moral dialogue that the situated self achieves a mutual understanding of the other.

Benhabib (1992) argues that only a moral dialogue "that is truly open and reflexive and that does not function with unnecessary epistemic limitations can lead to a mutual understanding of otherness" (p. 168). She continues to say that nothing can be known about the concrete other, "[n]either the concreteness nor the otherness" (p. 168) without opening the dialogue to the voice of the other. Thus, when we apply this concept to international business ethics, we see the need for the other, the marginalized voices within corporate communities, as well as international business communities and customer communities, to be able to participate in the moral dialogue.

Within the moral dialogue, marginalized voices can find a space to participate and the emergence of a shared understanding between self and concrete others can occur. Ideally, in this moral dialogue, corporate decision makers have a space to take all voices into consideration during the decision-making process. Thus, both internal and external community members will be given a chance to express their concerns-from the perspective of their own experiences. Greater mutual understanding of all parties' concrete otherness can then give rise to ethical decisions and a greater sense of corporate social responsibility. With more unlimited epistemological information available (including differing opinions stemming from different experiences), negotiation can potentially lead to greater understanding and a greater capacity for ethical decisions beneficial to all parties.

In addition, Benhabib (1987) discusses Gilligan's concept of moral maturity. When the self recognizes its construction within a network of relationships, moral deficiency evolves into moral maturity (Benhabib, 1987). Just as Walker (1989) defined ethics as "connected human beings searching for shareable interpretations of responsibility" (p. 20; cited in Hekman, 1995, p. 63), moral maturity stems from a relational self, constructed in a web of relationships with concrete others. Thus, moral maturity occurs during interaction between self and other-the construction of the relational self.

We believe these concepts of relatedness and moral maturity also can be applied to the development of a dialogic ethics in international business. Relatedness, or a sense of community, gives organizational decision makers a greater connection to both internal and external constituencies-multicultural organizational members, members of the town or city in which the organization is located, and a multicultural international work force. This connection can lead to an understanding of the concrete other's otherness through the dialogic process. With such an understanding of the other, exploitation is more difficult, and the potential for social responsibility is greater.

A Dialogic Stakeholder Model

Dialogic ethics has much to offer ethical discussions in general and in business ethics in particular. The development of a dialogic conception has certainly enriched communication theory. Still such conceptions remain relatively abstract and it is difficult to see how such communicative practices could be sustained within the structure of current commercial organizations. Their application becomes far clearer and more plausible by moving from an *owner/manager* to *stakeholder* model of organizations.

Freeman has provided the most widely discussed stakeholder theory or "constituency theory" (Freeman, 1984; Bruono & Nichols, 1990). This theory suggests that corporations are stewards or servants to the larger society. For Freeman (1984) the larger community to which the organization is wedded is defined in terms of two levels of stakeholders: those identifiable groups or individuals upon which the organization relies for survival, such as stockholders, employees, and customers, and those more generally classed groups or individuals who can affect or are affected by organizational policies and work practices. It is out of this web or network of relationships that the corporation establishes with the larger community, Freeman and Liedtka (1991) suggest, that these diverse groups have a "stake" in the corporation. Ethical conduct is, therefore, "obligatory and expected for maintenance of the relationships between the organizations and its constituents"(Freeman & Liedtka, 1991, p. 94).

This ethical conduct and maintenance of the organizations' relationships with the community, Freeman (1984) suggested, are accomplished through conversation. In this way of approaching organizational research, the organization is conceptualized as part of the community, not separate from it. Thus, when making organizational decisions, Freeman (1984) suggested that the values and ethical standards of the community should be both represented and considered. Economic information regarding the state of the marketplace is not sufficient when making organizational decisions that undoubtedly will affect the community. Thus, emotions, bodily processes and pleasures, factors which are individually based, and in part communally shaped, which are often thought to be outside of the organization, privatized, and limiting to rational decision making, become important concerns. As such, these factors which are marginalized in rational actor models, play a more central and critical role in stakeholder-based approaches to organizational ethics.

In addition to the aforementioned marginalized factors, many groups find themselves marginalized and thus, silenced within the commercial organizational site. Thus, in light of their public effects, corporations must be understood as complex political sites. The modern corporation has a variety of stakeholders, with competing interests within and between each of them needing to be resolved in internal decisions. Recognizing the existence of multiple stakeholders with competing legitimate interests suggests that corporate organizations are fundamentally political, rather than simply economic. The nature of the politics within corporate sites is increasingly significant as corporations have come to have powerful effects on social decision making. *Corporations could be positive social institutions providing a forum for the articulation and resolution of important social conflicts regarding the use of natural resources, the production of meaningful goods and services and the development of individuals.* However, these political processes are often closed, because a variety of practices exist which produce and privilege certain interests-principally managerial-in both public decision making and in the production of the type of person that exists in modern organizations and society.

Traditionally, stakeholders were considered external to the company and management groups strategically attempted to control them for the sake of "company" (though most often managerial) objectives. The standard approach of management is based on narrow values and strategic control processes. The key element of transformation is for management to consider stakeholders as legitimate parts of the company. The management role then becomes the coordination of the various stakeholder needs and objectives. With a concept of service to all, "good" management attempts to generate creative decisions which meet what otherwise might appear to be incompatible objectives. Evidence supports this as a wise, as well as appropriate change. The presence of diverse goals, rather than creating costly conflicts and impasses, creates the conditions whereby limited decisional frames are broken and the company *learns*. In the process the faulty basis of recurring conflicts are exposed and synergistic energy is created. Management groups need to make economically based decisions which have positive influences on profitability. But corporations are not only economic-based institutions. And, importantly, taking seriously the multiple goals of stakeholders fosters creative decisions that can improve economic viability. If the variety of stakeholder interests were considered, alternative goals would serve as a competitive measure of organizations.

Following stakeholder consideration, as well as enlightened economic interests, many companies have developed *forums* where stakeholders could be represented, but most of these have been contrived in ways that reduce the actual value representation-they lack an opportunity for *voice*. In order to realize dialogic ideals, both forums and voice must be considered in assessing representation.

Inventing Forums for Discussion. In traditional analyses, social values entered into corporations' decisions in four ways: Through consumer value representation in purchasing choices, through governmental tax guidance and regulation, through managers' voluntary commitment to social values, and through investment choices of workers and capital holders in employment and stock purchases. As shown, each of these is a weak form of representation because of structural limitations and social changes (investors want short-terms payoffs, managers have removed themselves from community, etc.). None of these foster the type of social interaction that leads to innovative solutions to conflicting stakeholder values and objectives, but additional forums are developing. In many companies the opportunities for employee participation in decision making are much greater today. The customer focus of many companies provides contexts for direct consumer representation in ways that have been missing for some time. Many companies have partnering arrangements with suppliers and large customers, while the growth of communication and information technologies allow for more frequent, sustained, and interactive contact among groups.

These activities have made companies more ethical, but each of these have been limited in important ways. For example, employee involvement plans have been developed more to increase compliance, commitment and loyalty than to broaden value debate and to increase innovation. Most often the involvement is limited to application decisions and does not include representation in company-wide planning and social goal formation. Customer focus groups often function more to solicit information on tastes and pricing to aid sales than to determine what consumers really want. Rarely are social values solicited at all except, again, as they might affect sales. The new technologies are being developed in most cases to extend the corporate influence outwardly rather than to provide the public with better information upon which to make their decisions, or to enable the public to participate in corporate decision making. *Most representation forums are used by management to suppress or to diffuse conflict arising from stakeholder groups rather than to foster genuine conflict and debate for the sake of company improvement.* Still, with concerted effort these mechanisms can be transformed and utilized for quite different ends. A first step to increasing dialogic communication and stakeholder representation is the expansion of these means-especially by increasing voice.

Increasing Voice. The current problem is not only the lack of sufficient opportunity for stakeholder representation, but often the interaction itself is systematically distorted. This is referred to as a lack of voice. The stakeholder can speak but, owing to contrived and flawed understandings, the representation is skewed. There are several ways this happens. In general, a prior social construction (a kind of image) stands in the place of real people in a real situation. Such constructions contain embedded values which are not disclosed. Since the construction is treated as the reality, it is not open to negotiation nor are alternative value premises considered. Generally, attention is directed away from the embedded values to shared "neutral" ones. A lot of attention has been directed to how this happens to employees, especially in professional (knowledge-intensive) workplaces, but a similar analysis would follow for other stakeholders.

Here we can consider four types of social constructions regarding employees which can limit voice and thus can be considered to limit ethical processes. Each of these social constructions *could* be the result of open interaction, held temporarily and continuously revised in ongoing micro negotiations. They limit voice, however, when they become fixed and taken for granted, hence they are closed to negotiation. They violate the Habermasian ideal in specific situated ways. When a stakeholder either wittingly or unwittingly accepts these constructions we have what is called *consent*. Consent designates those cases when a stakeholder enacts values which are not his/her own in what often appear to be free acts of self-representation. The stakeholder demonstrates complicity in his or her own disregard by others. In various studies of knowledge-intensive professional service groups, consent processes were a routine and costly part of much of daily work. Each type of consent was common.

The first type of social construction involves the construction of the actors. In general, voice is reduced through the fixing of roles and the reduction of personal complexity. For example, the division of labor has largely created separate realms of knowing and expertise. The success of "teams" indicate some of the price paid for this separation in traditional bureaucracies, but self-managed teams at best have overcome only part of the difficulty. The loss of voice is often even more subtle and pervasive. People have multiple identities and conflicting needs. An individual has many identities and conflicting aspirations arising from identities such as being a parent, citizen, softball player, as well as an employee. Corporations tend to sequester these other identities or elicit their support on behalf of managerial objectives. Thus, if considerations arise for the employee as a parent or citizen, they are to be suppressed in favor of the employee identity. This suppression is not only costly to the individual but also steals from the company the richer set of values that might guide corporate practices. A wide range of forms of thinking, emotions, moral principles and values are thus set aside. The employee stakeholder in these cases speaks as a "partial" person reducing representation and value debate. Women especially, but also gradually more men, are beginning to gain voice and to enrich decision making through challenging such limited conceptions.

Second, despite the moves toward decentralization and attacks on bureaucracy, most companies still have rather fixed structures, especially when it comes to major decisions. Workplaces that have shared authority have shown impressive gains even using most standard productivity measures. The ability to continuously renegotiate authority relations, based on shifting needs and points of expertise, is critical in changing environments. Voice is always limited if discussion happens within rules and authority relations rather than being about them. If stakeholders are to be partners in meeting the needs of all, it cannot be a partnership of unequals. Compliance, consent and loss of voice are characteristic of all fixed social relations.

Third, voice requires that stakeholders are informed. In most cases the information available to stakeholders is manufactured by management groups and is both limited and skewed. Even if management does not intentionally distort stakeholders' understanding, most options and data reported are produced from the same limited set of values and assumptions that more generally drive management decision making. If stakeholders are to overcome managerial limitations, they must challenge the values embedded in company information and knowledge. If this is understood, communication is no longer seen as the transfer of information or decision making with information (the standard views in most companies). Communication must be about the processes by which information is produced. Measurement is an increasingly dominant part of modern management with the impact of TQM and the general development of what Michael Power called the audit society. The temptation is to let measurable outcomes substitute for important discussions where, for example, "quality" is reduced to "standard" rather than "good." Efficiency measurements cannot replace discussions of values regarding what is being measured and what is being produced efficiently.

Accounting theorists and groups working with social accounting principles are becoming much clearer about the values embedded in standard accounting practices. But all information is fundamentally value-laden. The choice of linguistic distinctions producing categories of people (e.g., secretaries and administrative assistants), the euphemism for what things are called (business expenses or indirect salaries), the forms that are used for reports (including what is collected and what is not, as well as the categorical divisions), and the creation of spurious casual relations, are only the more obvious aspects of information creation. When people use information, they consent to the values on which it is based and voice is usually lost if these are not their own values. Opening information production activities to stakeholder discussion is a critical element of overcoming consent and gaining voice. Widespread sharing of information is of little help if the activities of information construction are left closed and invisible.

Finally, voice is hampered by discussion that focuses on the means rather than the ends. Many modern organizations have developed a logic that emphasizes efficiency or effectiveness based on measurable indices. The means of goal attainment often become goals in themselves. People often are treated as mere means of goal attainment rather than ends themselves. Unfortunately, in doing so, the actual outcome goals become increasingly fixed and invisible. One becomes fixed on increasing performance measures without asking what is sought, its value or alternative ways of accomplishment. The company operates like people who treat earning more money as an end without asking whether they are actually getting what the money is meant to give them, or whether there are better ways of goal accomplishment that require less money. The processes of goal and indices creation in most companies is not an open process and does not represent well the full set of stakeholder goals. Furthermore, the debate over preferred means of goal attainment reduces the possibility of finding ways that the goals of various groups can be attained simultaneously.

Thus voice is hampered through reduction of personal complexity, frozen social orders, contrived knowledge, reduction of value debate through "neutral" efficiency and performativity standards (including TQM standards). Much of what is considered stable is the result of social constructions; constructions accomplished under conditions of unequal power.

In order to overcome consent and to foster productive mutual decisions, we must change the way we think about human communication. A dialogic view of communication must replace the expressionist/information/adversarial view that dominates contemporary society. Influence centered, informational views of communication which focus on meaning transmission as if meanings were value neutral, must be replaced with views which attend to participation process in the formation of social meanings. In developing a dialogic practice, choices within politically defined contexts with fixed decisional alternatives need to be shifted to focus concern on the constitution of political contexts and other viable alternatives. Concern with effective use of language has to be changed to questions of whose language it is, its social/historical partialities, and a means of reclaiming alternative voices. Since corporate decisions are inevitably value-laden, they impact on what we will become as people and what kind of world we will live in. Thus, communication cannot be evaluated in effectiveness terms but rather appeals to moral criteria to grant all positions an equal right of codetermination. To achieve this, we need to first focus on the rights of decision makers to know over the rights of speakers to speak. The founders of American democracy thought they had accomplished this with the concept of freedom of speech, but they could not have anticipated the extent of the inequality of access to speaking forums and the difference in megaphone size. Also, of equal importance, their human rights philosophies were too primitive to understand the politics of experience and constraints on voice.

Freedom of expression is essential because good decision making requires that all relevant perspectives should be known by all. Unfortunately, in complex environments, like corporations, systems based on control do not assure that all perspectives are known. Freedom of expression is meaningless if there is no one to represent relevant positions or if the one with the biggest megaphone can drown out the chorus of free voices. However, the problem goes even deeper. Present organizational (as well as state and political) processes do not foster the development of all relevant positions. Freedom of expression neither specifies the right of being heard nor does it guarantee the expression of all positions. A form of "group-think" is a property of all modern systems even with freedom of expression. The desire for representation requires the building of processes that develops alternative perspectives, fosters their expression, and gives them an equal opportunity to influence decisions. The restrictions control systems place on representation may be direct-through freedom limitation or coercion-but are often unobtrusive and subtle through consent. Therefore, the process of representative decision making requires a means of overcoming these many restrictions.

Recreating Corporate Discussion. Creating corporations that are economically and socially sound begins with a mutual commitment to the whole, to the entire set of stakeholders. Self-interest pursuits, whether expressed in the name of profits, particular stakeholders or one's own strategic advantage, work against any genuine attempt at communication or productive joint decision making. To the extent that managers or any stakeholder can personally internalize the needs of others, they grow, they free themselves from routines and habitual positions, and they begin to reclaim suppressed needs and conflicts. Having conflicting needs and goals is a reality of being human at the individual and organizational levels. The answer to this condition lies in creative efforts to meet all needs rather than in preferencing some and suppressing others. Both the research on and practice of conflict negotiation have led to the same conclusion. If we focus on the many relevant goals rather than on our one, preferred means of obtaining them, then we have more creative options and conflicts can be solved more productively. This commitment to everyone's goals implies a risk, a risk for managers and all other stakeholders. To give up habitual and preferred ways of self-interest fulfillment is a leap of faith, but one that offers endless potential.

CONCLUSION

The international business situation poses unique and complex issues of ethics and responsibility. Rational and communitarian theoretical models of organizational ethics share a similar weakness in terms of the participation and representation of stakeholders in the decision-making process. Individualistic, rational models clearly place the power of ethical decision making within the reach of only a few organizational actors, thereby encouraging no efforts to represent the diverse ethics and values of community stakeholders at large. On the other hand, communitarian models emphasize collective participation in ethical and moral decision making in organizations, but they fail to provide a mechanism by which all of these voices in a community (including those which are marginalized) can be heard. Thus, in the end, communitarian models recognize the moral and ethical limits of rational actor models but are ill-equipped, both theoretically and practically, to provide representation to the diverse moral and ethical voices of community stakeholders. Communitarian models, by failing to provide a mechanism by which a universal, participatory ethical system can be created, fail to address concerns related to socially responsible decision making. This model is not equipped to offer power or privilege to those voices which are marginalized nor to those marginalized values, such as emotions, which organizations privatize.

Given the complexities of intercultural communication and building a world community, we suggest that a dialogic approach to organizational ethics is a more productive direction. Like communitarian approaches, our dialogic response would aim to recover those things that are feared by and excluded from rational actor models-emotions, the body, the feminine and pleasure. In so doing, conflict, argument and debate would not be avoided but would be embraced, for it is in conflict that we can begin to see a potential ethical path that may otherwise be hidden by our everyday routines and "taken-for-granted" ways of understanding the world. This framework suggests that ethics does not rest in agreement or consensus but in the avoidance of the suppression of alternative conceptions and possibilities.

Our challenge is the human hope for order rather than disorder, wrong order or opportunistic use of declining orders. We fear the future, hence, we hope to secure it today. Such fears are not overcome by control and holding on to traditional models, but by making edifying decisions together. We do not need to go back to the past for recovery of lost parts of self and a whole person; we must, instead, go forward to the selves hidden in each moment of opportunity and realize that the irreducible conflicts between our many legitimate selves are not different from the conflict with diverse others. Such conflicts show the potential in situations hidden in our routines. Creativity in response to the conflicts, rather than prior consensus, offer innovative, mutually satisfying, if temporary, arrangements. Ethics based on a dialogic model rest not on agreements to principles, but on avoidance of the suppression of alternative conceptions and new possibilities emerging in discourse. Discursive closures of different types need to be avoided. The central issue is not that merely people are treated as means rather than ends, but that all meaningful human ends-and all people's ends-are not given a place in decision-making processes.

The stakeholder model of corporations, suggested here, if it is complemented by adequate conceptions of communication and micro-practices of negotiation can lead to ethical daily practices in both national and international business organizations (see Deetz, 1995a). Many have already become part of similar approaches (e.g., Calás & Smircich, 1991, 1992; Martin, 1990, 1994; Linstead, 1993). The basic question shared by all of us is: How do we, together, create mutually satisfying worlds that are not yet known? The heterogeniety of the international community and the creative possibilities residing in intercultural communication provide possibilities that may have been overlooked in national cultures. Our current situation shows that we are both fundamentally different and interdependent.

Certainly such normative ideals confront contemporary organizations which have developed a discursive community where values are already inculcated into managerial decisions. These values-efficiency, performativity and effectiveness-shape today's organizational systems and in so doing limit the thinkable agency; the ability to redefine and to solve organizational issues creatively (Jackell, 1988; Burawoy, 1985; Knights & Willmott, 1989; Willmott, 1994; Deetz, 1995a, in press, have developed this idea in depth). Possibly, the discourse of organizations is so deeply entrenched in and limited to one particular way of seeing the world which is morally and ethically impoverished, that change from within such a weak discourse is virtually impossible (Benhabib, 1990). Simply put, members of organizations cannot envision ways of conceptualizing and addressing problems that are different from those of their existing organizational culture-a culture which, we have suggested, values and thus places an emphasis on economic efficiency with little regard for the impact that attaining such goals may have on the life of the community. If power is not equally distributed among various stakeholders and the voices of these groups are not heard, will the situated responses arrived at through this discourse reflect the interests of anyone other than those currently in powerful positions (i.e. organizational decision makers)? Still, the dialogic model offers our best hope, a hope guided by a model for action. At the end of our contemplations we cannot offer assurances, but we know better where to start as we strive to build the future.

REFERENCES

Alvesson, M. (1987). *Organization theory and technocratic consciousness: Rationality, ideology, and quality of work.* New York: de Gruyter.

Alvesson, M., & Deetz, S. (1996). Critical theory and postmodernism approaches to organization studies. In S. Clegg, C. Harding & W. Nord (Eds.), *The handbook of organization studies. (pp. 191-217).* London: Sage.

Apel, K.-O. (1979). *Toward a transformation of philosophy.* (G. Adey and D. Frisby, Trans.). London: Routledge & Kegan Paul.

Benhabib, S. (1990). Afterward: Communicative ethics and current controversies in practical philosophy. In S. Benhabib & F. Dallmayr (Eds.), *The communicative ethics controversy.* (pp. 330-370). Cambridge: MIT Press.

Benhabib, S. (1992). *Situating the self: Gender, community and postmodernism in contemporary ethics.* New York: Routledge.

Bruono, A.F., & Nichols, L.T. (1990). Stock-holder and stakeholder interpretations of business's social role. In W. M. Hoffman & J. M. Moore (Eds.), *Business ethics: Readings and cases in corporate morality* (pp. 170-175). New York: McGraw Hill Publishing Co.

Burawoy, M. (1985). *The politics of production: Factory regimes under capitalism and socialism.* London: Verso.

Buchholz, R.A. (1991). Corporate responsibility and the good society: From economics to ecology. *Business Horizons, 34*(4), 19.

Bullis, C. (1993). Organizational values and control. In C. Conrad (Ed.), *Ethical nexus* (pp. 75-102). Norwood, NJ: Ablex Publishing Corporation.

Calás, M., & Smircich, L. (1991). Voicing seduction to silence leadership. *Organization Studies, 12,* 567.

Calás, M., & Smircich, L. (1992). Re-writing gender into organizational theorizing: Directions from feminist perspectives. In M. Reed & M. Hughes (Eds.). *Re-thinking organization: New directions in organizational theory and analysis.* (pp. 227-253). London: Sage Publications.

Cameron, K., & Whetten, D. (Eds.). (1983). *Organizational effectiveness: A comparison of multiple models.* New York: Academic Press.

Carter, P., & Jackson, N. (1987). Management, myth, and metatheory-from scarcity to post scarcity. *International Studies of Management and Organizations, 17,* 64.

Chodorow, N. (1978). *The reproduction of mothering.* Berkeley: University of California Press.

Conrad, C. (1993). The ethical nexus: Conceptual grounding. In C. Conrad (Ed.), *Ethical nexus* (pp. 7-22). Norwood, NJ: Ablex Publishing Company.

Daly, M. (1990). *Gyn/Ecology: The metaethics of radical feminism.* (rev. ed.) Boston: Beacon Press.

Deetz, S. (1985). Ethical considerations in cultural research in organizations. In P. Frost, L. Moore, M. Louis, C. Lundberg, & J. Martin (Eds.), *Organizational culture* (pp. 253-269). Beverly Hills: Sage.

Deetz, S. (1990). Reclaiming the subject matter as a moral foundation for interpersonal interaction. *Communication Quarterly, 38,* 226.

Deetz, S. (1992). *Democracy in the age of corporate colonization: Developments in communication and the politics of everyday life.* Albany: State University of New York Press.

Deetz, S. (1995a). *Tranforming communication, transforming business: Building responsive and responsible workplaces.* Cresskill, NJ: Hampton Press, Inc.

Deetz, S. (1995b). Transforming communication, transforming business: Stimulating value negotiation for more responsive and responsible workplaces. *International Journal of Value-Based Management, 8,* 255.

Deetz, S., Fisher, B., & Power, P. (1995). Corporate control, the media industry, and society. Under review, *Business and Society*.

Deetz, S. (in press). Discursive formations, strategized subordination, and self-surveillance: An empirical case. In A. McKinlay & K. Starkey (Eds.), *Managing Foucault: A reader*. London: Sage.

Fischer, F. (1990). *Technocracy and the politics of expertise*. Newbury Park, CA: Sage.

Frederick, W. C. (1986). Toward CSR3: Why ethical analysis is indespensible and unavoidable in corporate affairs. *California Management Review, 28*(2), 126.

Freeman, R. E. (1984). *Strategic management: A stakeholder approach*. Boston: Pitman Publishing Inc.

Freeman, R. E., & Liedtka, J. (1991). Corporate social responsibility: A critical approach. *Business Horizons, 34*(4), 92.

Gadamer, H. G. (1975). *Truth and Method*. (G. Barden & J. Cumming, Trans.). New York: Seabury Press.

Gergen, K. (1992). Organizational theory in the post modern era. In M. Reed & M. Hughes (Eds.), *Rethinking Organization* (pp. 207-226). London: Sage.

Giddens, A. (1991). *Modernity and self-identity: Self and society in the late modern age*. Stanford: Stanford University Press.

Gilligan, C. (1982). *In a different voice*. Cambridge: Harvard University Press.

Gorz, André (1987). *Critique of economic reason*. (G. Handyside & C. Turner, Trans.). London: Verso.

Habermas, J. (1975). *Legitimation crisis*. (I. McCarthy, Trans.). Boston: Beacon Press.

Habermas, J. (1979). *Communication and the evolution of society*. (T. McCarthy, Trans.). Boston: Beacon Press.

Habermas, J. (1984). *The theory of communicative action, volume 1: Reason and the rationalization of society*. (T. McCarthy, Trans.). Boston: Beacon.

Habermas, J. (1987). *The theory of communicative action, volume 2: Lifeworld and system*. (T. McCarthy, Trans.). Boston: Beacon Press.

Habermas, J. (1990). Discourse ethics: Notes on a program of philosophical justification. In. S. Benhabib & F. Dallmayr (Eds.), *The communicative ethics controversy* (pp. 60-110). Cambridge: MIT Press.

Harding, S. (1991). *Whose science? Whose knowledge?: Thinking from women's lives*. Ithaca, NY: Cornell University Press.

Hartsock, N. (1983). *Money, sex, and power: Toward a feminist historical materialism*. New York: Longman.

Heidegger, M. (1961). *An Introduction to Metaphysics* (R. Manheim, Trans.). Garden City: Doubleday.

Hekman, S. J. (1995). *Moral voices, moral selves: Carol Gilligan and feminist moral theory*. University Park, PA: Penn State Press.

Jackell, R. (1988). *Moral mazes: The world of corporate managers*. Oxford: Oxford University Press.

Johnson, M. (1987). *The Body in the mind*. Chicago: University of Chicago Press.

Kant, I, (1959). *Foundations of the metaphysics of morals: And, what is enlightment?* (L.W. Beck, Trans.). New York: Liberal Arts Press.

King, S. S., & Cushman, D.P. (1994). High-speed management as a theoretic principle for yielding significant organizatonal communiation behaviors. In B. Kovacic (Ed.), *New approaches to organizational commmunication* (pp. 87-116). Albany: SUNY Press.

Knights, D., & Willmott, H. (1989). Power and subjectivity at work: From degradation to subjugation in social relations. *Sociology, 23*, 535.

Laumann, E., & Knoke, D. (1987). *The organizational state: Social choices in national policy domains*. Madison: University of Wisconsin Press.

Levinas, E. (1969). *Totality and Infinity*. Pittsburg: Dusquene University Press.

Linstead, S. (1993). Deconstruction in the study of organizations. In J. Hassard & M. Parker (Eds.), *Postmodernism and Organizations.* (pp. 49-70). London: Sage.

Lyotard, J. F. (1984). *The Postmodern Condition: A Report on Knowledge.* (G. Bennington & B. Massumi, Trans.). Minneapolis: University of Minnesota Press.

MacIntyre, A. (1984). *After virtue: A study in moral theory.* 2nd edition. Notre Dame: University of Notre Dame Press.

Mangham, I. (1995). MacIntyre and the manager. *Organization, 2*(2),181.

Martin, J. (1990). Deconstructing organizational taboos: The suppression of gender conflict in organizations. *Organization Science, 11,* 339.

Martin, J. (1994). The organization of exclusion: The institutionalization of sex inequality, gendered faculty jobs, and gendered knowledge in organizational theory and research. *Organization, 1,* 401.

McNay, L. (1992). *Foucault and feminism.* Boston: Northeastern University Press.

Noddings, N. (1984). *Caring.* Berkeley: University of California Press.

Rawls, J. (1971). *A theory of justice.* Cambridge: Harvard University Press.

Reich, R. (March-April,1991). Who is them? *Harvard Business Review, 77.*

Schmookler, A. (1992). *The illusion of choice: How the market economy shapes our destiny.* Albany: State University of New York Press.

Waltzer, M. (1987). *Interpretation and social criticism.* Cambridge: Harvard University Press.

Weber, M. (1958). *The prostestant ethic and the spirit of capitalism.* New York: Scribners.

Willmott, H. (1994). Bringing agency (back) into organizational analysis: Responding to the crises of (post)modernity. In J. Hassard & M. Parker (Eds.), *Towards a new theory of organizations.* (pp. 87-130). London: Routledge.

Wood, J. T. (1992). Gender and moral voice: Moving from woman's nature to standpoint epistemology. *Women's Studies in Communication, 15,* 1.

Young, I. (1990). The ideal of community and the politics of difference. In L. J. Nicholson (Ed.), *Feminism/postmodernism* (pp. 300-323). New York: Routledge.

Ethics in International Interaction: Perspectives on Diplomacy and Negotiation

Getinet Belay
Rutgers University

INTRODUCTION

Maxwell (1990) observes that the philosophy of international ethics is at an embryonic stage of development (p. 1) , and identifies a major gap in present-day conceptualizations of international interactions: "Certainly in the contemporary world of interdependent nations, the meager theoretical development of the concept of international morality presents a major intellectual challenge" (p. 2). As the occasions for ambiguity in moral reasoning and moral responsibility multiply in a culturally diverse but highly interconnected and interdependent global environment, ethics is a subject which confronts communication scholarship at a variety of levels of interactional analysis. Current communication research on the subject is confined, though, almost exclusively to international business interactions, particularly to those of transnational corporations (TNCs). There is relatively little research that directly addresses the ethics of diplomacy and negotiation in contemporary global interactional processes.

According to Fisher (1989), diplomacy is generally ignored in communication studies as a peripheral professional enclave with idiosyncratic norms and rules for conduct, i.e., as "an arena unto itself with its own culture" (p. 408). Indeed, despite its initial influence on the constitution of intercultural communication as a research field (Leeds-Hurwitz, 1990), diplomacy has not received significant research attention over the past thirty years. Conceptualizations of the interactional problematique of diplomacy as a specific communication institution are not available; nor have diplomacy's dependencies and influences on other areas of international and intercultural communication been systematically addressed. Consequently, there is little research knowledge to draw upon for analysis of contemporary trends and patterns in diplomatic interactional processes.

Dinh (1987) has pointed out yet another factor which may have eclipsed the significance of diplomacy as an area of ethical inquiry. This concerns "the popular belief that diplomacy is a secret bartering between governments, where the real intentions are hidden behind vague and flowery language" (Dinh, 1987, p. 3). State-centered perceptions of diplomacy hold, as I will discuss later, that the essential relationship among states is one of perennial competition, and diplomacy is moved by anything but considerations of national self-interest and material power. Hence, according to that view, moral considerations are irrelevant to diplomacy. The diplomatic profession has also often been defined in unflattering terms even from among its own practitioners. One of the most quoted definitions of a diplomat is that of Sir Henry Watton, himself an ambassador in the service of King James I, who remarked: "[A]n ambassador is an honest man sent to lie abroad for the good of his country" (McDermott, 1973, p. 37). Such definitional projections have fostered skeptical attitudes toward diplomacy, particularly one that does not view ethicality as being attributable to diplomatic interactions.

In this chapter, I argue that diplomacy is key to communication analysis of globalization and ethics. I also propose to develop an interactionist conceptualization of ethics and diplomacy. Three major reasons underscore the importance of diplomacy to a communication study of ethics. First, diplomacy is basically an exercise in international communication. Second, diplomacy is the oldest and historically most crucial institutional construct for the definition of norms, procedures and principles for international interactions. Third, this institutional construct is today undergoing profound ethical tensions and transformations, owing to the restructuring and redefinition of international interactions in the age of globalization, including the growing role of non-state actors and moral agencies. Understanding the tensions and transformations of moral reasoning, identity and responsibility which diplomacy faces today is invaluable for deeper conceptualization of the interactional challenges and opportunities that arise from the representation and negotiation of ethics in the globalization process.

The problem of ethics in diplomacy presents itself in two dimensions of analysis. The first relates to nations as cultural systems representing different constructions of moral codes and values. Central to this dimension of analysis are problems which arise from the cultural variation of moral reasoning in communicative transactions between diplomatic representations of any two or more units, i.e., nation-states, that comprise the international system. Some essential aspects of diplomacy pertaining to this first problem dimension of ethics will be addressed, but the primary focus of this chapter is a second dimension of analysis. This concerns diplomacy as a site for the interactional construction of ethical paradigms. Here, diplomacy will be conceptualized as a multilateral international institution for the constitution of norms and principles of morality for the international system as a whole.

DIPLOMACY AND ETHICS: A CONCEPTUAL FRAMEWORK

It is important to note that not individuals or groups, but countries constitute the primary interactional actors in diplomacy. The term *nation-state* is used in this chapter to refer to countries both as *cultural* and *political* entities. The terms *nation* and *state* are respectively used only when countries are referred to specifically as cultural or political entities. The tensions and transformations of ethics in diplomacy are connected with both the cultural and political profiles of the interactants. It is therefore useful to conceptualize first the specific constructions of diplomacy as a process as well as context of interaction between nation-states.

Diplomacy as Communication
Reston (1983) has reported an interesting episode about the communication hot line that was established between Washington and Moscow on April 4, 1963, following the Cuban Missile Crisis. The communication hot line was located in the Pentagon, between teleprinters that transmit messages from Washington in English and from Moscow in Russian, with human translators at each end. The first message on line was from Washington: "Testing: The quick brown fox jumped over the lazy dog's back. 1234567890." The Soviets were puzzled and wanted to know why the fox was jumping over the dog's back, and what those animals were all about. When it was finally established that this was just a keyboard test, the Soviets "began to describe, in a lyrical language the beauties of the Moscow sunset" (Reston, p. 24).

The episode illustrates the integral relationship between diplomacy, communication and interculturalism. The establishment of intensive, or rather more efficient communication was the response by both superpowers to their increasing sense of relational interdependence, i.e. their awareness of the disastrous consequences of misunderstanding or technological error in a nuclear age. Diplomacy was the interactional agency they utilized for meeting that communication need. The most up-to-date communication technology was put in place to enhance interactional competence—in this case to expedite exchange of messages—in crisis situations, and human translators were employed to overcome language barriers to communication.

But that episode also revealed, in a rather trivial way, the critical relationship between diplomacy and interculturalism. To verify the integrity of the technological system, the American side used a testing code—one that is standard in American typing classes. The American side assumed that the Soviets would understand the testing code for what it is. They did not. And once the code was explained to them, the Soviets felt that an elaborate lyrical description of the Moscow sunset would represent a match to the American act.

That diplomacy involves interculturalism is, as I will discuss below, quite a recent recognition. But from its very inception, diplomacy was understood to be a communication exercise. Briggs (1968) has classified the duties of the diplomat into three major categories: negotiation, representation and reporting (pp. 177-178). Those duties of the diplomat were already known in ancient times in a variety of world regions. Roy (1978) notes that, for example, Kautilya (322-298 B.C.), one of the leading writers on politics and diplomacy in ancient India, discussed the duties of diplomats as representatives, informers, communicators and negotiators. In Europe, the English word "diplomat" became current only at the end of the eighteenth century, and the title ambassador, derived from the Celtic word meaning "servant," only in the middle of the sixteenth century. In earlier times, diplomats and ambassadors were called messengers, heralds or orators. The communicational function of diplomacy was evident to the Venetians, who set the interactional patterns for the other Italian city-states. The Venetians initiated in the fifteenth century the practice of exchanging "resident ambassadors." Initially, they were not called ambassadors, but "resident orators." To conduct his profession, the "resident orator" had to be "an educated male versed in Latin, the lingua franca of the time. He had to be cultured, hospitable, have a good cook to entertain his guests, be above scandal in his private life and be eager to interfere indirectly in local politics" (Dinh, 1987, p. 14).

Communication is an integral component of diplomacy; communication also conditions diplomacy's existence, as well as its success or failure. This relates not only to communication as an interpersonal skill, but also to communication as a contextual construct, shaped by historical relational conditions, technologies, and cultural systems. The relational and technological factors which have influenced diplomacy will be discussed later in this chapter. The focus here is on the problematique of diplomacy as communication with the culturally *Other*. Before he summarized his observations and concepts in his widely read book *Man and Mankind: Conflict and Communication Between*

Cultures, Edmund Glenn (1981) actually became aware of the way cultural factors complicate communication while working as diplomatic interpreter. He interpreted for four Secretaries of State and also for Presidents Truman, Eisenhower, Kennedy and Johnson. Fisher (1989) recounts the frustrations that Glenn used to report from his role as interpreter in private meetings between heads of state,

> ... he often felt that the two principals were talking past each other, in effect not even talking about the same subject. Although one of the most skilled interpreters using English, French, Polish, and Russian, *there was nothing he could do about these mismatched meanings* short of going into a seminar about the subjective meaning of words, the relationship between language and thought, and the differences in the way that cultures lead people to order their reasoning processes. And, of course, that was not possible in such a situation (p. 413).

The task of diplomats is indeed analogous to that of interpreters. Like interpreters, diplomats face the challenge of intercultural communication going in both directions. At one level, their effectiveness as communicators depends on their proficiency in the cultural styles of their host countries. Only then can they accurately observe and interpret local developments, engage persuasively with their counterparts in the Foreign Office, influence the media and local public opinion. At another level, however, diplomats have also to be able to "translate" their knowledge about the realities of the host country in a manner that makes sense to their home-country officials. To the extent that the higher political leadership in the home-country generally operates in accord with ethnocentric perceptions and domestic political prisms, the cross-cultural communication challenge at this second line of interaction is not much easier than at the first one.

The intercultural communication challenge of diplomats is further complicated by the fact that diplomacy often involves communication about complex and value-laden subjects which require thought processes at higher degrees of abstraction. Fisher (1989), an anthropologist who has served the State Department in different diplomatic capacities, observes that "across a range in which one can apply intercultural communication analysis either to very concrete patterns of behavior on the one end, or to more abstract aspects of information processing that supply the meaning for communicating about abstract and complex subject matter on the other, diplomacy is much concerned with the abstract end of the range" (p. 412).

Diplomacy as Interactional Institution

Although diplomacy, like all other forms of interaction between individuals or groups belonging to different self-identifying human collectivities, is communication with the culturally *Other*, it also differs from all other forms of intercultural communication in one significant way: it is a system of communication between state governments. It is a formal means by which the self-identity of the sovereign state is represented and negotiated in interaction with other states. In its evolution as an institution for inter-state interactions, diplomacy has developed its own standardized codes, symbols, interactional rules and norms. Besides dialogue and persuasion, the compliance-gaining strategies of diplomacy include threats and promises, including economic cooperation or boycott, and military force—also called gunboat diplomacy.

For reasons that will be addressed later in this chapter, the current model of diplomacy as a global communication institution had its origins in Europe. The residential form of diplomacy began among the Italian city-states that eventually made its way into transalpine Europe (Mattingly, 1955). By the first half of the sixteenth century, the institution of permanent embassies became firmly established among the "new monarchies" of early-modern Europe such as Spain, France and England (Shennan, 1974). The establishment of permanent embassies and the codification of a secular system of immunities became the standard forms of diplomacy throughout the whole of Europe, particularly after the Peace of Westphalia which ended the Thirty Years War (1618–1648). During those years, a diplomatic body—later to be the `diplomatic corps'—was established "with its own names and titles, ceremonial procedures, and conventional language" (Dinh, 1987, p. 14). The publication of Francois de Callieres' elaborate treatise on diplomacy, *The Art of Negotiating with Sovereign Princes*, which is commonly referred to as the "bible of diplomats," also goes back to this early period of diplomacy.

It was not until late into the eighteenth century, though, that the meaning of diplomacy was extended to the management of international relations in general. This coincided with the emergence of the first non-monarchical state, France, in 1792—the year in which the word *international* itself was coined (Derian, 1993). It was also during this period that the interactional norms and protocols of diplomacy acquired clearer and more elaborate definitions and standardization. France emerged as the principal influence in the development of diplomatic theory and practice. Diplomatic ranks and titles were clearly defined in a protocol of the Congress of Aix la Chapelle on November 21, 1818. Latin was replaced by French as the verbal code of diplomatic interactions. In addition to a common language, diplomacy shared the common sociological origin of its practitioners: A homogeneous elite of aristocratic background made up the diplomatic corps of Europe from the eighteenth to early twentieth century (Derian, 1993, p. 245).

By the beginning of the twentieth century, diplomacy had evolved into a complex and highly organized international institution. The interactional norms and procedures did not change a great deal, and still remained modelled after those of the eighteenth and nineteenth centuries. However, diplomacy began to lose its aristocratic sociological veneer after WWI. The equality of English with the French language was also recognized at the 1919 Paris Conference. The role of Francois Calliieres treatise was substituted by Sir Harold Nicolson's (1950) *Diplomacy*, which, as the new handbook of diplomacy, "was read by aspiring diplomats from all countries" (Fisher, 1989, p. 408). Finally, the Vienna Convention on Diplomatic Relations, which incorporated the rules and norms of "diplomatic intercourse and immunities" in fifty-three elaborate articles of international agreement, was signed at the UN Conference in Austria on April 18, 1961.

Diplomacy is now considered an essential institution which has contributed to a relatively high degree of global cohesiveness. According to Fisher (1989), diplomacy was an early leader in creating a transnational cultural base by defining norms for addressing issues, by adopting customs for protocol, and by setting standard operating procedures (p. 410). Bull (1995) views diplomacy as "a custodian of the idea of international society" (p. 176).

Ethics: Institutional and International
Discussion of ethics and diplomacy must first address two conceptual problems, for which neither moral philosophy nor other disciplinary perspectives offer any solutions. Both problems are connected with the fact that diplomacy is an international institution. The first conceptual problem concerns whether institutions can be considered moral agents. The second relates to whether morality plays any role at all in international interactions. A communication approach to ethics offers productive perspectives for resolving both conceptual problems.

Following conceptualizations by Adler (1986), Buller et al. (1991), Churchill (1982) and Hofstede (1980), the term *ethics* refers in this study both to the moral codes and values used in the reasoning process, and to the actual behaviors or acts that result from the process. *Codes and values* include norms and principles which summarize the cognitive content of moral discourse as well as other genres, such as proverbs, metaphors, stories and songs, which, for most people, are powerful carriers of moral meaning. According to O'Conner (1994), those genres evoke not only the cognitive, but also the affective and imaginative depths of moral sensitivity and desire (p. 163).

Interaction is fundamental to any conception of a system, including a cultural system as an embodiment of an ethical paradigm by a self-identifying human community. Without interaction, the individual parts or units are disconnected and free-standing. Interactionist approaches view morality, like all other social values, as a product of communicative activity between the individual units that are involved in relational interdependence. In other words, ethical values are constituted in communicative interactions as part of the need by any human community for a stratified system of meaningful structures that are shared by its members (see Blumer, 1969; Fine & Kleinman, 1983; Geertz, 1973; Goffman, 1967; Mokros & Deetz in press; Stryker & Statham, 1984). Ethics is thus a cultural invention predicated by the necessities of social living. However, ethical constructions are dynamic and fluid, because ethical constructions, like the self-identity of a community, do not occur once and for all. They are constantly negotiated, confirmed, modified or changed in social interaction over space and time in accord with changes in relational contexts and identity parameters for community-building (Belay, 1996).

Institutions and ethics. The question as to whether institutions can be considered moral agents arises to the extent that ethical problems traditionally have been conceptualized in moral philosophy at the level of national society and in terms of interpersonal relations between individual human beings. Moral agency on the level of face-to-face interactions is thought to be embodied in the autonomous individual. In other words, human individuals represent the paradigm of moral agency. Institutions, on the other hand, are entities which do not have a mind, a will, a conscience in the way that human individuals do. Consequently, some authors have argued that institutions are not, and cannot be, moral agents (see, for example, Evans, 1981).

In examining whether and the extent to which institutions could be considered moral agents, it is important to note first that on the international level institutions are the most powerful and consequential actors. Most international interactions occur through institutional networks, such as diplomatic and corporate ones. The scope of international ethics would in fact shrink to triviality, if institutions were to be excluded from being considered moral agents.

Obviously, institutions as moral agents should be treated differently from human individuals. The acts performed by institutions, unlike the acts of single individuals, are far more complex, coordinated undertakings. Moreover, institutions are commonly comprised of human individuals who are related to one another and outsiders in certain fixed ways that are established by mutual agreement, law or common practice. The institution's existence may be justified by accomplishing specific ends, such as the creation of profits or the establishment of public order. These fixed relations determine what the various persons comprising the institution may do and how they may do it. In that sense, agents within institutions certainly are constrained by the fixed relations.

However, this does not warrant viewing institutions as mechanical entities. Maxwell (1990) correctly observes that rules of morality apply to all human interactions, regardless of whether those interactions involve single individuals, institutions or states (p. 144). This is firstly so because institutions are comprised of human individuals, or groups of individuals, who are bred to internalize moral thinking and moral scruples. In other words, institutions themselves are interactional sites for moral agents. These moral actors within institutions are often able to press for changes in goals or charters and achieve changes in the way the institution operates. Secondly, an institution is part and parcel of the *social living* schemes of the community within which it operates. It engages in multidimensional interactions with other institutions and the community at large, including the state. In that process, it influences and is in turn influenced by the moral norms and values of the rest of the community. In reference to this interactional social construction of morality, Maxwell (1990) emphasizes that no actor involved in human interactions is exempt from rules of morality. She observes: "The actor may make a loud statement about his right to be exempted from moral rules . . . but that will be ignored by most observers of his deeds" (Maxwell, 1990, p. 129).

It follows from this that institutions are moral agents. However, institutions become moral agents in a derivative sense, i.e., through those human beings that compose them, as well as in their interactional coexistence, i.e., *social living*, with other institutions and the larger community. With regard to diplomacy, the overall societal actors that influence its operations will be addressed later. Reference here is to the internal moral actors that shape its ethical constructions. Hoffmann (1981) identifies three internal agents in the diplomatic institution: the diplomatic corps, which gathers information relevant to policy and also locally implements policy decisions; intellectuals who develop conceptual models and/or help in designing policies, and statesmen who make policy-decisions (pp. 6, 7).

Morality and international Interactions It is often argued, as I will address in greater detail later in this chapter, that international interactions occur in an ethical vacuum. Only at the level of national society can a rough moral consensus prevail, which makes possible standards in law that rest on underlying values. In other words, standards of moral conduct in interactions at the level of a national society are clearly defined and enforced by cultural sanctions. According to that line of argument, no such elaborate constraints exist on the level of international interactions because the international arena is not a society of the sort required for nurturing consistent and moral action.

This line of argument confines the construction of ethics to interactions at the nation-state level alone. However, such an approach has little analytical validity. There is no historical or empirical reason to believe that the nation-state represents the only level of community for the interactional construction of ethics. Indeed, the nation-state as an organizing principle for self-identifying communities is historically quite a recent phenomenon. Constructions of ethical codes and values have occurred in the greater part of human history under conditions of non-nation-state community formations. Furthermore, the nation-state itself has incorporated many paradigms of morality that were constructed under pre-nation-state interactional conditions, such as, for example, the incorporation of the Judeo-Christian ethical paradigm by European nation-states.

In fact what matters for the formation of ethical paradigms is not the type of community at which interaction occurs, but rather the existence and degree of intensity of interaction itself. In that sense, it is reasonable to assume that communicative interactions which involve the whole world have opened the international arena as a site for ethical constructions. This statement does not imply that the international arena as an interactional site has been a moral one. It only means that interactions at the international level are not precluded from rules of morality. To the contrary, the international arena is a busy intersection with intense representations and negotiations of ethics. That morality does play a role in international discourse becomes evident when one considers, for example, the language in which statesmen justify their international engagement to the public. Stalin, when asked whether he was not concerned about the Vatican's influence, is reported to have responded: "How many divisions does the Pope have?" (Thompson, 1985, p. 2). But few statesmen, in public perhaps not even Stalin himself, would demonstrate such contempt for consideration of any other value than military force. Indeed, it is remarkable how statesmen throughout the world, even in instances when their acts may not be necessarily moral, cloak their reasoning and deeds in high moral purpose. It may be argued that hypocrisy is the tribute vice pays to virtue. But it is also important to understand why leaders feel the tribute needs to be paid. The first reason has already been mentioned in our discussion of institutions and ethics: Statesmen, like all other individuals, are embodiments of ethics. But more important for the discussions here: The international arena is not a morality-neutral interactional space. It consists of, among other things, moral reasoning-actors in the form of both national and international public opinion.

HISTORICAL CONSTRUCTION OF DIPLOMACY AND ETHICS: AN OVERVIEW

The historical beginnings of diplomacy are hard to ascertain. Thompson & Padover (1965, pp. 13-15) trace the origins of diplomacy in ancient Egypt to as early as the Eighteenth Dynasty (1580-1350 B.C.E). Several other authors, including Numelin (1950) and Watson (1982), also locate the beginnings of diplomacy in a variety of world regions such as pre-Columbian America, Greek city-states, ancient China and India. However, the transformation of diplomacy into a site for the construction and negotiation of international ethics is connected with a more recent interactional history.

Inter-State Institutional Construction

Buzan and Little (1994) distinguish between global interactional conditions before and after 1400 A.D., and identify two major developments that have given rise to an integrated global system in the post-1400 period. The first concerns the growth in interaction capacity as a result of the cluster of developments beginning with the perfection of oceangoing ships in Europe and China during the fourteenth and fifteenth centuries. These included the development of motorized sea, rail, road, and air transport during the nineteenth and twentieth centuries, and the parallel development of the printing press and electronic means of communication. The second development, which occurred after the Peace of Westphalia (1648) ended the Thirty Years War, concerns the emergence of a new interactional actor, the nation-state, as the dominant unit in the international system. In the ensuing interactional processes, "Europeans unquestionably created the first global international system by bringing all parts of humankind into regular economic and strategic contact with each other for the first time" (Buzan & Little, 1994, p. 234).

It is this much wider history that constitutes the real antecedent of diplomacy. In other words, the origin and development of diplomacy is connected historically with the process of integration and internal differentiation of the world into a single international system with Europe at the core. Diplomacy as an institution served basically the increased need to negotiate and stabilize the conflicting economic and military relationships in the multipolar power arrangement between European nation-states. In other words, diplomacy has evolved essentially as a mechanism in the exercise and rearrangement of power. In that regard, it is significant that permanent embassies arose at the same time as permanent armies were established (Dinh, 1987, p. 15).

In 1815, an attempt was made to set up a permanent organization of the great powers, the European Alliance, but by 1823 the Alliance had collapsed. In 1830, a system of "ambassadorial conferences" was created, and, following a series of wars on the continent, the European states were beginning to consider the possibility of eliminating war as an instrument of national policy and replacing it with peaceful negotiation and arbitration. A conference was called in the Hague by Tsar Nicholas II for the purpose of "outlawing war." But two consecutive Hague Conferences, held in 1899 and 1907, only succeeded in prescribing rules for arbitration and in revising the rules of war. (Dinh, 1987, p. 34). The guiding diplomatic principle until the end of WWI was instead the doctrine of the "balance of power." That doctrine meant, practically, that the various states created shifting alliances with one another, whereby a country or group of countries matched its military power against the power of the other side for self-protection. According to Morgenthau (1968) the European nations pursued that policy in two different ways, "by increasing their own power—and then they engage in an armaments race or in the competitive acquisition of territory—or by adding to their own power that of other nations—and then they embark upon a policy of alliances" (p. 1065).

The "balance of power" doctrine was revered as a quasi-ethical principle in diplomacy throughout Europe. It was considered an effective way of maintaining the continent's peace and stability. Both sovereignty and multipolarity were concentrated almost entirely in Europe until late into the nineteenth century, with Japan and America as late arrivals. In effect, European multipolarity was simply projected into the wider global system. Nicolson (1954) identifies five characteristic features of traditional European diplomacy:

1. Europe was regarded as the most important of all continents.
2. The Great Powers (France, Great Britain, Germany) were greater than the Small Powers (Italy, Belgium, Holland, Denmark, etc.) since they possessed a more extended range of interests, wider responsibilities, and, above all, more money and more guns.
3. The Great Powers possessed a common responsibility for the conduct of Small Powers and the preservation of peace between them. The principle of intervention was a generally accepted principle.
4. The establishment in every European country of a professional diplomatic service of a more or less identical model.
5. Sound negotiation must be continuous and confidential (pp. 99-107).

Between WWI and WWII several developments occurred which modified significantly the modus operandi of diplomacy as an interactional institution. Those developments are related to the growing international role of the United States and the then Soviet Union. Diplomacy as an interactional institution began to expand both in space and participating actors. For the first time in history, a worldwide permanent organization, the League of Nations, was founded in 1919. However, the relative weakness, at that point in time, of the values of an international society soon became evident, epitomized by the inability of the League to support a member state, Ethiopia, against Italian invasion. The League finally collapsed in 1941, after the major European states had broken into opposing sides. But the two world wars decisively weakened Europe's predominance in diplomacy. Morgenthau (1968) observes that by the end of WWII, the principal weights on each scale of the global power configuration were either entirely non-European, as in the case of the United States, or partly non-European as in the case of the then Soviet Union.

The effort to extend the scope of diplomacy to emerging global dimensions and institutionalize it as a constitutive vehicle of international society was finally realized, at least formally, with the creation of the United Nations in October 1945. The UN nurtured the global recognition of the concept of sovereignty. Neither the United States nor the U.S.S.R., the two global power centers after WWII, had an interest in maintaining the old colonial international order. Moreover, both the U.S. and the U.S.S.R. represented national systems of a new historical quality: Both were multiethnic and multiracial in their demographic and cultural make-up. The dominant role of the two states contributed to the collapse of the global colonial order. From the late 1940s to mid-1960s, a structural transformation took place below the equator. This change, called decolonization, comprised "the shift from the whole range of unequal relations and statuses that existed in 1850 to the nearly uniform system of sovereign equality that has existed since the end of the 1960s" (Buzan & Little, 1994, p. 253). The UN was particularly effective in drawing the newly independent states, which emerged out of the break-up of the colonial order, into the global diplomatic system as active interactants. That transformation of the international system also led to the proliferation of intergovernmental organizations both at regional and transcontinental levels.

The UN's real potential to become a constitutive vehicle of international society was stymied, however, by its complete reliance on the state-centric international system and by the ensuing Cold War. The UN structure was grounded in the paradigm that states are the central actors in global interactions. However, the system of autonomous nation-states, even in its new worldwide extension, had little sense of community and pursued divergent and conflicting interests. Moreover, the ensuing Cold War locked the entire nation-state system into a permanent conflict intensified by an East-West ideological and economic asymmetry and a "bipolar balance of power." From its very inception, the UN became a stage upon which the Cold War was fought. In addition to some direct interventions, the superpowers tested each other's reactions by proxy wars through the supply of arms and military advisers to their allies in the newly independent states. Bletz (1972) defines the Cold War as "a state of international tension, wherein political, economic, technological, sociological, psychological, paramilitary, and military measures short of overt armed conflict involving regular military forces are employed to achieve national objectives" (p. 42). This Cold War scheme of international interactions did not leave much space for diplomacy to evolve as a "custodian of international society." Dinh (1987) remarks that the diplomacy of the Cold War was "containment, and its communication policy was propaganda" (p. 42).

Nevertheless, in contrast to the Europe-centered international system, the Cold War also provided diplomacy with ethical projections which went beyond individual nation-states and were rather global in their orientation: anti-imperialism/anti-communism, good/evil, depending whose side one was on. This ideological model for legitimacy of governance and transnational "solidarity" neutralized tensions based on cultural and group-specific idiosyncracies, and it stabilized the nation-state system worldwide.

In addition, unlike the traditional scheme of European "balance of power," Cold war diplomacy was characterized by prudence in its approach to conflict in inter-state interactions. This relates to the recognition of the need to avoid war as a prime diplomatic objective. That historic shift occurred in direct relation to the radical redefinition of the conditions of human survival as a consequence of the atom bomb and the risk of a nuclear holocaust. First used by the United States in WWII, the atom bomb's evolution and its capacity for massive destruction geared diplomatic efforts toward avoiding a third world war. Both sides of the power balance understood that the arms race in which they were engaged was ethically problematic for the simple reason that the "good" which nuclear weapons sought to achieve was far outweighed by the "evil" that they might bring. Consequently, the Cold War was characterized by a mutually agreed upon objective—avoid war—and commonly accepted ways of acting—the creation of international institutions and the convening of international conferences to settle specific conflicts in inter-state relations. Thompson (1985, p. 6) characterizes international law as "the gentle civilizer" of inter-state interactions. In that regard, it is remarkable that, in spite of the intense global hostilities, a great deal of the norms and laws that regulate international interactions today were agreed upon during the Cold War years.

These include: State sovereignty is sacrosanct; aggressive war is always morally wrong; human rights must be protected, free flow of information promotes international understanding.

A major new development in the inter-state construction of diplomacy during this period was the gradual recognition of its interculturalism. Classical diplomacy consisted only of interactants who belonged to the same Judeo-Christian family of cultures. But as the European-centered structure of Classical Diplomacy weakened after WWI, cultural anthropological perspectives began to be accorded serious consideration in diplomatic policy-making. Margaret Mead had been invited to testify before the Senate Foreign Relations Committee, and according to Fisher (1972), even anthropological works on "primitive" groups and exotic cultures began to be followed rather avidly by members of the foreign affairs community. Leading anthropologists like Edward T. Hall (1959) were commissioned as diplomatic consultants and trainers. But anthropology has not had as substantial an impact on introducing serious conceptualizations of diplomacy as has intercultural communication. Fisher (1972) compares the mystic popularity of cultural anthropology among diplomats during this period with that which amateur psychiatry enjoys in certain urban social circles. The first serious effort to incorporate interculturalism as an integral component of diplomatic communication competency was not undertaken until the intensification of the decolonization process in the 1960s. At this time, Rossow (1962), in an article titled *The Professionalization of the New Diplomacy*, identified specifically the new global transformation which mandated diplomacy to take into account the relationship between communication and culture.

Ethics of Diplomacy as Inter-state Institution

Morality in diplomacy has been subordinated historically to the existential imperatives of the sovereign state, and consequently to the promotion of national interest by means of politics and war. Conceptually, the dialogics of ethics in international interactions was grounded in the philosophical treatise of Thomas Hobbes (1588-1679). Hobbes' (1887) primary concern was civil society at the intrastate level, and with establishing the obligation of the citizen to obey the sovereign. For this he developed in his *Leviathan* the notion of social contract. Hobbes (1887) wrote that, by contrast, the world of states has not made a contract, its members do not have above them a common power to keep them in awe, and they do not constitute a society. Hobbes (1887) observed,

> To this Warre of every man against every man, this ... is consequent:
> that nothing can be Unjust. The notion of Right and Wrong, Justice

and Injustice, have there no place. Where there is no common
Power, there is no Law: where no Law, no injustice. Force and
Fraud, are in Warre the two cardinal virtues (p. 65).

In other words, morality can exist only on the basis of the law of
established domestic order, i.e., with the positive legislation of a Leviathan in
which the enforcement of humane laws of self-preservation becomes possible.
Nations, by contrast, are in a state of nature—similar to individuals in pre-
Leviathan state. It is a state of anarchy, conflicting desires, and scarcity. There
is a general struggle for power, driven by "diffidence," and "glory." In such a
state there is no morality. The only concern in this competition is survival. This
means that the right of nature is the liberty to use one's power of self-
preservation; and those laws involve both self-defense and war.

This Hobbesian paradigm, which came to be adopted by all proponents of
the "Realist" school of thought in international politics, has been the
underlying ethical conception of diplomacy since the emergence of the state-
centered international system. It also constitutes the philosophical basis for the
Balance-of-Power doctrine. The Hobbesian ethical paradigm has had only a few
challenges throughout the history of diplomacy. The most important of these
was the Wilsonian approach. Woodrow Wilson believed that foreign policy
should be conducted with domestic moral standards, and, in the wake of WWI,
called for effective international institutions and "open covenants openly
arrived at" (see Rosenau, 1993; Thompson, 1985). The U.S. President's ethical
approach to diplomacy was the driving force for the creation of the League of
Nations.

Stimulated by Woodrow Wilson's diplomatic vision, a new school of
ethical thought, which came to be known as "Idealism," became predominant
during the period between the two world wars. As a term of description,
Idealism came into wide circulation in the 1920s. Its proponents included
prominent scholars on both sides of the Atlantic, among them Dickinson
(1926), who urged nations to forsake "their illusions, their cupidity, and their
pride" and build the League of Nations into "a working machine for peace" (p.
37). Proponents of idealism shared a belief in the essential goodness of human
nature, the primacy of ideas and education, and the ultimate power of an
aroused world public opinion (see Smith, 1993). They regarded fundamental
reform of the prevailing inter-state system to be possible as well as necessary.
They treated the power-drive and consequent aggressive impulses of national
states as a basic cause of war. They believed in the need to diffuse that drive
through a global democratic inter-state regime. The Idealists embraced the idea
of a United Nations later in the 1940s.

Although the international interactional realities of the 1920s to 1940s were neither dense with "world public opinion" nor with the sense of global community, the influence of Idealism on diplomatic ethical thinking was not insignificant. Owing to the influence of that school of thought, the phrase "power politics" began to bear "sinister connotations" (Thompson, 1985, p. 124). Indeed, the abolition of power as a factor of interstate interactions seemed to constitute, at least in public rhetoric, a central diplomatic engagement during the immediate years before and after the end of WWII. For example, U.S. Secretary of State Cordell Hull, upon returning in 1943 from the Moscow Conference, which prepared the way for the creation of the United Nations, proclaimed that the new international organization would lead to the end of power politics which had ravaged European society. In 1946, British Minister of State Philip Noel Baker said in the House of Commons that his government was "determined to use the institution of the United Nations to kill power politics ..." (see Thompson, 1984, p. 370).

The influence of Idealism on diplomatic ethics was short-lived, though. The collapse of the League and the international political circumstances that surrounded Hitler's instigation of WWII were widely interpreted in policy circles as discrediting to Idealism's diplomatic conceptions. Gaddis (1985) views the founding of the United Nations simply as a "deference" that postwar statesmen felt obliged to pay to the Wilsonian vision and its enormous public appeal. He notes: "At the level of actual policy, though, the Wilsonian approach was an early casualty of the Cold War" (Gaddis, 1985, p. 124).

In the early postwar years, a debate occurred between Idealists and Realists, in the wake of which Realism firmly established itself as the predominant paradigm of ethical thought in diplomacy. Realism is grounded in the basic Hobbesian philosophical notions presented above. For the Realist school, the international system is anarchic and based on the principle of self-preservation. Unlike interactions at the domestic level, which are regulated by private agreements and public law, international interactions lack any authority higher than the state. Hence, Realism treats standards of conduct at the international level as different from those governing behaviors within states.

Realists impugned Idealism's naïvete, and urged a study of the world as it is, rather than a study of the world as it might be. The writings of Morgenthau (1978) played a major role in the theoretical formulation of Realism's ethical conceptions. He noted that "statesmen think and act in terms of interest defined as power," which includes both material and psychological, military and economic capabilities. The "national interest" is to maximize power. Because power exists only relationally, it follows logically that the international arena is per definition conflictual—all countries cannot increase their power or satisfy their national interest simultaneously (Morgenthau, 1978, p. 5). Morganthau's (1978) ambiguity about power as a means and power as an end was clarified later by Waltz (1979). Waltz (1979) observed that at a minimum states seek their own preservation and, at a maximum, drive for universal domination. Only after survival is assured, he noted, "can they afford to seek other goals; consequently, states act, first and foremost, to maximize security" (Waltz, 1979, p. 118).

Morgenthau (1978) justifiably argued that the contest between Idealism and Realism was not tantamount to a contest between principle and expediency, morality and immorality, but rather a contest between one type of morality and another type of morality. Idealism located morality in the transsocietal arena, i.e., in a community of humankind. However, it did not, and under then prevalent global conditions probably could not, offer serious conceptual perspectives for interactive constitution of transsocietal community. The one it offered, namely, an international community of states, was ill-defined and not functional. This was the case with the League and, as I will discuss later, to a large extent also with the United Nations. For Realism, by contrast, morality in international interactions is situated in the domestic sphere—in the responsibility of leaders to their citizens. In other words, Realism's conceptions of morality was grounded in the empirical reality of a world in which the nation-state represented not only the only operative principle for organizing community, but also the predominant actor in international interactions. However, Realism was also oblivious to growing transsocietal configurations of interaction particularly after WWII, including the transsocietal nature of East-West asymmetries during the Cold War.

Societal and Transsocietal Construction of Diplomacy

The institutional and ethical constructions of diplomacy discussed here constitute only a part of the story, namely of its historical evolution as an institution for inter-state interactions. To fully understand its role in international interactions, it is equally important to examine the alternating effect between diplomacy and other areas of communication. Particularly relevant is the role of communication technologies in shaping the social construction of diplomacy as an interactional institution.

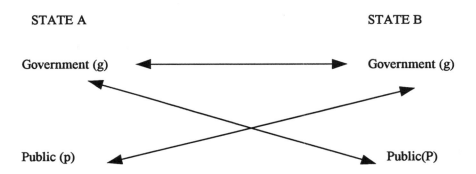

Fig. 7.1. Channels of International Communication (pre-globalization).

In its initial construction, diplomacy was basically communication between governments, i.e., Ag-Bg and Bg-Ag (see Fig. 7.1). A diplomat accredited to a foreign capital was a personal agent of his/her government, and all his/her interactions were restricted to his/her "opposite number" in the host country. This explains the traditional public perception of diplomacy as something mysterious. Diplomatic negotiations were conducted in secrecy, and treaties and agreements were kept secret. Interpersonal and face-to-face communication was the primary mode of diplomatic interaction, and *encrypted* or deceptive communication was developed as a uniquely diplomatic form of communication.

But to the extent that diplomatic policies became accessible to the citizenry, those patterns of diplomatic communication also began to change. This transformation of diplomacy is connected both with the mass media and the democratic reorganization of the nation-state. Thomas Paine (1792), in *The Rights of Man*, refers to Benjamin Franklin as "not the diplomat of a Court, but of MAN," thereby contrasting him with ambassadors of the European monarchies. Unlike the *ancient regime*, democracy put diplomacy under relatively great public accountability. Public opinion's influence on diplomacy became noticeable initially only at the level of individual nation-states, and was mediated by the print media. The role of the mass media as a societal interactional mediator between diplomacy and the citizenry first became evident during the Crimean War (1854-1856), in which England, France, Turkey and Sardinia defeated Russia. William Howard Russell, the war correspondent of *The London Times*, is reputed to have organized the first civilian effort to report a war to a civilian population. According to Knightley

(1975), Russell's dispatches about the Crimean War, and other conflicts, toppled the British government of the time. "His war reporting was considerably closer to the truth than anything the public had previously been permitted to learn ..." (Knightley, 1975, p. 5).

The emergence of *public opinion* as a factor in inter-state policy and decision-making expanded the interactional parameters of diplomacy. Besides the Ag-Bg and Bg-Ag line of communication, the Ag-Ap and Bg-Bp lines of communication were included in all diplomatic interaction processes. Airflight was the first tangible technology which heralded the shrinking of time and space relations in international communication. The influence of airflight on diplomacy was by no means insignificant. It facilitated the major technological factor for the creation of the League of Nations and later the United Nations. Besides its role in the proliferation of other international intergovernmental organizations (IGOs), airflight also has facilitated the so-called *shuttle diplomacy*, including Summitry or face-to-face communication between heads of states or their highest representatives. But in influencing the social construction of diplomacy, another transborder technology, namely radio, was far more consequential. Radio made it possible for the first time in history for leaders of one country to communicate with citizens of another country over the head of their own leaders—a factor which may explain why that broadcasting medium for a long time, and in most countries of the world, was put under government control. The interactional significance of the new mass medium was that it introduced a far more complex construction of diplomatic communication: Ag-Bg, Ag-Ap, Ag-Bp and Bg-Ag, Bg-Bp, Bg-Ap (see Fig. 7.1).

Radio technology offered diplomacy a powerful means of communication for pursuing its traditional statist goals. Martin (1958) has analyzed the enormous role of that medium during WWII and its subsequent incorporation into the Cold War scheme of international communication. But the new busy transborder web of wireless communication, together with the domestically operating visual medium, television, also produced for diplomacy the most profound challenge in its history. In other words, the new configuration of diplomatic communication unleashed a dynamic of its own. This is related to the emergence of *international public opinion*, which heralded the transsocietal constitution of the *public*, and the growing role of ordinary citizens as autonomous actors in global interactional processes. The mass media made it possible for the public to relate to the human dimensions of inter-state interactions and conflicts. The new interactional construction marked the transition from Classical Diplomacy to New Diplomacy (also called Public Diplomacy), which incorporates mass media campaigns, cultural affairs, aid programs, student exchange or scholarship programs, and people-to-people programs such as the Peace Corps. Fisher (1972) accounts for the emergence of Public Diplomacy with the governments' realization that "the actual consequences of a given policy initiative or overseas program are determined not only by that policy's logic as understood in government-to-government relations, or by the skill used in presenting and executing the policy in traditional diplomatic ways, but also by how both the domestic and the foreign public perceive the issues and the policy offered" (p. 8).

The growing influence of ordinary citizens in international affairs, marked in particular by the proliferation of local and international nongovernmental organizations (INGOs), also called *Citizens' Forums*, constitutes one of the most decisive developments since WWII. It has radically altered, as I will discuss later, the configuration of participants in international interactions. Already in the early years after the end of WWII, several dozen nongovernmental organizations were engaged in international civic activities in various countries, mostly in the United States—the country with the richest tradition of grassroots civic action. For example, in 1945 no less than 42 American non-governmental organizations (NGOs) attached to the U.S. delegation took part in the UN Conference in San Francisco. According to Archer (1983), 20 of those NGOs were concerned with broad social problems and the attendant issues of human rights and peace.

Local nongovernmental organizations (NGOs) and international nongovernmental organizations (INGOs) continued to proliferate throughout the world in the postwar years. By the late 1970s, an intricate web of NGOs and INGOs, interlinked through a variety of central agencies such as the "Conference of Nongovernment Organizations in Consultative Status with the Economic and Social Council of the United Nations," commonly known by its acronym "CONGO," were campaigning around the globe for a variety of causes, including human rights, disarmament, environmental policies and gender equity (see Wood, 1981). According to Boulding (1988), most nongovernmental organizations came into existence because of some shared concern for human well-being that crosses national borders. It is important to note here that not even authoritarian control in the communist-ruled part of the world could entirely stifle civic action, as was illustrated by the persistent human rights activities of dissident groups and personalities in the 1970s and 1980s. In an irony of history, the atom bomb was perhaps the single most important factor that enhanced an increasing sense of global interdependence and moral responsibility for many ordinary citizens worldwide. The two world wars had already created some of the narratives and stories that commonly contribute to self-awareness, as well as to moral sensibility and desire among human beings as members of an interdependent community. The global interactional conditions of the post war years produced countless such symbols, narratives, songs, and metaphors. A random list of symbols and events that, in an array of images and associations, began to shape the "global mind" includes the human landing on the moon, Chernobyl, John F. Kennedy, pop music, Martin Luther King, the Vietnam War, Andrei Sacharov, Band Aid, Afghanistan, We-the-People, Mahatama, Ghandi, green house effect, Nelson Mandela and the Berlin Wall.

THE DIPLOMACY AND ETHICS OF GLOBALIZATION

Global interactional processes before and after WWII differ in one major way. Global interactional processes before the Second World War were centered around the nation-state, while those of the postwar years have acquired increasingly supranational characteristics. This was already the case, as mentioned earlier, with the Cold War, which had given rise to a dichotomous global configuration on the basis of identities, values and interests that transcended those of the nation-state. This is particularly the case today, where global interactional processes have assumed far greater complexity in terms of both context and interactant actors. Along with this shift in the conditions of interaction, the issue of international morality has ceased to be an abstract idea. Instead, it has become a real challenge and opportunity, necessitated by multifaceted factors that have led to global projections of the notions of society and, especially, of community.

From Cold War to Globalization: Shifting Conditions of Interaction
Since the collapse of the Europe-centered global arrangement between the two world wars, the end of the East-West ideological dichotomy in the late eighties no doubt represents a radical shift in the conditions of international interaction. But that shift has also given rise to a variety of unjustified interpretations and projections about the emerging patterns of international interaction. For example, Halal (1989), much in the tradition of Idealism, writes: "Until recently the very idea that the Earth would be integrated into a single whole was so monumental that it was almost universally regarded as radical, unworkable, or utopian. Now a unified planet suddenly seems possible" (p. 555). Interestingly, two leading proponents of the Realism school also have come up with divergent models of interpretation, which are being widely debated in academic and policy-making circles. Fukuyama (1989), the deputy director of the US State Department's policy planning staff, characterizes recent world events as the "end of history," and observes,

The twentieth century saw the developed world descend into a a paroxysm of ideological violence, as liberalism contended first with the remnants of absolutism, then Bolshevism and Fascism, and finally an updated Marxism that threatened to lead to the ultimate apocalypse of nuclear war. But the century that began full of self-confidence in the ultimate triumph of Western liberal democracy seems at its close to be returning full circle to where it started: not to an 'end of ideology' or a convergence between capitalism and socialism, as earlier predicted, but to an unabashed victory of economic and political liberalism (p. 3).

By contrast, Huntington (1993), another prominent Realist, forecasts the beginning of a new volatile history. Whereas Fukuyama (1989) sees the end of history in the universal acceptance of liberal democracy, Huntington (1993) implies that liberal democracy has reached its natural borders and, in reference to the increasing transsocietal cultural constructions of the so-called Pan Identities in various regions of the world, writes, "... the 'kin-country-syndrome' is replacing political ideology and traditional balance of power considerations as the principal basis for cooperations and coalitions"(p. 35).

Huntington (1993) believes that this "syndrome" will inevitably lead to conflict. He notes,

... the fundamental source of conflict in this new world will not be primarily ideological or primarily economic. The great divisions among humankind and the dominating source of conflict will be cultural. ... The clash of civilizations will dominate global politics. The fault lines between civilizations will be the battle lines of the future (p. 22).

It is important to note that Fukuyama (1989) evaluates contemporary global developments on the basis of a strictly ideological approach, while Huntington (1993) simply substitutes culture for ideology as a paradigm for a new Cold War. That Fukuyama (1989) equates the end of Hegelian conception of history with the end of history itself is apparent. But, Huntington's (1993) deterministic assumptions about cultural diversity and conflict lack theoretical justifications. He does not explain, for example, why cultural diversity at the international level should *inevitably* lead to conflict any more than does cultural diversity in multiethnic and multiracial nations like the United States.

The ethical conceptions which underlay Fukuyama's (1989) and Huntington's (1993) respective models of interpretation are also remarkable.

Fukuyama (1989) laments the passing of the ideologized nation-state as the decline of nobler human virtues,

> The end of history will be a very sad time. The struggle for recognition, the willingness to risk one's life for an abstract goal, the worldwide ideological struggle that called for daring, courage, imagination and idealism, will be replaced by economic calculation, the endless solving of economic problems, environmental concerns, and the satisfaction of sophisticated consumer demands (p. 18).

Huntington (1993) does not believe that it is possible to conceptualize shared values of international morality under conditions of cultural diversity. He observes: "A world of clashing civilizations is inevitably a world of double standards: people apply one standard to their kin countries and a different standard to others" (Huntington, 1993, p. 36).

However, an interactionist conceptualization suggests that current global processes by no means represent anything like an "end of history" or an inevitable clash between cleanly demarcated and antagonistic cultures. Nor do these processes justify assumptions that a unified planet "suddenly seems possible." The conditions of international interactions have been altered radically, though, by the *globalization* process, of which the end of the East-West ideological dichotomy itself is, in large parts, a consequence (Belay, 1993; 1996). In that process, sub-nation-state, nation-state, and post-nation-state actors compete, interact and conflict in complex, but predictable ways. Closer examination of the essential features of globalization is crucial for understanding the evolving social construction and ethics of diplomacy.

From an interactional perspective, one may conceptualize *globalization* as an historically unique condition for international interaction. This new interactional condition is characterized first by growing interconnection of the world with converging satellite, computer, cable, VCR, telephone, fax, television, and radio technologies. Global communication networking has introduced a radical restructuring of time-space relations, which various authors have described as the shrinking of space (Agnew, 1987), time-space compression (Featherstone, 1990), or the temporalization of space (Hall, 1989). The communication revolution has undermined the role of space as a barrier to global interactions. Along with the collapse of spatial barriers, diminished costs of communication, including transportation, have made not only goods and ideas, but also people much more geographically mobile than ever before (Harvey, 1993). Important to note is that the new technologies have also introduced what Thompson (1990) has called quasi-mediated interaction. In contrast to previous mass-mediated communication, quasi-mediated interactions are not impersonal, nor do they presuppose passive receivers (Belay, 1996).

Interconnectedness, which makes fast and intensive transsocietal communication possible more than ever before, goes hand in hand with yet a second aspect of globalization that drives those transsocietal interactions. This relates to the reality of interdependence between nations, due to growing transnational interests and concerns in the areas of capital, natural resources, trade, ecology, health and the like. Ionescu (1991) defines interdependence as the effect of the scientific information revolution of the mid-twentieth century on the conduct of human, domestic and international affairs which links those affairs so closely that "they become, by synergy, a circumbience or superior to, and different from, their sum total" (p. 5). According to Parry (1993), communication and transport technologies were the necessary conditions for worldwide political interdependence. But he also emphasizes a rather pluralistic account of the origins of interdependence and notes: "... what we are experiencing is not something which is totally unprecedented but, rather, a transformation of quantity into quality. The elements of interdependence which earlier authors had identified—such as trade and capital movements—have, through the new technologies, vastly increased in size and velocity" (Parry, 1993, p. 145). As Buzan & Little (1994) observe, the organization of trade, production and finance, the process of diplomacy, and networks of transportation and communication all operate on a global scale. In other words, economic, strategic and communication technologies have become global not only in reach, but also in organization. Furthermore "national" security has become increasingly inseparable from "international" security, whereby both assume, going beyond the narrower military concept, a much broader definition, including drug trafficking, terrorism and the like (Kennedy, 1993, p. 130). Soediomoto (see Campanella, 1993) suggests that the dynamics of interdependence might better be understood if we think of the globe "not in terms of a map of nations but as a meteorological map, where weather systems swirl independently of any national boundaries and low and high fronts create new climatic conditions far ahead of them" (p. 195).

The globalization process has diminished the predominant historical role of the nation-state as an organizing principle for self-identifying human communities. This becomes evident when one considers contemporary subnational and postnational trends which Belay has discussed as *intrasocietal* and *transsocietal* shifts of identity (Belay, 1996). *Intrasocietal* shifts refer to the redirection of identification from national culture to that of subnational groups as contrastive parameters of cultural self-definition. It represents an inward, disintegrative reconstruction of identity in the age of globalization. A particular case in point is the growing role of ethnic identification, especially its politicization, in various parts of the world (Belay, 1996).

Transsocietal shifts concern the redirection of identification from national to supranational cultural constructs. Two types of identity constructions are apparent today at the supranational level. The first relates to the growing globalization of occupational as well as sociological identities such as gender and environmentalism. The transnational passage of *environmentalism*, owing to its emphasis on the planetary nature of ecological interdependence, caters to global networks of identity and involvement (Belay, 1996). Equally significant is the globalization of gender, specifically female, cultural identification. Boulding (1988) evaluates the transsocietal representation of female cultural identity as one that is less emotionally invested in existing ways of doing things and can visualize alternative approaches to problems more easily, because women "have lived at the margins of the public sphere for so long" (p. 136).

The *transsocietal* passage of "geobasic identifications" represents another major redirection of identity. This refers to the so-called Pan identities that attempt to unify in a single political community several, usually contiguous, states on the basis of common cultural characteristics or a "family of cultures." Examples of such transnational identity constructions include Pan-Arabism, Pan-Europeanism and Pan-Africanism (Belay, 1996).

Together with the transsocietal shifts of cultural identity, the fact that economic, strategic and communication technologies have become global both in reach and organization have brought to international interactions relatively new and powerful actors other than the nation state. Indeed, nation-states, once deemed the only actors on the international stage, have now become only one of several players in the emerging global environment. This is connected with the institutionalization of globalization through an increasing number of intergovernmental and international nongovernmental organizations. Already in the late eighties, there were roughly 10,000 transnational corporations (TNCs) with 90,000 affiliates. Sixty percent of the affiliates of the top 500 TNCs were located in Organization for Economic Cooperation and Development (OECD) countries. But subsidiaries of TNCs are also spread over forty-five African countries, twenty-four Latin American countries, sixteen Middle Eastern countries, and twenty-two countries in East and South Asia (Boulding, 1988, p. 52).

The data on the number of intergovernmental and international nongovernmental, non-corporate organizations vary greatly, but all sources indicate a rapid increase. In 1909, there were only 37 intergovernmental organizations (IGOs), and 176 international nongovernmental organizations (INGOs). According to Held (1990), the number of IGOs increased from 280 in

1972 to 365 in 1984, while that of INGOs increased from 2173 to 4615 during the same period. Based on a broader definition of both types of organizations and rather extensive research, Boulding (1988) identified 2000 IGOs and 18,000 INGOs by the late eighties.

Current Institutional Orientations and Ethical Dialogics

In an address given shortly before his departure from office, former American Secretary of State, George Shultz, described some of the consequences of globalization in diplomacy. He remarked that, undermining the ancient constraints of geography and borders, globalization is "challenging established institutions and values, and redefining the agenda of political discourse" (see Roberts, 1991, p. 13). Accounts by several professional diplomats reflect radical challenges and transformations which confront diplomacy today. For example, Roberts (1991), a former US ambassador to Yugoslavia, writes, "Nowhere have the changes wrought by the information revolution been more profound than in the world I know best—that of American diplomacy .... The information revolution has compressed the time and distance which once separated one's own country and others in all parts of the globe" (p. 113).

STATE A STATE B

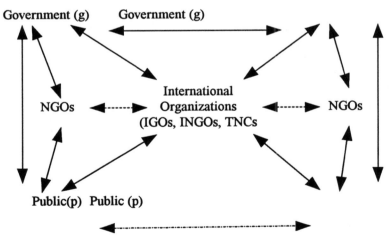

Fig. 7.2. Channels of International Communication (globalization).

Figure 7.2 shows the complex construction of the channels of international communication in the age of globalization. To the extent that globalization has radically restructured the patterns of international interactions in space, in density as well as in participating actors, diplomacy finds itself under enormous pressure to adjust. Changes in three major aspects of its traditional modus operandi require particular focus. Firstly, diplomacy has gone, more than ever before, far beyond being merely an institution for government-to-government interaction. It involves growingly interaction with publics, both foreign and domestic. In other words, the influence of publics on interstate negotiations has been enhanced by globalization—a development which, in turn, has also redefined the role of diplomats as communicators. As Roberts (1991) notes, "(u)nless we communicate effectively with the public of foreign countries about our policies, we will be unable to cope adequately with the problems of our age ..." (p. 113).

The increased public influence on diplomatic processes, and, consequently, the growing role of diplomats as public communicators magnify the intercultural problematique of diplomacy. As a result of their socialization to the norms and procedures of the diplomatic institution, diplomats in the past had become more like each other than were the countries they represented. But to the extent that globalization mandates a direct link of diplomacy with foreign publics, and that, as I will discuss below, more and more professionals not trained in diplomatic skills are being drawn into the diplomatic process, the potential for misrepresentation and misattribution cannot be overemphasized. Communication challenges derive not simply from lack of intercultural "sensitivity" or from contrasting forms of nonverbal behavior. More importantly, the diplomatic process requires managing complex intercultural communication processes. This is so because diplomacy often involves complex subjects which are deeply influenced by the cultural variation of moral reasoning. According to Fisher (1989), the challenge that diplomats must face most urgently is "communicating interculturally about abstract, value-laden subjects, where comprehension depends on interpreting the style and social meaning of communication, and appreciating the implicit assumptions and habits of perceiving and reasoning that go with culture's conditioning" (p. 418).

Secondly, career diplomats no longer exercise, in the now archaic phrase, the same `extraordinary and plenipotentiary' powers they used to in negotiations with their host-country governments. Fisher (1989) observes that the number of people who get involved in a nation's diplomatic activity increases enormously as the world becomes more interdependent. The communication and transportation technologies of globalization make it possible for heads of government or senior ministers to speak or meet with their counterparts without the use of ambassadorial intermediaries. Moreover, instructions are obtained from the top home-country political leadership instantaneously by cable or telephone, and ambassadors "have little leeway (and seldom much influence) in policy matters" (Roberts, 1991, p. 114). In addition, negotiations on specific issues of bilateral interest are now conducted by specialists and technicians who fly in directly from their home countries. Consequently, "[I]t is not uncommon to hear ambassadors complain that they have become little more than glorified innkeepers for the large number of VIPs, Congressmen, and other visiting firemen who expect to be put up at the ambassador's residence" (Roberts, 1991, p. 114).

Thirdly, globalization has changed the character and dimension of the problems that confront diplomats. The demands which diplomats must consolidate and act upon, such as security, trade, investment and the like, are often not confined within the borders of a single country. Rather, they are international in scope, requiring joint measures by diverse national governments and the rallying of public support and involvement across national borders.

The latter two trends mentioned above, suggest that globalization has enhanced the movement of diplomacy away from bilateral government-to-government to multilateral, both regional and transcontinental, intergovernmental spheres of interaction. Today, a great deal of diplomatic interaction occurs already in specialized international agencies such as the General Agreement on Tariffs and Trade (GATT), the International Monetary Fund (IMF) and the World Bank, or regional ones such as the European Community and NAFTA. In other words, the construction of diplomacy as an interactional institution is becoming more and more global both in purpose and organization, much like that of corporate and nongovernmental institutions.

Along with the globalization process, the dialogics of ethics and diplomacy is gradually evolving out of its nation-state and Cold War ideological conceptual orientations. Consistent conceptualizations of ethics similar to the Idealism and Realism paradigms are not (yet) available. However, the new dialogics of ethics and diplomacy indicates distinctive conceptual orientations, which could be described as "globalism." Figure 7.3 summarizes the patterns and agencies of contemporary international interactions. Intergovernmental organizations (IGOs), transnational corporations (TNCs) and international nongovernmental organizations (INGOs) comprise the major interactional actors. The interaction of these agencies with nation-state and global communities as well as the interaction between these agencies with one another build the reference points for Globalist theorization on diplomacy and ethics.

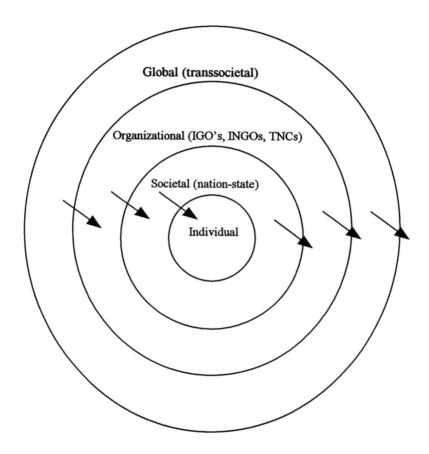

Fig. 7.3. Relationship among the Four Levels of Ethics.

There is a consensus among Globalists that the nation-state has been weakened, and that globalization mandates some sort of supranational morality. Buzan (1991) summarizes the Globalist moral consensus on diplomacy, when he writes, "The ideological content of interdependence is, in effect, that the art of good government needs to include a substantially higher element of responsible external behavior than has hitherto been the norm" (p. 24).

Globalists also agree that as the nation-state becomes weaker, so also is the configuration of international interactants shifting from the predominance of governmental to that of nongovernmental actors. Many Globalists accord, in particular, INGOS enormous role as agents of the emerging international morality. These organizations, which have campaigned for transborder concerns with human and ecological well being throughout the postwar years, have been instrumental for the moral and legal recognition of common values. Many of them, such as Greenpeace or Doctors Without Borders, often undertake or participate in international intervention, which infringes upon state sovereignty. INGOs also provide a continuing lobby in support of constructive international policies directed at individual governments or IGOs, such as the United Nations. In particular, they develop models for new policies drafted in resolutions at conferences organized to occur simultaneously with congresses of major IGOs (Boulding, 1988). The presence and influence of INGOs has today increased so significantly that, according to Lyons & Mastanduno (1993), "it no longer makes sense to speak of states as the exclusive or even primary actors in the international system" (p. 525).

Globalist dialogics of ethics is divided, however, on the question of sovereignty. The question is significant at the level of both theory and praxis. Conceptually, any claims of, and proposals for, international morality would, despite globalization, be meaningless, if Globalist theorization does not resolve the constraints sovereignty imposes on such claims and proposals. At the practical level, sovereignty has constituted the legal foundation of the international system since the end of WWII. The principle of sovereignty, as incorporated under nine points in the United Nations Charter (see Jones, 1992, pp. 44-45), stipulates that nations have an inviolable right of control over their territories. The purpose of the international intergovernmental structure that was created in the postwar years was merely to serve as a link between sovereign states.

In the on-going Globalist dialogics of sovereignty, one may distinguish, in a very broad sense, between two different approaches. A group of Globalist authors contends that the principle of nation-state sovereignty has become anachronistic to present-day realities. Kratochwil (1995) argues that, in terms of responsibilities and obligations, sovereignty has evolved largely in response to developments in Euro-centric international society, but is now most likely to change under the influence of globalization. Rosenau (1995) contends that the lines of sovereignty have long been crossed. He identifies a number of signals and argues that they point to a decline in the effectiveness of states, an erosion of their authority, and a corresponding increase in the competency of international organizations. Rosenau (1995) refers in particular to the fact that IGOs, which were initially established, as mentioned earlier, only to link sovereign states, are now being commissioned to regulate social matter formerly managed at the national level. The critique of sovereignty which Onuf (1995) presents is in fact a critique of the state itself because he claims that the state no longer holds a monopoly of respect from those it serves.

Jackson (1995) believes that *international community* has already become a meaningful concept. He distinguishes between the "community of states," which includes citizens as well as sovereigns as 'right and duty bearing units' and the "community of humankind," i.e., humans as "right and duty bearing units" (Jackson, 1995, pp. 61-64). Jackson (1995) views the United Nations as "one obvious operative community of sovereign states," in which citizens of at least some states are members once removed (p. 62). Lyons & Mastanduno (1995) contend that the members of the international community already share a sense of rights, duties, values and obligations. They refer specifically to attitudinal changes with regard to international intervention, and observe: "In the past, great powers have often arrogated this authority to themselves. What is distinctive about the present period of history, characterized by the global expansion of international society, is that such derogations of authority are increasingly difficult to justify.... What appears to be required, increasingly, is what might be called collective legitimation" (Lyons & Mastanduno, 1995, p. 8). Because it has become imperative for intervenors to legitimize their actions, the shifting patterns of justification for intervention can, according to Lyons & Mastanduno (1995), tell a great deal about the extent to which the balance between state autonomy and the authority of the international community is in the process of fundamental change. Lyons & Mastanduno (1993) observe that widely recognized justifications in contemporary international society fall in the middle of the legitimacy spectrum summarized in Figure 7. 4.

Pure realism			Contemporary international society			Pure globalism
1	2	3	4	5	6	7
Might makes right	Self Preservation	Consent of host government	Consensus in the international community	Collapse of governing authority in host country	Universal values or principles	Global governing authority

Fig. 7.4. Justifications for International Intervention.
From Lyons and Mastanduno. (1993). *Models of justification for international intervention* (p.528).

However, another group of Globalist theoreticians argues that it is not justified to underestimate the role of the nation-state, or to overrate the importance of international organizations such as the United Nations. For example, Kennedy (1993) admits that there has been a certain erosion of the powers of the nation-state in recent decades, but observes that the nation-state remains the primary locus of identity of most people, "regardless of who their employer is and what they do for a living, individuals pay taxes to the state, are subject to its laws, serve (if need be) in its armed forces, and can travel only by having its passport" (p. 134). I argue elsewhere (Belay, 1996), that while its historical role has been significantly eroded as an organizing principle of community, the nation-state is still salient, "This is because there is nothing archaic about citizenship.... The project of `world citizenship' must appear premature for a long time to come" (pp. 340-342).

Sid-Ahmed (1990) and Hamelink (1993) emphasize that the question of sovereignty should be treated in the context of the unequal relationship that exists between the various units of the international system. They contend that great powers frequently articulate their particular interests in the language of universal moral principles in an effort to persuade the others to accept them. They point out, in particular, that the so-called Third World states are most vulnerable to external pressure, which explains the sensitivity of those states toward the concept of a `right' of international intervention. Sid-Ahmed (1990) observes: "... the question of curtailing national sovereignty raise[s] a still more important question, namely, that of depriving weaker states of prerogatives which protect them from stronger states in a world still marked by uneven development" (p. 91). Other authors have observed that whether or not globalization is in, effect, a form in which the hegemony of the great powers can assert itself, or a process which results in equitable global integration, will depend on the institutionalization of globalization through protective and democratic bodies (see, for example Mowlana, 1993; Parry, 1993). Held (1993) emphasizes the need to reform the UN Security Council and its veto system in order to strengthen the Third World voice.

Ionescu (1991), Parry (1993), and Smouts (1993) have introduced far more radical perspectives for addressing ethics and diplomacy in the age of globalization. Smouts (1993) is skeptical that the organizations set up immediately after the Second World War, such as the United Nations, are capable of meeting the challenges of globalization. Ionescu (1991) also has developed the concept of *elite political cognition* to explain the limitations of IGOs, such as GATT and the IMF, to serve as forums in which a common consensus on approaches to interdependence policy-making will emerge. By *elite cognition*, Ionescu (1991) means both knowledge and judgment. Parry (1993) concurs with Ionescu (1991), and observes: "Concentration on elite cognition would lead to questions about how the network of managers of globalization are able to formulate the kinds of judgment to handle issues of quite staggering complexity, whether these concern the environment, health or security" (p. 148). He proposes that those engaged in managing the interdependent world be subject to a measure of accountability if only as some protection against the severe dangers consequent upon any mismanagement. "... the need for compensatory protective democracy both above and below the level of the nation-state becomes all the more pressing" (Parry, 1993, p. 148).

CONCLUDING REMARKS

The globalization process has rendered obsolete some longstanding perceptions about international interaction and morality. It is no longer realistic to view the world in terms of a pre-Leviathan anarchy, in which nation-states are trapped in a "prisoners' dilemma"—none trusting the other states, each pursuing power for itself as an end as well as a reassurance against what other states would do with untrammeled power. Today, international interactions occur under conditions of complex global interdependency, where multiple channels connect societies. Growing recognition of common human and ecological concerns has also opened the way to processes for construction of global ethics.

The growth of an international culture and ethical principles has gone far beyond the diplomatic institution. To the extent that the nation-state has been weakened, other interactional actors have appeared to influence—both as agencies and as reference points—evolving international moral perspectives. However, it is premature to write off the nation-state. No other substitute exists today for defining the rights and duties of citizenship. In spite of interconnectedness and interdependence, the world of globalization is still a far cry from being an operative global moral community. Globalization has given rise not only to global integration, but simultaneously to various forms of regional and sociological asymmetries and discontinuities, including a prospect for further marginalization of the southern hemisphere, where four-fifths of the world's population lives. As Kennedy (1993) points out, globalization is driven primarily by the market rationale, and the "rational market, by its very nature, is not concerned with social justice and fairness" (p. 56).

By the same token, it is interesting to note that the nation-state itself is actively engaged in strengthening the international regulatory structures of globalization, even though this means for the nation-state further erosion of its control over domestic affairs. In other words, the nation-state has adopted a globalist orientation, and through its regional and transcontinental IGOs, such as NAFTA and GATT, is operating increasingly at the supranational level—in a manner similar to TNCs and INGOs. These IGOs, which constitute the focal point of the nation-state's most recent diplomatic efforts, also possess decisive international competency as "legislators" of globalization.

In this international locus of engagement of the nation-state rest both the challenges and opportunities that diplomacy as an international institution faces today. This locus of engagement also could be used as a specific reference point for formulating concrete proposals for transforming diplomacy from its traditional nation-state-centered moral orientation to an internationalist one. IGOs, which are currently the most powerful centers of international diplomatic activity, could play an instrumental role, particularly in two problematic areas of globalization. First, they could help mitigate the wide gap between international legality and morality. Thompson (1985) has argued that one of the gravest errors of contemporary perceptions about international processes is the separation of law and morality. Several authors stress the need for IGOs to pay as much attention to helping shape a moral consensus for an interdependent global order as they do to creating the regulatory structures for globalization. Kung (1991) observes that the international community of states has created trans-national, trans-cultural and trans-religious legal structures, and asks, "... but what is a world order without a binding and obligatory ethic for the whole of humankind—for all of its time-conditioned nature—i.e., without a world ethic?" (p. 34). Thompson (1985) also cautions, "But law cannot speak if there is no underlying moral consensus" (p. 1).

Second, the processes of integration and fragmentation generated by globalization could lead to several conflictual developments. Globalization may be viewed as an interactional condition that gives rise to the proliferation of intersecting cultural identities, each trying to win its existential right in place and/or space (Belay, 1996). Aggressive forms of disintegration could result from efforts to impose cultural homogeneity. Moreover, the regional and sociological asymmetries of globalization also could produce serious challenges to economic and political governance, as those regions and population groups which feel dislocated embrace a variety of nativist and fundamentalist appeals. The tensions could become uncontrollable, if those nativist and fundamentalist forces assume political power and attempt to reinvigorate the nation-state in an historically regressive crusade against the integrationist influences of globalization. Diplomacy at the level of IGOs could help circumscribe these tendencies, through greater engagement on behalf of a moral agenda which incorporates five central challenges for the evolving global community. These are human rights, social justice, gender equity, environmental preservation, and cultural pluralism. Engagement on behalf of such a moral agenda could transform the traditional state-centered role of diplomacy into one of international ethical agency. In other words, a diplomacy that views itself as social mediator between the market forces (TNCs) and the moral forces (INGOs) of globalization, could certainly move the world in a positive direction.

REFERENCES

Adler, N. (1986). *International dimensions of organizational behavior*. Boston, MA: Kent Publishing Company.

Agnew, J. (1987). *Place and politics*. London: Allen and Unwin.

Archer, A. (1983). Methods of multilateral management: The interrelationship of international organizations and NGOs. In T. T. Gati (Ed.), *The U.S., the U.N., and the management of global change* (pp. 303-325). New York: New York University Press.

Belay, G. (1993). Toward a paradigm shift for intercultural and international communication: New research directions. In S. Deetz (Ed.), *Communication Yearbook* (pp. 437-457). Newbury Park, CA: Sage Publications.

Belay, G. (1996). (Re)construction and negotiation of cultural identities in the age of globalization. In H. B. Mokros (Ed.), *Interaction and Identity. Information and Behavior*, 5, 319-346.

Blumer, H. (1969). *Symbolic interactionism: Perspective and Method*. Englewood Cliffs, NJ: Prentice-Hall.

Bletz, D. F. (1972). *The role of the military professional in U. S. foreign policy*. New York: Praeger.

Boulding, E. (1988). *Building a global civic culture: Education for an interdependent world*. New York: Columbia University Press.

Briggs, E. (1968). *Anatomy of diplomacy: The origin and execution of American foreign policy*. New York: David McKay.

Bull, H. (1995). *The anarchical society*. New York: Columbia University Press.

Buller, P. F., Kohls, J. J., & Anderson, K. S. (1991). The challenge of global ethics. *Journal of Business Ethics*, 10, 767-775.

Buzan, B. (1991). Interdependence and Britain's external relations. In L. Freedman & M. Clarke (Eds.), *Britain in the world* (pp. 10-41). Cambridge: Cambridge University Press.

Buzan, B., & Little, R. (1994). The idea of international system: Theory meets history. *International Political Science Review, 15*(3), 231-255.

Campanella, M. L. (1993). The effects of globalization and turbulence on policy-making processes. *Government and Opposition, 28,* 190-204.

Churchill, L. R. (1982). The teaching of ethics and moral values in teaching: Some contemporary confusion. *Journal of Higher Education, 53*(3), 296-306.

Dinh, T. V. (1987). *Communication and diplomacy in a changing world.* Norwood, NJ: Ablex.

Derian, J. D. (1993). Diplomacy. In J. Krieger (Ed.), *The Oxford companion to politics of the world* (pp. 244-246). New York: Oxford University Press.

Dickinson, L. (1926). *The international anarchy, 1904-1914.* London: Century Company.

Evans, W. A. (1981). *Management ethics: An intercultural perspective.* Boston: Martinus Nijhoff.

Featherstone, M. (1990). Global culture: An introduction. *Theory, Culture & Society, 7*(2-3), 1-14.

Fine, G. A., & Kleinman, S. (1983). Network and meaning: An interactionis approach to structure. *Symbolic Interaction, 6,* pp. 97-110.

Fisher, G. (1989). Diplomacy. In M. K. Asante & W. B. Gudykunst (Eds.), *Handbook of international and intercultural communication* (pp. 407-422). Newbury Park, CA: Sage.

Fisher, G. (1972). *Public diplomacy and the behavioral sciences.* Bloomington: Indiana University Press.

Fukuyama, F. (1989, Summer). The end of history? *National Interest,* 3-18.

Gaddis, J. L. (1985). Morality and the cold war: The American experience. In K. W. Thompson (Ed.), *Ethics in international relations: Ethics in foreign policy* (pp. 109-126). New Brunswick, NJ: Transaction Books.

Geertz, C. (1973). *The interpretation of cultures.* New York: Basic Books.

Glenn, E.S. (1981). *Man and mankind: Conflict and communication between cultures.* Norwood, NJ: Ablex.

Goffman, E. (1967). *Interaction rituals: Essays on face-to-face behavior.* Garden City, NY: Anchor Books.

Halal, W. E. (1989). A unified planet suddenly seems possible. *Futures, 21*(6), 555-561.

Hall, E. T. (1959). *The silent language.* New York: Doubleday.

Hall, S. (1989). Ethnicity: Identity and difference. *Radical America, 23*(4), 9-21.

Hamelink, C. J. (1993). Globalism and national sovereignty. In K. Nordenstrang & H. I. Schiller, *Beyond national sovereignty: International communication in the 1990s* (pp. 371-393). Norwood, NJ: Ablex.

Harvey, D. (1993). From space to place and back again: Reflections on the condition of postmodernity. In J. Bird, B. Curtis, T. Putnam, G. Robertson, & L. Tickner (Eds.), *Mapping the Futures* (pp. 3-29). New York: Routledge.

Hegel, G. W. F. (1973). *The phenomenology of mind* (J. B. Baillie, Trans.). New York: Harper & Row.

Held, D. (1990) The decline of the nation state. In S. Hall & M. Jaques (Eds.), *New times: The changing times of politics in the 1990's* (pp. 191-204). New York: Verso.

Held, D. (1993). *Prospects for democracy.* Cambridge: Polity Press.

Hobbes, T. (1887). *Leviathan.* London: George Routledge.

Hoffmannn, S. (1981). *Duties beyond borders: On the limits and possibilities of ethical international politics.* Syracuse: Syracuse University Press.

Hofstede, G. (1980). *Culture's consequences: International differences in work related values.* Beverly Hills, CA: Sage.

Huntington, S. (1993). The clash of civilizations? *Foreign Affairs, 72*(3), 23-49.

Ionescu, G. (1991). *Leadership in an interdependent world: The statesmanship of Adenauer, de Gaulle, Thatcher and Gorbachev.* London: Longman.

Jackson, R. H. (1995). International community beyond the cold war. In G. M. Lyons & M. Mastanduno, (Eds.), *Beyond Westphalia? State sovereignty and international intervention* (pp. 59-86). Baltimore: The Johns Hopkins University Press.

Jones, D. (1992). The declaratory tradition. In T. Nardin & D. Mapel (Eds.), *Traditions of international ethics* (pp. 42-61). Cambridge: Cambridge University Press.

Kennedy, P. (1993). *Preparing for the twenty-first century.* New York: Random House.

Knightley, P. (1975). *The first casualty: From the Crimea to Vietnam—the war correspondent as a hero. Propaganda and myth maker.* New York: Harcourt Brace Jovanovich.

Kratochwil, F. (1995). Sovereignty as dominium: Is there a right of humanitarian intervention? In G. M. Lyons & M. Mastanduno (Eds.), *Beyond Westphalia? State sovereignty and international intervention* (pp. 21-42). Baltimore: The Johns Hopkins University Press.

Kung, H. (1991). *Global responsibility: In search of a new world ethic.* New York: Crossroad Publishing Company.

Leeds-Hurwitz, W. (1990). Notes in the history of intercultural communication: The foreign service institute and the mandate for intercultural training. *Quarterly Journal of Speech, 76,* 262-281.

Lyons, G. M., & Mastanduno, M. (1995). Introduction: International intervention, state sovereignty, and the future of international society. In G. M. Lyons & M. Mastanduno (Eds.), *Beyond Weastphalia? State sovereignty and international intervention* (pp. 1-20). Baltimore: The Johns Hopkins University Press.

Lyons, G. M., & Mastanduno, M. (1993). International intervention, state sovereignty, and the future of international society. *International Science Journal, 45,* 517-532.

Martin, L. J. (1958). *International propaganda: Its legal and diplomatic control.* Minneapolis: University of Minnesota Press.

Mattingly, G. (1955). *Renaissance diplomacy.* Boston: Houghton Mifflin.

McDermott, G. (1973). *The new diplomacy and its apparatus.* London: The Plum Press Ltd.

Maxwell, M. (1990). *Morality among nations.* Albany, NY: State University of New York Press.

Mokros, H. B., & Deetz, S. (in press). What counts as real? A constitutive view of communication and the disenfranchised in the context of health. In E. B. Ray (Ed.), *Communication and the disenfranchised: Social health issues and implications.* Hillsdale, NJ: Lawrence Erlbaum Associates.

Morgenthau, H. (1968). Balance of power. *Encyclopaedia Britannica. 2,* (pp. 1064-1065). Chicago: Encyclopaedia Britannica.

Morgenthau, H. (1978). *Politics among nations: The struggle for power and peace.* New York: Alfred A. Knopf.

Mowlana, H. (1993). The new global order and cultural ecology. *Media, Culture, and Society, 15,* 9-27.

Nicolson, H. (1954). *The evolution of diplomatic method.* London: Constable & Co. Ltd.

Nicolson, H. (1950). *Diplomacy.* London: Oxford University Press (Original work was published in 1939).

Numelin, R. (1950). *The beginnings of diplomacy.* London: Oxford University Press.

Onuf, N. (1995). Intervention for the common good. In G. M. Lyons & M. Mastanduno (Eds.). *Beyond Westphalia? State sovereignty and international intervention* (pp. 43-58). Baltimore: The Johns Hopkins University Press.

O'Connor, J. (1994, April). Does a global village warrant a global ethic? *Religion, 24,* 155-164.

Paine, T. (1792). *The rights of man.* London: H. D. Symonds.

Parry, G. (1993). The interweaving of foreign and domestic policy-making. *Government and Opposition, 28,* 143-151.

Reston, J. (1983, April 5). U.S. hot line to Soviet: Little use for 20 years. *The New York Times,* April 5, 1983, p. 24.

Roberts, W. (1991). The media dimension II: Diplomacy in the information age. *The World Today, 47,* 112-115.

Rosenau, J. (1993). International relations. In J. Krieger (Ed.). *The Oxford companion to politics of the world* (pp. 455-460). New York: Oxford University Press.

Rosenau, J. (1995). Sovereignty in a turbulent world. In G. M. Lyons & M. Mastanduno (Eds.). *Beyond Westphalia? State sovereignty and international intervention* (pp. 191-227). Baltimore: The Johns Hopkins University Press.

Rossow, R. (1962). The professionalization of the new diplomacy. *World Politics, 14*, 561-575.

Roy, S. L. (1978). *Diplomacy in ancient India.* Calcutta: Charu Publishing Co.

Shennan, J. H. (1974). *The origins of the modern European state 1450-1725.* London: Hutchinson.

Sid-Ahmed, M. (1990). The coming global civilization. *IFDA Dossier, 77*, 89-92.

Smith, M. J. (1993). Idealism. In J. Krieger (Ed.), *The Oxford companion to politics of the world* (pp. 408-409). New York: Oxford University Press.

Smouts, M. C. (1993). Some thoughts on international organizations and theories of regulation. *International Social Science Journal, 45*, 443-498.

Stryker, S., & Statham, A. (1984). Symbolic interaction and role theory. In G. D. Lindzey & E. Aronson (Eds.), *Handbook of social psychology* (pp. 311-378). Reading, MA: Addison-Wesley.

Thompson, J. B. (1990). *Ideology of modern culture.* Cambridge: Polity Press.

Thompson, J. W., & Padover, S. K. (1965). *Secret diplomacy: Espionage and cryptography 1500-1815.* New York: Frederick Ungar Publishing Company.

Thompson, K. W. (1984). The ethical dimensions of diplomacy. *Review of Politics, 46*(3), 367-387.

Thompson, K. W. (1985). Ethics and international relations: The problem. In K. W. Thompson (Ed.), *Ethics in international relations: Ethics in foreign policy* (pp.1-17). New Brunswick, NJ: Transaction Books.

Waltz, K. (1979). *Theory of international politics.* Reading, MA: Addison-Wesley Publishing Company.

Watson, A. (1982). *Diplomacy: The dialogue between states.* London: Eyre Methuen.

Wedge, B. (1968). Communication analysis and comprehensive diplomacy. In A. S. Hoffmann (Ed.), *International communication and the new diplomacy* (pp. 24-47). Bloomington, IN: Indiana University Press.

Wood, D. (1981). Patterns of international collaboration among nongovernmental organizations. In N. A. Sims (Ed.), *Explorations in ethics and international relations* (pp. 121-143). London: Croom Helm Ltd.

Conclusion

Fred L. Casmir
Pepperdine University

The work on the book is finished, and as I sit here contemplating what we have accomplished, many thoughts rush through my mind. Foremost, because I am first of all a teacher, is the question of whether or not we accomplished what we set out to do. Actually, as the editor I had several purposes. First of all, I did not want to deal with ethics as an abstract subject matter—something which required no personal response or feeling of responsibility on the part of teachers and students using our book in a classroom setting, or for that matter, on the part of anyone who would read it. Since I am really not sure how anyone can adequately study human interactions, or more specifically intercultural and international communication, from an uninvolved, supposedly objective, *outsider's* point of view, that orientation was one of the bases for bringing together the chapters you have read.

As I result, and I am sure you noticed it, we all did more than describe or identify. We made choices, we made decisions and we took stands. Our purpose, however, was not to simply instruct you in norms of ethical behavior. As communication scholars, one of our purposes was to engage you in a kind of *long distance dialog*. To me, that word *engage* includes more, however, than whatever you, I and the other authors might do within the setting of reading written words. Having you engage the ideas presented, and assuming a stance of active, thoughtful and responsible personal participation, is even more important when one considers the role of ethics in human lives.

We also did not want to produce a book which represented an abstract kind of survey of ethics as an academic, intellectual or philosophical exercise. I am sure there is value in learning about the history of ethics, as it were, in the Western world. It provides a framework, and insights which could prevent us from assuming that ethical challenges are very recent, or only related to the world in which we live today.

But that was not our intent. In spite of the fact that this is a book which centers on intercultural and international communication as these two areas relate to ethics, we chose not to turn this book into some kind of comparative study of various culture-related ethical systems. The reason is actually quite simple. Once again, as scholars who are concerned with culture and inter-cultural interactions, we certainly were very cognizant of differences in cultures and the resulting problems when representatives of different cultures seek opportunities to think, plan and work together. By the same token we felt that what holds probably true of all surveys of ideals, values or philosophical issues, applies to our book as well. It is difficult to come up with some sort of statistical average as a basis for the development of applications of value- or ethic-systems in human lives. Of course, we also recognized the fact that while culture plays a significant role, it by no means pre-determines all human reactions or responses. In the longrun, ethics and values are either absorbed, *lived* or dealt with by individuals (probably on the basis of whether or not they appear to have value to them), or they become mere shibboleths, often repeated but really not producing significant consistency or thoughtful changes in our behavior.

All that brings up an important issue. My students often ask me, usually before examinations or at the beginning of a course I offer, whether the material covered will be *cumulative*. I must admit to some problems with that question, since I am nor sure how anyone learns anything without *accumulating*. In relationship to our subject matter in this book, I thus need to ask myself what should be involved in a learning process that takes ethics as its subject matter. In other words, how do we learn what we learn—basically an epistemological question. You probably have just completed this book as part of an active, involving, challenging course in which you, your teacher and our book played some significant interrelated roles. Now, the question is what have you learned, and, just as importantly to a teacher, how can we determine what you have learned? Teaching and learning are complex processes, and, frankly we do not know enough about either one to be secure in producing consistently predictable results.

Some of the thoughts which are on my mind today, are the direct result of my reading the work of others. In other words, I am debtor to a lot of individuals. I have forgotten some of their names; in the case of others in only remember very clearly the main ideas they shared, while many of the details are no longer clear in my mind. In all cases, those things I remember best are the result of my thinking about what I read in various attempts to engage the ideas presented to me. Such active processing commonly had enough of an extended influence that even the writing and editing of this book has been influenced by it. For instance, I remember running across a discussion by Martin Buber dealing with his attempt to instruct others in ethics. I believe that he considered it a fatal mistake, and certainly one which had little or no impact. Among Nietzsche's essays there was one which dealt with values, specifically with values as measures, not as an ever-changing human activity. As I remember he used the word, on purpose, not as a verb but as a noun to make his point. I do know that much of what Edmund Burke wrote had an impact on my thinking, especially as far as my work as a communication scholar is concerned. His insistence on seeing all societies as partnerships of past, present and future generations certainly makes me think of values and ethics as more than a matter of momentary concern. I am also challenged that my concerns about teaching have been a subject matter for the writings of many others before me. G. K. Chesterton, to mention only one example that I remember, addressed a question which is often raised today as well. Should a teacher merely draw out what is already present in students, young and old, so that they can develop their own values and ethical standards (or ignore the subject), or is teaching based on the authority and impact of a teacher? Chesterton, I recall, drew the conclusion, one with which I agree, that the very presence of a teacher always introduces authority into any learning situation. That makes sense to me, since I also believe that it is not possible for any of us to deal with anything in our environment only in, what we have often called and valued as, an *objective* manner.

Have I reached any conclusions based on these thoughts? I think I have. Certainly there are two points I would like to make at the end of this project, process and effort. The first is that I believe ethics should not merely be a subject matter to be studied, but rather that values and ethics require a response from us—even if it is the rejection of a specific instance or concept. I think all of us who cooperated in writing this book took an *ought* stance or perspective, one which is based on an orientation which requires thoughtful, responsible response to ethical and value challenges in our age and in our world. I do not mean to imply that we do not, or should not respect value- and ethics-systems which are different from our own. However, I do not believe that one can take an ethical stance which in effect does not allow rejection of concepts that our own standards for living and acting require us to reject if we are to remain true to what we call *important* or *significant* in our lives.

Secondly, I have tried to make clear that the engagement of ideas requires *thinking* about the matters which are brought to our attention. To me that is probably the most important foundation for learning. What I have written in this conclusion reminds me of reading Jesus' instruction to his disciples that they should act towards others the way they would like to be treated—it has been called the Golden Rule. There is also the Apostle Paul's injunction to Christian's facing the very difficult environment of their times, not merely to accept as correct, but *think about* all those things which are praiseworthy, including all that is true, honorable, just, pure and lovely. I consider that to be not a bad conclusion when it comes to the actual role we want ethics and values to play in our lives.

The Authors

Getinet Belay (PhD, 1988 Free University of West Berlin) is interested in globalization, interaction, and cultural change, focusing especially on the representation and negotiation of cultural identity in the globalization process. His other publications include, "Toward a Paradigm Shift for International and Intercultural Communication: New Research Directions," *Communication Yearbook* 16 (1993), 437-571; "(Re)construction and Negotiation of Cultural Identities in the Age of Globalization," *Information and Behavior*, 5 (1996), 319-346. He is currently Assistant Professor of Communication at Rutgers, the State University of New Jersey.

Fred L. Casmir (PhD, 1961 The Ohio State University) is Distinguished Professor of Communication at Pepperdine University, and author of publications on five continents, including *Communication in Development* (Ablex, 1991), *Building Communication Theories: A Socio/Cultural Approach* (Lawrence Erlbaum Associates, 1993), and *Communication in Eastern Europe: The Role of History, Culture, and Media in Contemporary Conflicts* (Lawrence Erlbaum Associates, 1995). Consulted, lectured, and taught in the areas of intercultural and mass communication in various countries in Europe, Asia, Africa, Australia, and North America. He has served at Pepperdine University as coordinator of the International Studies major.

Deborah J. Cohen (PhD Candidate, Rutgers University) is a doctoral student in communication at Rutgers University. In addition to ethical issues, she is pursuing research in the area of health communication as it pertains to storytelling as a place for identity construction in infertility support groups.

271

Stanley Deetz (PhD, 1973 Ohio University) is author of *Transforming Communication, Transforming Business: Building Responsive and Responsible Workplaces* (Hampton, 1995), *Democracy in an Age of Corporate Colonization: Developments in Communication and the Politics of Everyday Life* (SUNY, 1992), and editor or author of 8 other books. He has published numerous essays in scholarly journals and books regarding stakeholder representation, decision making, culture, and communication in corporate organizations and has lectured widely in the U.S. and Europe. In 1994, he was a Senior Fulbright Scholar in the Företagsekonomiska Institutionen, Göteborgs Universitet, Sweden, lecturing and conducting research on managing knowledge-intensive work. He has served as a consultant on culture, diversity, and participatory decision making for several major corporations. He will also serve as President of the International Communication Association in 1996-97. He is currently a Professor of Communication at Rutgers University, New Brunswick, New Jersey, where he teaches courses in organizational theory, organizational communication and communication theory.

Paige P. Edley (PhD Candidate, Rutgers University) is working toward completing her dissertation entitled *The Construction of Culture/Identity within Interaction in a Woman-owned Small Business: A Feminist Ethnography*. She is also the co-author of *Women Candidates Going Public: The 30—Second Format* (*Argumentation and Advocacy*, Fall, 1994).

Deni Elliot (EdD, 1984 Harvard University) is University Professor of Ethics at The University of Montana and Director of the Practical Ethics Center there. She is also Director for the M.A. in Philosophy with a Specialization in Teaching Applied Ethics Program. Elliott is also Professor, Department of Philosophy and Adjunct Professor, School of Journalism at The University of Montana. she was the founding director for the Institute for the Study of Applied and Professional Ethics at Dartmouth College, which she directed for five years. Elliott has written numerous articles, book chapters and encyclopedia entries for the scholarly, trade and lay press, on the subject of ethics.

Bradford J. Hall (PhD, 1989 Communication University of Washington) is interested in cultural communication, intercultural conflict, organizational culture, and how people establish and maintain membership within a variety of communities. He has published in such journals as *Communication Monographs, Human Relations, The International Journal of Intercultural Relations* and *Human Communication Research*. He is currently an associate professor in the department of Communication and Journalism at the University of New Mexico.

Folu F. Ogundimu, (PhD, 1991 Indiana University) is Assistant Professor, School of Journalism, Michigan State University, East Lansing. He also holds a diploma in mass communication from the University of Lagos, Nigeria. His research and publications include work on Africa's media image, development communications, mass communication training in Africa, political liberalization and broadcast media privatization in Africa. Dr. Ogundimu is a former award-winning journalist and principal editor with the Nigerian Television Authority. His academic awards and fellowships have included grants from the Rockefeller Foundation, The Hewlett Foundation, the Poynter Institute, the St. Petersburg (Fla.) Times, and the Shorenstein-Barone Center for Press and Public Policy at Harvard University.

Scott R. Olson (PhD, 1985 Northwestern University) is Professor of Communication and Associate Dean of Arts and Sciences at Central Connecticut State University. His articles have appeared in *Critical Studies in Mass Communication*, the *Journal of Communication*, and the *Journal of Film and Video*. His most recent book *Komuikacjz w organizacji I zarzadzaniu* (1996, Wroclow, Poland: Polythechnika Wroclawska Press).

Cornelius B. Pratt (PhD, 1981, University of Minnesota) is professor in the College of Communication Arts and Sciences at Michigan State University. Before joining the faculty at Michigan State in 1991, he taught at Weber State University, Utah, and at Virginia Polytechnic Institute and State University, Blacksburg. He has received awards for excellence in research on ethics. Pratt is co-author of *International Afro media: A reference guide* (Greenwood, 1996).

Linda Steiner (PhD, 1979, Institute of Communications Research, University of Illinois at Urbana) has published on feminist theorizing and its applications for communications ethics; the history and structure of feminist media in the U.S., and the evolving conceptions of women journalists. Her articles have appeared in *American Journalism, Journalism Quarterly, Journalism Monographs, Critical Studies in Mass Communications, Journalism History*. She taught at Governors State University for twelve years before going to Rutgers University, where she is currently an assistant Professor of Journalism.

AUTHOR INDEX

SUBJECT INDEX